# Toy Monster

# Toy Monster

## *The Big, Bad World of Mattel*

Jerry Oppenheimer

**WILEY**

John Wiley & Sons, Inc.

For general information on our other products and services or for technical support, please
contact our Customer Care Department within the United States at (800) 762-2974,
outside the United States at (317) 572-3993 or fax (317) 572-4002.

Wiley also publishes its books in a variety of electronic formats. Some content that appears
in print may not be available in electronic books. For more information about Wiley
products, visit our web site at www.wiley.com.

*Library of Congress Cataloging-in-Publication Data:*
Oppenheimer, Jerry.
    Toy monster : the big, bad world of Mattel / Jerry Oppenheimer.
      p.  cm.
    Includes bibliographical references.
    ISBN 978-0-470-37126-8 (cloth)
      1. Mattel, Inc.  2. Toy industry—United States.  I. Title.
  HD9993.T694M386   2009
  338.7'688720973—dc22
                                             2008051535

Printed in the United States of America
10  9  8  7  6  5  4  3  2  1

*For Caroline, Cuco, Trix, Max, Louise, Jesse, and Toby*

# Contents

# Part One

# THE BARBIE WAR
# AND THE
# HANDLER-RYAN ERA

# Chapter 1

# Barbie's Untold Heritage

After consummating yet another evening of compulsive sex—this night with the tall redhead who is Mattel's top-secret voice of the first talking Barbie doll—Jack Ryan, the "Father of Barbie," looks up at the oak ceiling of the boudoir in his Hefneresque Bel-Air Tudor mansion known as "The Castle," turns to voluptuous, brown-eyed, breast-enhanced Gwen Florea, who, besides thrilling millions of little girls by having their favorite doll speak, helps run Mattel's high-tech recording studio and acoustics lab, and says, "You know something, Kid, I should cut a hole in the ceiling so when I make love I can look up and see the stars and the moon. Wouldn't that be just delightful?"

Even in bed, where he spends many evenings with one or more real-life beautiful dolls, most possessing the attributes of his fantasy doll, Barbie—the long-legged, slim-waisted, pointy-breasted, 11½ inch plastic one that is making him a fortune—the Father of Barbie can always conjure up new ideas; the corny romantic bedroom sunroof is just one. He usually talks his ideas into a tape recorder he carries, or jots them down on a pad he keeps next to his toilet.

3

While Barbie and other iconic Mattel playthings he's developed—Chatty Cathy, Ken, Hot Wheels, not to mention the Optigan music-maker, among others—are earning him millions in royalties, his very favorite toy is The Castle. This private kingdom, on more than four acres of expensive turf, underscores the Father of Barbie's hyperactive narcissism and singular quirkiness and eccentricity.

Literally following the old adage that "a man's home is his castle," Ryan transformed what had once been Bel-Air's second oldest stately home, the staid (by Hollywood standards) 16,000-square-foot manse and grounds of silent-to-talkies Oscar winner Warner Baxter (who underwent a lobotomy to "cure" his arthritis and died not long after), into the Father of Barbie's own private "once-upon-a-time" theme park.

There's the high Greek Revival Moorish archway. There's the wood bridge over the moat that protects the entrance. There are battlements. There are the massive arches guarded by knights in armor. There are the giant stone fireplaces, the leaded glass windows, and the rich wood paneling. There is the massive ballroom with marble floors. There's the scallop-edged swimming pool with cabanas, and the open dance pavilion with a gazebo top. There's the tennis court and tennis house (which often is home to one or more ladies of the moment). There's the circular staircase leading to the tree house, which can serve eight under a chandelier, where the likes of CBS chairman William Paley often enjoys a repast.

The Tom Jones Room, in the lower level of the main house, is reserved for intimate Thursday-night no-utensils dinner bacchanals at which the Father of Barbie presides from an enormous throne that once belonged to the Prince of Parma. (Ryan had originally bought the throne to cover the toilet where he jots his ideas, but it was disappointingly too big for the loo.) His Queen, a different beauty chosen each week, wears the crown used in commercials for Imperial Margarine.

Curiously, many of the adornments in the immense house are fake, like a movie set, because Ryan tends to not finish many of the numerous renovation projects he starts. The pillars supporting the temporary roof of the dance pavilion are made of plywood and are hollow and house playful gofers; the drapes in the main house are made of inexpensive canvas, but painted with ornate gold trimming to give the appearance of being costly; at the end of one room is a big faux fireplace that is skillfully dummied up to look authentic; and some of the asphalt drive-way is painted in such a way as to give the look of stone. On some projects, he had the assistance of a Disneyland designer. "The idea that something was finished would mean that he wouldn't be able to do anything more with it," observes a close friend Annie Constantinesco. "So many things were a mockup, and if it went further than that, it stopped being interesting to him because he could always improve on a mockup."

At one point during the never-ending renovation, the Father of Barbie had ordered expensive oak paneling from the estate of William Randolph Hearst, and had delivered to The Castle spectacular lime-stone blocks imported from a 15th-century French abbey, but never got around to installing any of it.

Because of the immense size of The Castle, the Father of Barbie has the help of about a dozen bright, handsome students from the nearby campus of UCLA. These unpaid interns, known as "Ryan's Boys," receive free room and board in exchange for sundry services, such as keeping the grounds and house in tip-top shape and offering security and valet services for the huge parties the Father of Barbie throws. *Look* magazine wrote a feature about the intriguing setup, headlined, "The Butler Goes to College."

Since Ryan is in constant and often-frenzied communication with col-leagues and friends, he installed 144 telephones throughout The Castle and grounds. Some of the phones are even in trees, and for those he changed the ring tones to sound like the chirping of birds. The entire phone system is switched through a highly sophisticated communications system that he bought as surplus from a U.S. Navy destroyer and reengineered.

A car buff, he has some 18 autos in various states of customiza-tion, and even owns a mint-condition 1935 Reo fire engine. It's not unheard of for Ryan to invite a group of revelers to jump aboard and, with siren wailing, race from The Castle through the gold-paved streets of Beverly Hills to party at the latest "in" disco.

For first-time guests, awe-inspired by the mind-boggling layout, Ryan put together a guidebook of his playground, appropriately enti-tled, *It's a Party*.

■ ■ ■

During his lifetime, the Father of Barbie had his name on more than a thousand patents, and was a man of seemingly as many personas—inventor, designer, and serial Casanova, to name just a few. The *Los Angeles Times* once characterized him as "a strange mixture of the new technologist and the old playboy." Zsa Zsa Gabor, the second of his five wives (he was the sixth of her nine husbands), had a somewhat different view. She described the Father of Barbie this way: "[M]y knight in shining armor, the inhabitant of a fairy-tale castle, Jack my new husband . . . was a full-blown seventies-style swinger into wife-swapping and sundry sexual pursuits as a way of life." Most of her assessment was accurate, except for the wife-swapping part, unless she meant he swapped one old wife for one new one with rings and weddings, like she did with her mates.

Except for a small circle of confidantes, few knew that the Father of Barbie was a mass of treatable and untreatable emotional problems and addictions, including what later became known as *hypersexuality*, a manic need for sexual gratification, which was one of the symptoms of his bipolar disorder—a well-kept secret and an illness that explained his compulsive womanizing.

Barbie has quite an untold heritage.

■ ■ ■

As Barbie's 50th anniversary on March 9, 2009 loomed, the first Voice of Barbie reminisces nostalgically about her relationship with the Father of Barbie—one she says "was just a brief fling as far as bed was concerned."

Observes Gwen Florea: "Jack was fun-crazy. That night when he wanted to cut a hole in the ceiling so that he could see the starlight, I had to talk him out of it, or he would have done it. He'd do things like that on the spur of the moment."

They were an oddly matched twosome, but so was the Father of Barbie with all of his other women—the ones he knew biblically, and those he courted and charmed socially.

While most playboys used their proverbial Little Black Books to list the vital statistics and other intimate details about their women, the Father of Barbie's method was far more advanced. He adopted the

McBee Keysort System, used by librarians before the advent of small computers, to list the Barbie-like physical attributes and sometimes sexual interests and appetites of the women he knew. Most of that data was gathered at Hollywood parties and Beverly Hills society and charity functions. It was entered into the system by his coterie of beautiful social secretaries, such as statuesque Gun Sundberg, a former Miss Scandinavia, and Swedish Tanning Secrets TV commercial knockout.

Along with gathering all the details, his secretaries photographed certain guests and attached the prints to the data cards. The information in Ryan's eight address books was also added to the mix. If the Father of Barbie required a statuesque Barbie doll lookalike with certain kinks for one of the Castle revels, or if he needed 60 chic couples for one of his enormous celebrity parties, his beautiful assistants had no problem gathering the precise card sort.

■ ■ ■

Whereas the Voice of Barbie was six-foot-one in heels, the Father of Barbie was a diminutive five-foot-eight—and that was in his custom-made elevator shoes imported from Church's of London, which gave him at least three more inches. "My being taller than him was always something that he loved, like a real-life Barbie doll," relates the Voice of Barbie. "He once said to me he loved me being tall so he could stick his nose in my boobs when he hugged me."

Derek Gable, a star designer and executive at Mattel for 16 years who was part of the company's "brain drain" from the United Kingdom, says Ryan fancied himself a sort of funny-looking Hugh Hefner. Hefner had his own Barbie doll–like Barbi (no e on the end). Benton, the Playboy founder's longtime playmate who, with a singing career in mind, once recorded a dud called "Barbi Doll."

Recalls Gable: "The first time I ever heard of Jack Ryan was in a newspaper back in England, one of the scandal ones, probably, and the headline said, "Jack and His Dolly Birds," with a picture of him having dinner under a chandelier in his tree house on his estate, and the story was about this whacked-out guy who has all these dolly birds."

Despite his success in bedding a chorus line of beauties, the Father of Barbie was no handsome Ken (the boy doll developed by Ryan and his crack team of Mattel designers and engineers that was brilliantly promoted as Barbie's main squeeze). Besides Jack Ryan's height, or lack thereof, his hair was cut and dyed an odd orange-red by famed "stylist to the stars" Jay Sebring (who, along with actress Sharon Tate, was one of cult leader Charles Manson's victims); his speaking voice sounded as if he had inhaled laughing gas; his forehead was overly large and alien-like; he had a Humpty Dumpty build—his chest puffed out like a rooster in heat and he had skinny arms and spindly legs; and his complexion was a Bela Lugosi–like pale because of his genetic Irish-American pallor as well as the fact that he rarely ventured into the southern California sun.

A dandy of sorts, he sported custom-tailored suits from Mr. Guy in Beverly Hills, wore safari jackets with a silk ascot, and often arrived at a party wearing a full-length fur coat. Many considered him a blast, while others thought he was Napoleonic—in size and demeanor. His IQ was in the genius range.

The Father of Barbie was also considered a sensuous lover.

"Jack was very good in bed," Gwen Florea attests years later. "He was very, very considerate. But it was the whole aura of his personality that was so attractive."

As with so many others in Jack Ryan's orbit, ranging from the creative geniuses at Mattel to Hollywood's celebrity A-list, she was referring to his charm, brilliance, inventiveness, eccentricity, and life-style. However, those are some of the same characteristics that have relegated Ryan to virtual anonymity in the long and storied history of Mattel and the mythology surrounding the Barbie doll as she entered her second half-century.

The press courted the Father of Barbie and praised his intellect and talent. "Under his supervision, the Barbie Doll and all her friends and wardrobe demands were born," declared the *Los Angeles Times.* "He is an inventor who has already patented . . . the most successful toys ever sold."

■ ■ ■

While the media extolled Ryan's intellectual and creative virtues, a far more powerful figure in the Father of Barbie's life criticized, begrudged, and denied them—especially when it came to who actually conceived, or invented, or devised the biggest-selling, most-iconic doll in the universe.

Her name is Ruth Handler, Mattel's driven, ambitious, and cutthroat co-founder. After Ryan's death in 1991, and before her own passing in 2002, she publicly waged what many in Ryan's circle believe was a deliberate campaign to diminish, if not altogether erase, his role as the Father of Barbie, and take full credit as the billion-dollar doll's inventor and as "Mother of Barbie."

Privately, within the hallowed halls of Mattel, the two had been at each other's throats for almost two decades. It was a backroom and boardroom drama that eventually exploded into what one high-powered Beverly Hills lawyer describes as "a scorched-earth legal battle," as in *Ryan v. Mattel.*

"Ruth Handler came in after Jack died and started a whole PR campaign about her being the creator of Barbie," maintains Stephen Gnass, founder of a serious, prestigious seminar program for inventors called Invention Convention, and a close friend of Ryan's. "Enough propaganda, enough promotion and you can make anybody believe anything. Ruth Handler really marginalized anything that Jack had to do with Mattel. She was making her case after he was dead and he was in no position to defend his legacy."

To Gnass, Ryan seemed possessed by Barbie.

"When Jack talked about creating Barbie, or improving Barbie, he would light up and describe the breasts and the legs and how tall she needed to be. He was intrigued by that," recalls Gnass. "When he talked about Barbie it was like listening to somebody talk about a sexual episode, almost like listening to a sexual pervert talk about creating this doll. He got a little glow, was animated, had a twinkle in his eye. Barbie was the number-one toy at Mattel that he would talk about creating. I often think about the expression on his face when he described the doll's voluptuousness."

An expert at media spin and self-promotion, and once described in the *New York Times* as a "one-woman sales-merchandising-promotion-administrative force, a sort of industrial Orson Welles," Ruth Handler was enormously successful at getting her story across—and her rendition of Barbie's birth became an integral part of the Barbie myth and phenomenon.

As she once stated bluntly, "One of my strengths is that I do have the courage of my convictions and the guts to take a position, stand up for it, and make it happen. I can be very persuasive in getting others to see the light."

Hints of the Handler-Ryan feud became public on rare occasions, such as when the *New York Times*, in a profile of the toy company in 1968, described Ryan as "Mattel's real secret weapon," and noted that Ruth and her husband and Mattel co-founder, Elliot Handler, were "reluctant to credit any single person with the invention of new toy 'principles.'" The story pointed out that early publicity about Mattel that had credited Ryan with the development of Barbie had "caused a top-level chasm" between him and the Handlers, especially Ruth, whose vendetta only intensified.

When the *Times* ran a caption-sized feature item in 1994 about Barbie's 35th anniversary, and named the then-deceased Jack Ryan as "Barbie's creator," Ruth Handler went as ballistic as the realistic toy missiles that were designed for Mattel by Ryan, which sold in the millions, and were even featured in *Life* magazine. Ryan had helped design real missiles for use by the military before he joined Mattel. In a letter to the *Times*, Handler stated that the story "contained an inaccuracy. The late Jack Ryan was not Barbie's creator. My husband Elliot, and I were the founders of Mattel Toys, and I was the creator of the Barbie doll. Jack Ryan, in his role as head of the research-and-development department, managed some of the design work relating to the doll and her accessories."

Mattel was Ruth's show, they were her toys, and no one else was going to get credit. Those in the creative end were thought of as "technicians," literally and figuratively.

Ruth was considered "ruthless, a real hatchet man who was completely oblivious to design," asserts Fred Adickes, who came from designing tailfins at General Motors to serve as chief industrial designer at Mattel under Ryan. Adickes helped spearhead the development of Hot Wheels and worked on the "World of Barbie," which included the doll's first car, a Corvette, and her home and furnishings. The project was Ryan and the Handlers' way of expanding Barbie beyond just clothing and fashion accessories.

"Ruth and Elliot's word was law," says Adickes, years later. "They were exalted. They were Mattel's God and Holy Spirit—and they had a competitive, adversarial relationship with Jack Ryan. In the end, Ruth was designated as the inventor of Barbie. This was done not only for ego, but probably for good business reasons. It wouldn't be good business to identify anyone else who contributed."

Adickes notes that after he left Mattel, unhappy with the politics and culture, Elliot Handler began taking credit for Hot Wheels. As Adickes observes, "It wouldn't be good business for the Handlers to say, 'Well, the man who actually came up with the idea for Hot Wheels was an automotive designer who left the company.'"

Salaried Mattel designers such as Adickes who were big producers sometimes received bonuses and stock options, but were barely compensated for their lucrative ideas. After signing a mandatory document turning over all patent rights to a toy that might generate hundreds of millions of dollars in revenue for Mattel, he says they received in return a crisp one-dollar bill. "Sometimes I got it," notes Adickes, "sometimes not."

Because the world-famous Barbie brand has been the most significant product in Mattel's extraordinary lifetime, the unvarnished story of the doll's conception and implementation offers a candid snapshot of Mattel's founders and their complex relationship with their employees, and of the company's curious corporate culture. It underscores how Mattel became an international juggernaut—the biggest, baddest toy company in the world.

Placing Barbie's plastic DNA under a microscope, one finds contradictions in Ruth Handler's story of Barbie's conception. It also reveals the very private war the Handlers were waging against Jack Ryan, which subsequently so debilitated him emotionally and physically that at the age of 64 he had a tragic end. His manner of death has long been kept secret.

# Chapter 2

# A Shocking Cover-Up

Ruth Handler's account of Barbie's creation became formally etched in stone with her autobiography, *Dream Doll*, published in 1994, three years after Ryan's death. What Walt Disney was to Mickey, Ruth Handler essentially declared she was to Barbie—and Jack Ryan was virtually nowhere in sight. Her campaign worked. Subsequent articles and books about the doll took her at her word that she was the "the creator of Barbie."

Written with the help of Jacqueline Shannon, a journalist (who declined to be interviewed for this book), *Dream Doll*, published by Longmeadow Press (a small, long-defunct house), and widely reviewed at the time, mentions Jack Ryan only briefly, with little more than a dozen short references in the 227-page book, and gives him little or no credit for his lucrative and creative role. Her one concession to Ryan was his development of the "Twist 'n' Turn Barbie," a major breakthrough, that gave the doll natural movement by allowing little girls to bend her at the waist and legs, and twist her at the hips—with no visible joints.

But Handler went on to complain: "Because these technological innovations were among the few Barbie features we were able to patent, Jack Ryan would later tell people that he was the inventor of the Barbie doll. You can imagine how annoying this was."

She may have been annoyed, but, in fact, Ryan held the only U.S. patents related to the Barbie doll, while the Handlers, neither of whom were engineers, had none involving Barbie, a key fact to which Ruth didn't fess up in *Dream Doll*, among many other things. Ryan's first patent, filed seven months before Barbie's debut at the 1959 International Toy Fair in New York, was for doll construction; his second was for doll construction, natural movements, and positions; his third was for a doll having an angular adjustable line; and the fourth was for natural movements and positions—the breakthrough involving the Twist 'n' Turn development.

Ryan was also involved in designing the tiny mechanisms that permitted Barbie, Chatty Cathy, and Larry the Lion, among other Mattel classics, to speak. For about two years, leggy Gwen Florea had been recording Barbie's voice, two-second sound bites, on records smaller than a quarter that fit inside under the doll's breasts. Among the first words Barbie spoke were, "I love being a fashion model." When a more sophisticated voice unit was in development by Ryan and his team, Florea interviewed and recorded dozens of actresses to become the potential new voice. But when she made the final presentation to Jack Ryan and the Handlers they wanted only her voice. "I was told that they did not want anybody on the outside to know who the voice was, that it would be counterproductive to have an actual human in competition with Barbie."

According to retired chief designer of Barbie Collector Dolls & Collectibles, Carol Spencer, a 36-year Mattel veteran, and an internationally known Barbie expert and author, the Handlers changed the design of Ryan's last patent to avoid paying him royalties. "Jack Ryan had the patent for the twist waist," says Spencer. "After Jack left Mattel, the Handlers broke his patent. They merely stopped using features that Jack had patented, which is an easy way to 'break' a patent. Mattel went from his angular twist waist to a horizontal twist waist."

Ryan's defenders assert that Ruth Handler ordered the changes as part of a campaign to disparage and denigrate him. And Mattel would eventually stop payment on all of Ryan's royalties, leading to a legal battle royal.

"Jack got the short end of the stick," declares Annie Constantinesco, a Masters graduate at the Sorbonne and a Fulbright scholar who became an integral part of Jack Ryan's world in the late 1960s and remained a lifelong close confidante.

> It was after Jack died that it was no-holds-barred, with Ruth Handler taking all the credit for Barbie. She probably always did claim credit for inventing Barbie to a degree, but after Jack died there were quite often articles, or interviews where she was featured, and she basically totally ignored him, or his name, or his contribution, and said it was all her doing.

> But Jack addressed every feature of the doll. He had all the patents. To analyze the success of Barbie is to analyze what the features of the Barbie doll are that made it such a success, and one is the bendable waist that didn't exist before. Nobody had that feature and it was one of Jack's most prominent patents. When you look at a little girl playing with Barbie, that's one of the things that they love, and that was one of Jack's big contributions.

> And the concept of Barbie was so in keeping with Jack's concept of a woman—the long legs, the small waist, the big tits. That was his take on women.

The Barbie doll introduced to the world in March 1959, sheathed in a tight black-and-white-striped bathing suit, fit Ryan's profile of the perfect fantasy woman; her real-life vital dimensions were a Pamela Andersonesque 39–18–34.

*The Women's Review of Books*, billed as a "serious, informed discussion of new writing by and about women," then published by the Wellesley Centers for Women, an organization closely tied to Wellesley College, severely panned *Dream Doll*. "Handler's autobiography," wrote the critic, "is nakedly self-serving, an attempt at auto-canonization. . . . Sadly, Handler's real achievement—as a woman who started an enormously important company—is obscured by her own account."

The review pointed out Handler's unrelenting boasts, such as describing herself as "a fiercely independent woman, one who has always felt the need to prove myself," and the critic noted that Handler ends *Dream Doll* with an appendix titled "Awards and Honors," but "leaves out her rap sheet," a reference to Handler's white-collar crimes in the 1970s that forced her (along with her husband) from Mattel, and almost landed her in prison.

The shocking case of how she and a few colleagues finagled Mattel's books and cashed in on insider information (detailed later in this book) demonstrated Ruth Handler's ability to twist facts and dodge the truth. If she prevaricated with hard-nosed investigators from the Securities and Exchange Commission and federal prosecutors, as she did, is it difficult to make the leap that she'd take full credit for Barbie over Jack Ryan, whom she deeply resented, and who wasn't around to defend himself?

■ ■ ■

In mid-2008, as Barbie's 50th anniversary approached, Ruth's widower, Elliot Handler, was, at 92 years old, in relatively good health. Well-liked by his former Mattel employees as the soft-spoken, creative member of the Handler team, while "mannish" Ruth, as Gwen Florea described her, was the one who took care of business, Elliot had recently completed painting portraits of his six great-grandchildren in his Century City penthouse overlooking Beverly Hills. An artist, he had just undergone a second surgery for carpal tunnel syndrome on his right hand, making painting difficult.

Mattel, and how he and his wife were forced out more than three decades earlier, are subjects he's loath to discuss. However, he acknowledges that Jack Ryan "was a talented designer, a talented engineer who created a good engineering and design department for us. We brought him in working for us and we gave him a small royalty to go along with the product that he worked with." He concedes that there was an ongoing feud between Ryan and Ruth. "They had arguments on a number of things. He and Ruth did not get along too well. It was just personality. Ruth had a strong ego and so did Jack. If you put two people with big egos together they bounce around a little bit."

Still, he defended Ruth against Ryan when it came to the subject of Barbie. "The doll was completely Ruth Handler's idea," Elliot declares. "She always wanted a teenage doll, and this thing kind of came together. Jack Ryan had nothing to do with the original creativity of the doll. His work had to do with the mechanical things."

According to Ruth's book, the Barbie doll was her concept from start to finish.

She stated that in the early 1950s, she had watched her daughter, Barbara, then approaching adolescence, and her friends, playing with cutout dolls—paper renditions of young career women, nurses, secretaries, all very feminine and sexualized. She saw how the girls dressed them and fantasized about their make-believe lives. As Handler saw it, "They were using these dolls to project their dreams. . . . So one day it hit me: Wouldn't it be great if we could take that play pattern and three-dimensionalize it so little girls could do their dreaming and role-playing with real dolls and real clothes instead of the flimsy paper or cardboard ones?"

Handler believed that a more adult-looking doll, one with breasts, could be a huge seller for her and Elliot's growing company. But when she presented the concept within Mattel, none of the men could see it, she bemoaned.

In 1956, the Handlers, already reaping substantial profits from their decade-old Mattel (thanks in part to being one of the first toy companies to shrewdly gamble advertising dollars on TV commercials), took a month-and-a-half European vacation. In Lucerne, just a few days before leaving for home, Ruth spotted a plastic doll in a shop window that was "the embodiment" of the adult-looking doll she had been unsuccessfully advocating back at headquarters. She stood "transfixed" with 15-year-old daughter Barbara at her side, gazing at the 11½-inch plastic rendition dressed in a tight miniature ski outfit.

"I was gripped," Ruth Handler recalled.

Called Bild-Lilli, the doll had everything she claimed she had been envisioning for a marketable, money-making product—long legs, thin waist, perky breasts—the same female attributes that Jack Ryan fantasized about, lusted after, and eventually engineered into Barbie. Over the years, that supermodel-like body in doll form would be one of the few things on which Ruth Handler and Jack Ryan ever agreed.

Bild-Lilli had the look of an erotic Deutschland dominatrix with arched eyebrows and a tightly pulled-back ponytail rather than the Doris Day, girl-next-door image that Ruth had envisioned. In the latter part of the first decade of the twenty-first century, Lilli's real-life counterpart might be the pinup and burlesque entertainer Dita von Teese. Lilli was based on a sexy, popular cartoon character whose floozy lifestyle was depicted in a hugely popular strip in *Bild Zeitung*, a garish German tabloid. Because of Lilli's immense popularity, the newspaper had commissioned a well-known German doll designer, Max Weissbrodt, to turn her into an adult novelty, a doll that men hung from their rearview mirrors or gave as suggestive gifts to their women.

Ruth snapped up Lilli and brought her back home. With a makeover, she believed Mattel could sell millions to America's Baby Boomerettes. Jack Ryan was just the man to handle the project.

# Chapter 3

# From Weapons of Mass Destruction to Barbie, and the Knocking Off of a German Doll

John William (Jack) Ryan was a Yalie who designed high-tech weapons for America's Cold War machine before joining Mattel.

Born in New York City, November 12, 1926, the future Father of Barbie grew up in elegant surroundings in a sprawling house filled with antiques and beautiful hand-carved furniture in the Manhattan commuter-suburb of Yonkers. He was the second son of James J. Ryan, an Irish immigrant from a farming family, who became a fashionable Manhattan contractor to the rich and famous, specializing in opulent store facades, and the paneled interiors of fancy homes for the likes of Katherine Hepburn, Helen Hayes, June Havoc, and hoi polloi like the Hearsts. Annually, he was commissioned to do the Bride's House for *House Beautiful*, and when the World's Fair came to New York in 1939, he designed model homes for the great exhibition. He was a drinker, sportsman, and dapper dresser who wintered in Florida two months out of the year and, like his son, was a roué. Even in his last years he liked to pinch and rub up against the beauties who populated The Castle.

Lily Urqhart Croston Ryan, his wife, who brought James Ryan Jr. into the world seven years before his famous brother, Jack, worked for a time in *Life* magazine's art department and, according to Ryan family lore, was with her English pedigree the proprietor of a fancy tearoom across the street from Radio City Music Hall.

As a mother, however, Lily was an odd duck, with child-rearing ideas that would never pass Dr. Spock's muster—such as refusing to allow Jack to have any friends. That alone would have a devastating psychological impact on his adult life, and on virtually everyone around him.

"When my father was growing up, his mother didn't let him play with other children because she felt they weren't good enough to play with him, and others weren't good enough to come to the Ryan home, and when the Ryan boys were invited to other people's homes, well, those people weren't good enough, either," recounts Diana Ryan, the second of Jack Ryan's two daughters. "My father's mother didn't want other kids to come to the Ryan home because she felt like her home, while beautiful, wasn't ready, wasn't finished. So it was both 'they're not good enough,' and 'we're not good enough.' So that was my grandmother's issue."

Emotionally crippled by the memory of his lonely childhood, the Father of Barbie as an adult required constant attention, crowds of people, nightly parties, innumerable lovers, and a succession of wives. But he claimed loneliness was never a problem for him, although he acknowledged he had "a tendency to be sensitive in that direction. To like to be with people is important to me, to be part of a group, accepted, liked, respected and to share in the mutual feelings people have. Human feelings are important to me. I'm sensitive to them."

Because of his mother's fears and phobias, Jack Ryan's only play-mate, pal, and mentor growing up was his big brother, Jim, which might have been a blessing in disguise. "My father and Jim got a little ingrown," observes Diana Ryan, a divorcee with two sons. A committed Christian, she started a business to help people organize their lives "to have time for the people they love."

Besides barring Jack from having friends, Lily Ryan was also blind to the fact that her youngest son had a major but undiagnosed learning disability. The future Father of Barbie—the much-hailed inventor and intellectual—was severely dyslexic. He could not read, but was able shrewdly to hide his infirmity, one of a number of serious emotional problems—ranging from being bipolar to suicidal, alcoholic, and cocaine-addicted—that would surface over the years.

"My Uncle Jim was the bookworm and so when they were growing up he would do the reading and then Dad would debrief him," says Diana Ryan. "My dad was introduced to high school work when he was in elementary school, and college work when he was in high school. Jim taught my father most of his high school stuff because they were very close and always together, and my father just absorbed things like a sponge from Jim. In those days there weren't people who could diagnose learning disorders, but my dad figured out on his own what these days would be called a learning disorder."

When Jack was seven, for instance, Jim taught him high school German. When Jack was in high school at the exclusive Barnard School, in the fancy enclave of Riverdale in the Bronx, he was permitted to skip biology in order to teach physics, which his brother had taught him—without Jack having once read a book on the subject. It was during the early years of World War II, and all of the regular physics instructors were in uniform.

Jack was a junior mad scientist with a seriously dangerous mischievous streak. The future Father of Barbie boasted that he made dynamite in the Ryan's basement, and detonated the charges to frighten the neighbors. On a tamer note, when he spotted neighborhood boys riding three-speed bikes, Jack designed and built a nine-speed. Often bored at school, he built a crystal radio set and customized it so it was hidden in his desk, with the earphones stashed in the inkwell. A born entrepreneur, he sold more than a dozen to classmates.

He taught himself how to take apart and put together an automobile engine, and later, when he was earning millions at Mattel, he had dozens of cars, many he redesigned, such as grafting Mercedes-Benz grills on to old Studebakers, or slicing new Rolls Royces in half and putting another make's body in the middle—the first unofficial stretch limousines. So it was not a great leap for him to become a key figure in the design and implementation of another of Mattel's iconic huge sellers, Hot Wheels, which is for boys what Barbie is for girls.

In his senior year of high school, he was elected class president, and was so advanced in his studies that he was allowed to attend classes just one day a week, spending the rest working in an electronics laboratory for a disciple of the famed inventor and industrialist Vincent Hugo Bendix, where Ryan devised a better way to test radio crystals—and won a $25 war bond for his breakthrough.

After graduating from high school, with the war still on, Ryan was easily accepted at Yale, and enlisted in the university's Naval officer training program, serving from July 1944 to July 1946, at the New Haven campus and in the Pacific, where he was assigned to an ammunition ship.

Still, he couldn't handle reading books, so he found a way around the problem.

"When Dad went to Yale he told me that he put together a study group for each of his classes, and appointed himself moderator of each of the study groups," says Diana Ryan. "He doled out the reading assignments and then he'd have people read the chapters and report back to him, all of which he absorbed. Since he was the moderator, he didn't assign chapters to himself, so he got through Yale pretty much without having to do *any* reading."

While majoring in electrical engineering and industrial administration, he undertook an extra term of independent research work in personnel psychology with the E. Wight Bakke Foundation at the Institute of Human Relations at Yale. He was also active on campus as a sharp-shooting member of the Yale pistol team; he'd have a lifetime fascination with guns, developing successful toy guns and rifles for Mattel.

He joined Dramat, Yale's dramatic society, where he was known as an outgoing, attention-getting exhibitionist. Rather than act, he volunteered for the less glamorous job of production manager after he discovered that the Dramat's musical, "In the Clover," was scheduled to tour women's colleges—women were always his favorite form of recreation. Throughout his lifetime he believed that the female brain, not just the body, was superior to that of the male.

Even before graduation, he got a job as a technical consultant at a White Plains, New York, plastics company, which was invaluable experience when he got to Mattel, where plastic ruled.

He graduated with a BS degree from Yale's School of Engineering in 1948, announcing plans to assist his brother, Jim, in the development of electronic inventions. However, his first job out of school was managing the Square Root Manufacturing Company for a friend, J.J. Root, who was producing TV antennas for postwar-American couch potatoes. Ryan also took some graduate courses at Harvard.

While there, the future Father of Barbie fell in love, or so it seemed. Her name was Barbara Harris, a pretty, stiff-lipped Brahmin, the daughter of a Texas Company executive and a concert violinist and teacher. A Parsons School of Design graduate, the future Mrs. Jack Ryan worked as a designer of chic scarves for the Vera brand—a company formed by Vera Neumann, an artist who became a noted textile designer whose popular scarves were signed VERA in small print.

Jack and Barbara dated for a year or two and got married in August 1950, in what would become an ill-fated, unconventional union after Ryan joined Mattel.

"Because Dad was in a hurry, and Mom was too shy to have a big wedding, they eloped," says Diana Ryan. "They were married in a friend's living room in New Rochelle, New York—just with friends and the minister—and that was it."

For the next two years, they lived with Jack's parents and brother in his boyhood home in Yonkers, a decision in which the bride had no say. Through the years she'd have little input in anything her dominant and controlling husband decided. The reason he moved back home was his lifelong issue of loneliness. He felt more comfortable with lots of people around. For Barbara Ryan, it would get much worse.

It was during this time that Jack was offered a plum job with a high security clearance at one of America's premier defense contractors (and inventor of the microwave oven), Raytheon (which means "light from the gods"). It was 1952: General Dwight David Eisenhower was elected President; U.S. troops were battling the Communist North Koreans; French soldiers were fighting the Communist Viet Minh in Vietnam; and the United States dedicated the Nautilus, the world's first atomic submarine, to fight the Reds, if needed. And in Waltham, Massachusetts, 26-year-old Jack Ryan was doing his part for America's so-called military–industrial complex.

He was assigned to work on preliminary design for the ground-to-air Hawk missile, and was performing reliability studies for the air-to-air Sparrow III missile, both of which were ordered by the Cold War Pentagon. "I was in charge of the work of seven-hundred engineers and scientists developing the Hawk system—I wasn't their boss but I was the young guy who ran it," Ryan revealed years later.

It was during missile test-firing trips to the Point Magu Naval Air Missile Test Center, just north of Los Angeles, that the future Father of Barbie heard about a prosperous, up-and-coming toy company called Mattel.

■ ■ ■

"I used to go to California every six weeks," Jack Ryan once explained, "and I had to be accompanied at all times by the project officer, a Navy commander, just to make sure that certain secrets were protected."

He sold ideas to toy companies because he wasn't making much money as a commander, and he introduced me to people from Mattel and I met them and they made me an offer I couldn't refuse.

I'm no Einstein but I recognized serendipity when I saw it and I latched on to it. I said, these people are the right kind of people, going in the right direction. So I left all the missiles behind me. I was an independent inventor collaborating with Ruth and Elliot Handler, who were just a nice young couple that started the Mattel Toy Company. It was being in the right time at the right place and realizing I was lucky.

Jack returned to Boston and told Barbara, who had recently given birth to their first child, Anne, that he'd found nirvana in southern California. Once again he gave her no options. The Ryans were L.A.-bound.

Ryan joined the Handlers around 1955, just as Mattel, with annual sales of $6 million, was about to skyrocket. Earlier that year, the Handlers were made an offer *they* couldn't refuse, courtesy of Walt Disney, ABC-TV, and a mouse named Mickey. At the time, the Handlers had retained their first advertising agency, Carson/Roberts, and had a $150,000-a-year advertising budget, which was considered high for the toy industry back then. The money went for newspaper, magazine, and chain-store catalog ads, which was the way companies hawked their products in the golden age of toys, with most of the hype beginning around Thanksgiving and culminating at Christmas.

But now, the Handlers were being offered a different opportunity to get their message across to kids and tap their parents' pocketbooks. If the Handlers were willing to put up $500,000, their entire current net worth, and sign a contract for 52 weeks, they could be the sole sponsor of a 15-minute segment on a new, untested show called the *Mickey Mouse Club*. The Handlers considered their fate, and took the risk.

"Ruth was always a gambler," notes Derek Gable. "She loved Vegas." The Handlers figured that with Disney connected to the program, they couldn't lose. They decided to advertise a new product brought to them by an outside inventor, called the Burp Gun. Toy guns and replica rifles like the Winchester were lucrative for Mattel's boys' toys line through the 1950s and the very early 1960s, thanks to the popularity of TV shows featuring Gene Autry, Roy Rogers, and The Lone Ranger. The Handlers' gamble paid off. They sold a million Burp Guns, and forever changed the way the toy industry advertised.

Toy commercials in those days were often incredibly deceptive—the products made to look or sound far different from what they actually were in order to mislead kids and their parents. In the early 1960s, the National Association of Broadcasters introduced tough guidelines for toy advertising in response to public criticism about misleading commercials by Mattel and others. For instance, Mattel was ordered by the

Federal Communications Commission to pull a Hot Wheels commercial from the air because it misrepresented the toy.

Jack Ryan watched the Handlers' successes and how they operated and was even more impressed. As he stated later, "Ruth has a mind like a steel trap and Elliot has a sensitivity of product that is uncanny."

The Handlers had never publicly revealed their financial arrangement with Ryan, but in mid-2008, the surviving co-founder agreed to divulge aspects of their agreement. "We needed someone to help come up with new products," says Elliot Handler. "Ryan came to us highly recommended as a very good designer, and we made a deal with him. We put him in charge of design. We gave him a small percentage of products that he was involved with, like a royalty."

Ryan was overjoyed. He initially asked for $25,000 a year, which he knew the Handlers, who were tight with money, wouldn't pay. Instead, haggling back and forth, he made a far better deal.

Marvin Barab, Mattel's first marketing director, who worked under Ryan and considered him "one of the most brilliant men I've ever met—and he thought so, too," says the Handlers gave Ryan such a lucrative deal because they had not expected the kind of growth Mattel suddenly experienced, most of it attributable to Barbie. As a result, the Handlers were forced to pay Ryan huge royalty fees, which drove them crazy. Barab, who was hired several months before Barbie's debut at the toy fair, notes that when he came aboard Ryan was "in the hierarchy" at Mattel, one of the key decision makers.

> In the original deal, as I understood it, Jack was getting a percentage of the company's gross sales. Later, the Handlers renegotiated his royalty level because it got to be too big of an item. They felt they were paying him way too much. As I understood it, it was not just on Barbie that he got his percentage, but every patent issued by that company was in his name.

According to a number of Ryan colleagues, the amount of his royalty was a whopping 1.5 percent, soon generating him sometimes more than $1 million a year, which he spent as fast as it came in on his high living style.

"The Handlers did some crazy things in the early days involving Jack because they thought he walked on water, and they were scared to

death of a competitor getting a contract with him, so they were ridic-
ulously generous in the deal they struck with Jack, who was excellent
at selling himself," observes Denis V. Bosley, a former Mattel engineer
and vice president, who was recruited by Ryan in London.

"The Handlers were still bootstrapping it when suddenly along
comes this Raytheon engineer who's obviously brilliant, who says,
'I know you can't afford my salary, so I'll be generous; just pay me
a small percentage,'" adds Fred Adickes, who was hired at Mattel by
Ryan and remained a lifelong friend and colleague.

But Adickes doesn't think that Ryan hoodwinked the very shrewd
Handlers, who had never gone much beyond high school, but were
self-taught, street-smart businesspeople. "It wasn't a conning, one way
or the other," he says.

> It was just simple math. The Handlers knew their pricing
> structure could absorb 1.5 percent without any problem. And
> if Jack gave them a truly interesting product they would get
> quite a boost in the marketplace, so they were basically hir-
> ing his technology for a bargain, and from Jack's standpoint he
> knew what he could do. He knew his potential, and was bet-
> ting on that, and Ruth and Elliot were just very content with
> their simple math and simple accounting. It was a good deal
> on both sides.

> His agreement called for him to give his services and creativity
> in exchange for the royalty, yet he was in charge of all the crea-
> tive people at Mattel, so there was a blur as to who did what.

While Ryan was acting as a vice president of R&D, he was neither an officer, nor an employee, but rather an independent contractor,
essentially a full-time consultant, which allowed him much freedom.
This also alienated the Handlers as time passed, because Ryan liked to
play as much as he liked to create.

Although he wasn't an official employee, Ryan considered himself
to be "a third of Mattel"—*Ruth, Elliot, and Jack* was the way he saw it.
"I invented the products and they sold them." And he made it quite
clear in public: "I designed the Barbie doll—if that's any claim to fame,
but at least it shows some kind of interest in art, or in women."

■ ■ ■

When the Handlers returned to Mattel headquarters from Europe with the Lilli doll, they began serious discussions with Ryan about how to proceed in terms of design and manufacturing.

One decision, though, already was made. Ruth claimed in *Dream Doll* that Barbie was named after her daughter, Barbara. But Ryan intimates contend that Barbie was named after both Barbara Handler *and* Barbara Ryan, the latter at Jack's insistence. Over the years, however, Barbara Handler Segal, a divorcee, has claimed the title, even making a guest appearance in 2007 on *Oprah*, billed as the real-life Barbie, and giving press interviews, though she was often embarrassed when compared to the doll, especially when she was a teenager. At least one other Ryan family name had been attached to another popular Mattel doll, Baby First Step, a walking doll powered by batteries. During the development stage involving Ryan, it was called the "Diana Project," named after Ryan's youngest daughter.

"One of the first things I heard from Ruth Handler was that she did a lot of sales traveling and out of guilt brought home the most expensive doll she could buy [for Barbara] at FAO Schwartz, in New York," Ryan confided years later at an Invention Convention gathering.

They [the Handlers] spoke a lot of Yiddish, so I picked up a lot of their Yiddish expressions. She used to say things about her children like, "That cockamamie kid is potchking around with paper dolls." So I said, "Well, Ruth, we have these market research psychologists that work for me now. They really go into depth about what motivates children and why they're doing what they're doing."

So I said, "Why don't I go home with you and I'll just watch the kids and talk to them." So I did and I went there and she and the neighbor girl were busy playing with paper dolls just like the mother predicted—cheap paper dolls, and I said to them, "Gee, you're having a lot of fun, but what about those beautiful dolls up on the shelf there. They're very expensive." And Barbara said, "The dresses are pretty but when you take the clothes off, they've got dopey figures."

So I looked at the paper dolls they were cutting out, and they were more voluptuous than any drawing in the popular magazines of the time. *Esquire* had the drawings of a man named [George] Petty, and a man named [Alberto] Vargas, both of whom had a different vision of the feminine figure, but they both were quite beautiful.

These little girls were saying they wanted a doll that didn't have a dopey figure. They were very aware of those things. . . . If a child wanted to be something and identify with something and project from there we provided all the tools—starting with a beautiful body. The kid wanted a beautiful body, so we gave her a beautiful body, and we gave her all the tools to act out and practice what she wanted to do.

Ryan and the Handlers agreed that the Lilli doll would be used as the model for Barbie. Ryan would oversee a creative team and implement it all—from her engineering to her makeover to her manufacturing.

With his education and missile background, Ryan brought rare expertise to the project, and instituted ideas that had an enormous impact on the toy industry as a whole. "Jack brought real scientific vigor to how you design, develop, manufacture, and market toys," observes Roger Coyro, a longtime business associate and confidante, who would play a key role when the Father of Barbie and Mattel's relationship went south.

Jack transformed the toy industry by bringing scientific standards and new materials and processes to manufacture products that hadn't been done before. The Handlers wouldn't have had the knowledge or the inclination to pursue that. Jack brought real analysis—cost analysis—to how a toy's manufactured. He developed formulas for how many you had to sell to break even, the manufacturing time, the material cost. He was one of the first guys to take products overseas for manufacturing.

■ ■ ■

Years before, Mattel did the bulk of its manufacturing business in China (which would result in the company's global image–tarnishing toy recall scandal of 2007), the Handlers and Ryan decided to outsource the production of Barbie to Japan in 1956. "We couldn't make it in the United States because the labor costs were too high," explains Elliot Handler in a 2008 interview with the author. "We wanted to make a three-dollar doll. If we made it here, it would have cost seven or eight dollars, and it wouldn't have been successful because no one would have paid that much. It's the same reason Mattel goes to China today."

Three dollars was the cost of the doll alone. The Handlers and Ryan decided that there would be many outfits and accessories to follow—just like Barbara Handler's cutout dolls had. It was a shrewd business plan.

As Marvin Barab observes, "It's the Gillette razor approach. Give away the razor and sell the blades."

In *Dream Doll*, Ruth Handler wrote: "I handed Ryan the Lilli doll and said, 'Jack while you're over there [Japan], see if you can find someone who could make a doll of this approximate size. We'll sculpt our own face and body and design a line of clothes and accessories, but see if you can find a manufacturer.'"

Ryan found a company called Kokosai Boeki, and he had the help of a small dream team in preparing Barbie for her debut into society. There was one-time Seventh Avenue fashionista Charlotte Johnson, who for years would oversee design of the dolls' endless wardrobe— she even designed some of the fashions in her own personal style. For the doll's face, Ryan enlisted veteran Universal Studios makeup artist Bud Westmore, who was under strict orders to make her look like an American teenage fashion model. Because Lilli was a bit too anatomically correct for the U.S. market, Ryan personally handled the breasts, since he was such an expert. "I filed the nipples off the mold," he later acknowledged.

■ ■ ■

What Ruth Handler didn't reveal in her autobiography was that they had ignored one very important step in the process of bringing the Barbie doll to market. Mattel, playing fast and loose, never bothered to secure licensing permission from Greiner & Hausser GmbH, the manufacturer of Bild-Lilli, to remake her into Barbie. This would lead to court battles in the United States and Germany, beginning in the early 1960s and going into the twenty-first century. For years, Mattel kept Lilli, Barbie's one-and-only ancestor, under tight wraps.

Along with his market research duties, Marvin Barab was in charge of the archives of Mattel's design projects. One afternoon, while taking inventory, he discovered a doll hidden in a box that closely resembled Barbie, but was dated much earlier than Mattel's.

> I was kind of shocked looking at it, so I marched into Jack's office. I said, "Jack, look." He said, "Yeah." I said, "Look at the date on it, Jack." He said, "Yeah." I said, "Well, what does it mean?" And he stared at me and said, "Plagiarize, plagiarize, that's how God made your eyes. Now put it back, and I don't ever want to hear you mention that doll again."

> As I interpreted it, he was saying, "Yes, that's the origin of Barbie." He was admitting that Barbie was copied off of that doll. It was not known at the time, and for a number of years in the future, that Barbie was based on Lilli, or was the reincarnation of Lilli.

"Ruth is the one who came up with the basic concept and adopted it when she first saw the Lilli doll," he believes. What he did know for certain was that "she *didn't* invent it."

> Ruth was no engineer and never tried to be. She did not have the capability of carrying the engineering and design through to the level that Jack did, and as quickly as Jack did. Jack took it and brought it into a state to be turned over ready for production.

> But in the process of producing Barbie, neither one of them gave it a thought that maybe they should buy the rights to Lilli, or even that it was necessary to buy the rights.

■ ■ ■

By 1960, a year after Barbie's introduction at the toy fair, she was minting gold for Mattel. The Handlers couldn't keep up with the incredible demand.

"To get Barbie, you had to have influence because there was such a shortage," recalls Jay Horowitz, owner of American Classic Toys, and the third generation in the toy business. "I was 13 and working in my father's toy store in Great Neck on Long Island. He was also a wholesaler, so he may have received 3,000 pieces from Mattel. Then he would say, who are my best customers, and he would assign—he gets three dozen, he gets two dozen. At the store, people came off the street all day long—'Do you have Barbie?' 'No, no; sorry, we don't have it.' But if a good customer came in and bought something, we'd say, 'I have a Barbie for you.' When Barbie came in I put it on the shelf and it was gone in five minutes. It was insane."

Kokusai Boeki, the chosen factory in the Land of the Rising Sun, was soon stamping out more than 100,000 dolls a week—peanuts compared to what would happen in the future, when Mattel would claim *one billion* sold. A headline in the *Saturday Evening Post* declared, "Barbie Is a Million-Dollar Doll." Barbie fan clubs were started. According to a Hollywood columnist, Barbie was getting more fan mail than Elizabeth Taylor and Audrey Hepburn *combined*.

Seemingly unaware of all this action, or rather because of it, Rolf Hausser, managing director of Greiner & Hausser, which manufactured the Lilli doll in Germany, received a patent in the United States for the doll hip joint used in Lilli, which had moveable legs and arms, and a head that could be turned to the side.

More competitively, Hausser made an exclusive licensing deal with a major Mattel rival, the very aggressive New York City toy producer, Louis Marx, who had a reputation for knocking off products by Mattel. "He was the big bully on the block," maintains Fred Adickes. "He'd go to a toy fair, see what was there, and he'd knock it off quickly." Adickes had it happen to him. He had designed a low-slung, quality three-wheeler for Mattel, but it bombed because Marx quickly turned out a cheap, blow-molded plastic version. He called it Big Wheels, which became a classic, and virtually overnight made a bundle, underscoring his credo: "Give the customer more for less money."

Envying Mattel's big score with Barbie, Louis Marx, hailed in a 1955 *Time* magazine cover story as "The Toy King," secured from Hausser the rights to license Lilli, and introduced her with some minor touches to the American market as the Miss Seventeen doll—one of

Barbie's first competitors for the hearts and minds of the free world's little girls, and for their parents' pocketbooks. A taller, less attractive Barbie knockoff, the doll did use the Bild-Lilli head mold, which was manufactured in Hong Kong.

The first salvo in what would become Mattel's Teutonic War had been fired.

■ ■ ■

On March 24, 1961, two years after Barbie's introduction, as the Handlers and Ryan were reaping the profits, G&H and a gloating Louis Marx quietly sued Mattel in federal court in California, alleging that the House of Barbie had infringed on G&H's patent for Bild-Lilli's hip joint, and further claimed that Barbie was "a direct take-off and copy of" Bild-Lilli. Moreover, they charged that Mattel "falsely and misleadingly represented itself as having originated the design," according to court records.

Mattel denied the infringement, claiming the G&H patent was invalid, or if valid was not infringed by Mattel. And in a counterclaim, Mattel accused G&H and Marx of "unfair competition" and alleged a "campaign of harassment of [Mattel's] customers and potential customers." With incredible chutzpah, Mattel even claimed that the inspiration for Barbie came from a wooden doll dating back to 19th century Vermont—based on research by Jack Ryan's brother, Jim, who also was a Mattel executive.

Marx claimed Mattel had copied the "form, posture, facial expressions" and appearance of Lilli, "perpetrating a hoax upon the public." Mattel shot back, alleging that Marx's Miss Seventeen was "an inferior doll . . . of confusingly similar appearance" to Barbie, and even brought the Father of Barbie into the case by alleging Marx had made a knockoff of a cap gun mechanism Jack Ryan had devised.

The case, which received little, if any, press attention at the time, sat idle for more than a year when, on March 4, 1963, both sides suddenly agreed to stop fighting, and the case was dismissed.

But that was far from the end of Hausser's claims against Mattel. All appeared peaceful in 1964, when a curious deal was struck between Mattel and G&H.

For the small sum of 85,000 deutsche marks, which translated into just $21,600—in three lump-sum payments, no less—Mattel bought G&H's Bild-Lilli copyright and its German and U.S. patent rights. And for another 15,000 deutsche marks, or $3,800, G&H gave Mattel the rights to Marx's marketing territories when its license expired in 1970. (In 1972, Marx Toys was sold to Quaker Oats and subsequently went out of business.) Aside from what appeared to be a giveaway to Mattel, G&H, represented in the negotiations by managing director Rolf Hausser, agreed not to produce any dolls similar to Barbie or Bild-Lilli, or to produce or sell any doll with the names Bild-Lilli, Lilli, or Barbie. Mattel affirmed it would not use the names Lilli, or Bild-Lilli. And why would it? Barbie already was its star.

While Mattel continued generating enormous profits from Barbie, G&H floundered. In 1983, bankruptcy proceedings were initiated, and the firm was essentially out of business two years later.

But in May 2001, in Germany, Rolf Hausser's wife, acting as the court-appointed liquidator for G&H, took new legal action against Mattel. The lawsuit alleged that fraud was involved in the 1964 agreements. G&H claimed it "had been induced to accept a flat fee for the 1964 licenses based on material misrepresentations by Mattel regarding the number of Barbie dolls it was selling in Germany and internationally," according to court records. "G&H asserted that it would have insisted on a per doll royalty had it known the actual volume of Barbie sales."

G&H asked the German court to declare the 1964 agreements nonbinding, and sought damages "based on an appropriate royalty for every Barbie doll sold by Mattel since 1964," which would amount to hundreds of millions of dollars or more.

Germany has always seemed to play a pivotal role in the genealogy of Barbie. One of Mattel's first forays into the international market was in Bild-Lilli's homeland in the early 1960s, through the licensing of distributorships. "We found out the things we were doing were wrong," Ruth Handler told the *Los Angeles Times*. "Then we set up to penetrate the markets in a more businesslike way." For instance, Mattel purchased a small, vacant doll factory in the West German town of Barbenhausen, and nicknamed it "Barbiehausen."

In response to the latest G&H lawsuit, Mattel initiated its own action against the company, Rolf Hausser, and his wife, Margarethe-Lilly Hausser. Mattel stated in federal court in Los Angeles that the

1963 dismissal of the lawsuits and the 1964 G&H licensing agreements protected the company, and it asked for injunctive relief barring the German action, as well as a preliminary injunction to keep the Germans from moving forward with the lawsuit in the Fatherland.

Mattel's motion for the preliminary injunction was denied, and its entire lawsuit was soon dismissed. Mattel appealed. In late 2003, the 9th U.S. Circuit Court of Appeals in San Francisco affirmed the denial of the preliminary injunction, but disagreed with the entire dismissal, reinstated Mattel's lawsuit, and remanded the case for further proceedings without ruling on the merits.

Meanwhile, a court in Germany dismissed G&H's case "with prejudice" citing statute of limitations, and because the company had been liquidated. G&H appealed the decision.

In the U.S. appeals court's written opinion, it was noted that "Barbie, the ubiquitous doll produced by Mattel, has been a regular visitor to our court. . . . Today Barbie generates over $2 billion in wholesale revenues each year, a sum which helps to explain why Barbie comes to visit us so frequently. It presumably also helps to explain why a lawsuit was filed in Germany in May 2001 by G&H, claiming that it had been defrauded by Mattel. . . ."

Asked in 2008 whether Barbie was a knockoff of the much-disputed and much-litigated Bild-Lilli doll, Mattel co-founder Elliot Handler admitted to the author, "Well, you might call it that, yes. Ruth wanted to adapt the same body as the Lilli doll with some modifications. Changes were made, improvements were made. Ruth wanted her own look [for the doll.] And Jack Ryan put it all together."

Former Mattel executives and designers assert that Hot Wheels also was a knockoff of sorts. "On a trip to Europe, the Handlers brought back a few Matchbox cars," according to former Mattel engineer Janos Beny. "Elliot told Ryan that he would like to get in that same business, and Jack told us guys to start coming up with some schtick that would make ours special."

Hot Wheels became one of Mattel's biggest-selling and most iconic brands next to Barbie. In 2008, Hot Wheels celebrated its 40th year, with Mattel boasting that more than 15 million boys ages 5 through 15 were "avid collectors," with the average boy collector owning more than 41 of the little cars.

# Chapter 4

# Putting the "Matt" in Mattel, and How the Toymaker Became a Hotbed of Aggressive Hotheads

Unlike Jack Ryan's classy albeit strange and lonely upbringing, and his Ivy League education, the founders of Mattel came from a completely different world.

While the Ryans were part of upscale Yonkers society, the Handler and the Moscowicz tribes were struggling for survival, like so many of the tired, poor, huddled masses who had come from all over Europe via Ellis Island in the early 1900s. As happened with many ethnic groups whose surnames were Greek to harried U.S. immigration clerks, Moscowicz was shortened to Mosco.

Like Jack Ryan, Ruth Mosco was a Scorpio, born on November 4, 1916, the last of her mother Ida's brood of 10, who last gave birth when she was 40. Unlike Ryan's sophisticated mother, however, Ida Mosco was an illiterate Polish peasant, a baby-making machine.

It was from Ruth's street-smart, hustler father, Jacob, that she inherited her shrewd business sense, her intense entrepreneurial drive, and her love of gambling. The Polish patriarch had been a foot soldier in the Russian army, and had gone over the hill, most likely to escape gambling debts, according to Mosco family lore. The "Mother of Barbie" later acknowledged that she had a proclivity for rolling the dice and maintaining a poker face, which no doubt accounts for a good part of Mattel's early winning streak.

While many eastern-European Jewish immigrants found themselves living in the crowded tenements of New York's Lower East Side, the Moscos fortuitously landed in the West—Denver, probably because Jacob fibbed to immigration that he was a blacksmith, a trade needed for the dozens of rail lines carrying gold and silver ore from the Rockies into the Mile High City's smelters. Ida and her six children (four would be born in the United States) had been left behind in Warsaw; she arrived in steerage with her babies a year after her husband. They spoke only Yiddish at home, and Ida remained illiterate until her death. In their early years in America, the family had little money, made worse by the patriarch's gambling addiction, according to Ruth's account in *Dream Doll*.

Because her mother was in poor health, Ruth was raised from the age of six months by an older sister, Sarah, and her new husband, Louie Greenwald. Ruth considered Sarah, a 3rd-grade school dropout but shrewd and street-smart, the "greatest influence on the woman I was to become." In *Dream Doll*, Ruth pooh-poohed the possibility that her mother's "supposed rejection" triggered her lifelong need to "prove herself."

The Moscos had a knack for making a buck. With little or no education, they had the ability to start what became successful businesses. Ruth, of course, would co-found the biggest and most famous. But her father did well, too, building custom bodies for trucks, which provided jobs for five of her brothers. Liquor stores, pharmacies, food markets, used-car lots—those were the kind of businesses the Moscos got into and did well with, although one brother practiced law, an ambition that Ruth had for a time.

Driven to make money and by a fear of losing it all, an immigrant mentality that stayed with her throughout her life, Ruth was holding down an after-school job as early as the age of 10 in the drugstore that Sarah and Louie owned at the time.

"I preferred working over playing with other kids," she stated. She was a loner who never had a close friendship; the future Mother of Barbie was a tomboy who considered girltalk "stupid." For the woman who has taken credit for conceiving the most feminine and sexualized doll ever, she admitted, "I didn't like dolls and never played with them." Always tough and business-minded, she considered women weak. It wasn't until the age of 40, she stated, that she began "to truly appreciate and enjoy female companionship."

Ruth was a cute brunette of 16 when she discovered her first and last real-life dream doll—17-year-old Isadore (Izzy) Elliot Handler, whom she said she met while he and his chums were searching for a crap game on Denver's West Side—shades of her father. As a roll of the dice would have it, one of her brothers had a game going at the Mosco homestead.

Years later, Elliot, the son of a house painter, recalls the romantic scene of their meeting somewhat differently. "It was at one of those Jewish charitable affairs where they did dancing and stuff, a social thing. One of my friends knew her, and we started dancing, and we didn't stop."

Like Barbie and Ken, it was "love at first sight," Elliot acknowledges years later in an interview with the author. "I was attracted to everything about her—the face, the body, the style. She was real cute, kind of a roundish, cute face, and dark hair. Everything worked. We just hit it off and kept going together."

One of America's great mergers—romantic and corporate—was in the cards.

■ ■ ■

With the assistance of a social service agency called the Jewish Consumptive Relief Society, Elliot Handler's family landed in Denver from Chicago after emigrating from the Ukraine. During America's great flu epidemic of 1918, which ravaged the country, Elliot's father, Sam, had gotten ill and contracted tuberculosis. "I was like three years old. It was just one of those things and quite a few Jewish families came to Denver because of that epidemic," recalls Handler, who was one of four in his mother Frieda's brood.

When he met the Mosco girl, the Handler boy was a senior in high school, with artistic talent and ambitions of becoming an artist. A kid with a creative bent, he already had a part-time job working for a small lighting fixture company. "They needed somebody to do some detail work—graphics and detail construction work."

Ruth and Elliot began going steady in 1932, around the same time that future competitor Louis Marx was operating a Pennsylvania toy factory known as "The Monkey Works," nicknamed for a Depression-era metal plaything called the Climbing Monkey.

Theirs was not a love match made in Heaven, at least in the eyes of Ruth's parents. "My family lived on the West Side and her family lived on the East Side, which was more upscale. Her family had businesses. My father made a little money. So the families were in two different worlds," says Elliot. "There really was no connection between them in any way. Even later, the parents weren't close, other than the children."

It only got worse when Elliot and Ruth started dating seriously, because the Mosco family had visions of Ruth marrying well—maybe even a doctor. Says Elliot, "They thought I was a poor schlep."

But Ruth had a different view. In *Dream Doll*, she noted, "None of the other guys I dated came close to sparking the feelings in me that Izzy did."

The summer she was 19, the young lovers had a heated argument. To spite him, she and a girlfriend took off for Hollywood, where a Mosco family acquaintance worked as a secretary at Paramount Pictures. Ruth was hooked by the glamour and almost immediately snagged a job as a studio stenographer, which offered lots of overtime. Years later, showing off her Mattel corporate acumen in *Dream Doll*, she noted, "[T]he emerging businesswoman in me was appalled at the waste of money and poor management this represented."

The Moscos were overjoyed that Ruth had put distance between herself and the Handler boy, praying their romance was over. Maybe in Hollywood, working at Paramount, she'd meet and marry a rich producer, which was even better than a doctor, or even a lawyer.

"But I went to Los Angeles and we were together for quite a while," says Elliot. "But then her family insisted that Ruth come back home because we were getting too close—and I was a poor artist, and what was she going to do with a poor artist?"

Over her parents' objections, Ruth became Mrs. Elliot Handler on June 26, 1938. By then, the Mosco family was in the money—the wedding was at Denver's fancy-schmancy Park Lane Hotel, and the bride's wedding gift from her siblings was a new car, a Chevy coupe, which the newlyweds drove back to L.A., where they would make their home and start a little business of their own.

■ ■ ■

On the Sears & Roebuck installment plan, the Handlers purchased power tools that Elliot, then taking part-time courses at L.A.'s Art Center College of Design, needed to fashion decorative tchotchkes out of a new form of plastic called Plexiglas, which was being used in the wartime defense industry. He began turning out the accessories in a garage the Handlers shared with a neighbor, who soon complained about the mess he was making.

Forced out, but knowing they were onto something, the young entrepreneurs rented inexpensive space in a former Chinese laundry. They also brought in a partner, an older, easygoing chap by the name of Harold "Matt" Matson, a shop foreman and craftsman, to help with the manufacturing. Before long, Ruth, a five-foot-two dynamo, was making sales calls, successfully hawking what Elliot and Matson were making. The first time out, she later boasted, she got a $500 order.

For a time, the Handlers and Matson were involved in a relatively successful costume jewelry business with a pushy Russian immigrant jeweler and his abrasive investors. During that period, Ruth became a mother, giving birth to Barbara in May 1941, seven months before Pearl Harbor, and Kenneth (for whom the Ken doll was later named) in March 1944, when the allies began bombing Berlin. By then, Elliot and Matt were fed up with their Russian partners, and decided to make a go of it on their own again, producing plastic picture frames— Elliot designing, Matson making them in his garage, and Ruth selling them. Her first sale was for $3,000. When plastic was banned during the war effort, the team made the frames out of inferior wood, the defects hidden with decorative flocking.

Nevertheless, Ruth's next sale to the same customer was for $6,000. To celebrate, the Handlers and Matson decided to formalize their partnership, to make a real business and give it a name. Needing a catchy moniker, they combined Matt's name with Elliot's.

They called their little company "Mattel."

Mattel's first venture in the toy business was making dollhouse furniture from picture frame plastic and wood leftovers. Toward the end of the war, Elliot was drafted, but that didn't stop Mattel's production. With his Army basic training at a camp near Los Angeles, Private Handler spent weekend leaves working on new toy ideas and helping Matson with the doll furniture, which had started selling briskly on consignment. Before long, with Ruth running the business end, they had sales reps on both coasts, and soon in the Midwest and Southeast.

In 1945, Mattel's first full year in business, the company turned a healthy profit of $30,000 on $100,000 in dollhouse furniture sales.

Incorporated in California 1948 and reincorporated in Delaware in 1968, Mattel had its first best annual sales of about $6 million on a hugely popular item called the "Uke-A-Doodle," a $1.49 plastic ukelele, of which more than 10 million were sold thanks in part to radio and TV personality Arthur Godfrey, who had revived the ukelele's popularity by strumming it on the air. That was followed by a plastic piano, the first with raised black keys, which quickly sold more than half-a-million units. More musical toys came off the Mattel assembly line—the "Cowboy Ge-Tar," the "Musical Merry-Go-Round," the "Jack-in-the Box," all thanks to an inventor who approached the

Handlers with a cheap, simple, rubber-band version of the complex and expensive Swiss music box mechanism.

The Handlers and Mattel thrived.

Ruth loved the adrenalin rush of doing business in the high-pressure postwar toy world; she savored the hustle, the pitch, and especially the sale. Elliot, the artist, was just happy to put his ideas and design talents to work, and see the money begin to roll in.

But Matson, the second half of what had become a lucrative partnership, was a different story. Older than the Handlers, married, with children to support and a mortgage to pay, he was a gentle, talented, hardworking, decent guy—someone Ruth would likely call a *mensch*—who was nowhere near as aggressive or hungry for riches and power as his colleagues.

"He invested about ten thousand dollars, which was his life savings at the time," the aging Elliot Handler told the author in 2007. "As time went on, he got pretty nervous about the business and said he'd like to get his money back, so we bought him out. He asked if he could make some of the things we used to make like the picture frames and jewelry and I said by all means go ahead. I have no problem with that."

In *Dream Doll*, Ruth painted a schmaltzy scene of finding Matson "hunched over his desk, his head buried in his arms. . . . He looked up at us with miserable eyes. 'I can't take this pressure-cooker business anymore,'" she quoted him as saying. "Elliot and I felt sorry for him," Ruth asserted, so they made him an offer the poor guy couldn't resist.

The Handlers arranged for Ruth's sister, Sarah, and her husband, liquor store owner Louie Greenwald—both savvy investors, to buy Matson's end of the business for what must have been a relative song. Unlike Matson, the Greenwalds had confidence in the Handlers' vision and "were excited about Mattel's future." At the time, the deal put the ever-increasingly valuable Mattel firmly in the hands of Handler and Mosco family members.

Matson and his family surely must have watched with envy as Mattel grew into the biggest and most successful toy company in the world, worth hundreds of millions of dollars in stock to the Handlers at one point.

Asked by the author if he thought Matson's decision to cash-out at Mattel's beginnings some six decades earlier might have been a great disappointment to him, Elliot Handler says, "Oh, I'm sure it was. But I don't know why it's worth zeroing in on what happened with him because it was a very minor little thing in the history of the business."

As Ruth put it in *Dream Doll*, "We never heard from Matt again."

■ ■ ■

With Matt Matson out of the picture, Jack Ryan became the Handlers' go-to guy and principal collaborator.

As vice president of Research & Design (R&D), "Jack had autonomy to run the department how he wanted to and that was magic," notes former veteran Mattel engineer, designer, and inventor Derek Gable.

But Ryan's genius and expertise meant much more to Mattel than just toy ideas and design. Because of his education and experience, the Handlers gave him free reign to establish the R&D corporate culture. On his own, he created a first in the toy industry—a think tank known as Preliminary Design, considered to be Mattel's most important department, where all future toy products were hatched.

"Jack also created Mattel's acoustics department [headed by his brother, Jim], the chemistry lab, all the various departments that he created in order to produce the very best toys in the world," notes Janos Beny. "The Handlers created Mattel, but Jack Ryan made it big for them."

His role involved everything at Mattel from security to recruitment to testing children.

As Fred Adickes, one of Hot Wheels' key developers under Ryan, observes, "To Ruth and Elliot, Jack was the hero who came from Raytheon. The Handlers had no corporate background. They had never really worked for other companies. They never worked particularly as employees, but they had a great intuitive drive. They needed someone with Jack's brilliance to get the company jumpin' and bumpin.'"

Secrecy was a high priority. Mattel needed to protect its ideas in an industry where industrial espionage was a way of life. The toy business, as the *New York Times* once noted, is "one of the world's most secretive and fiendishly competitive industries."

Under Ryan, who had been schooled in security at Raytheon, an impenetrable wall was established around Mattel's Research & Development department, with the assistance of Jack's sibling mentor, Jim Ryan, a brilliant engineer who had also become a key player at Mattel as head of the recording-acoustics laboratory, from whence the doll voices emanated. Jim had served in Army intelligence and, according to a close colleague, had ties to the Central Intelligence Agency and therefore was skilled in the ways of espionage.

There was only one way in and one way out of R&D, and that checkpoint was guarded 24 hours a day, seven days a week by a uniformed, armed security guard. R&D employees—the designers, engineers, model makers, assistants, and secretaries who reported to Ryan—were required to show a coded, numbered badge, and had to go through a turnstile to gain entrance. For others, a warning sign at the guard station read: YOU MUST BE SIGNED IN AT THE R&D TURNSTILE & ESCORTED BY AN R&D EMPLOYEE FOR ENTRANCE INTO THE MODEL SHOP WITH A STRIPED BADGE. Virtually every nook and cranny of Mattel was constantly being checked for electronic bugging by the enemy; shredders took care of confidential documents and plans, and prototypes and models were crushed into dust to keep them from falling into the hands of the competition.

"We were literally locked up," says Derek Gable, who had worked in the aerospace industry in Great Britain. "Security at Mattel was tighter than aerospace. Industrial espionage was very serious. The money that could be lost by any of our ideas getting out was very significant. We were sworn to secrecy. We weren't even supposed to talk to our families about what we were working on. It was very hush-hush."

The Father of Barbie's involvement went far beyond keeping the secrets safe. Intensely interested in the psychology of marketing—how children play with a toy and why—Jack Ryan established the use of testing rooms with one-way mirrors so he and his designers could surreptitiously watch youngsters at play, especially girls with dolls. He soon learned that "the first thing they almost invariably do is to undress the doll. It's a fact of life, like gravity. Sometimes they'll feed it. When they get bored they put it to bed, like parents. There's another division of play where they're imagining something they want to do—if there's even a toothpick there, they'll put it in the doll's hand and pretend she's leading a band, or she's an orchestra leader."

Ryan worked closely with Elliot Handler on the selections from the 2,000 toy ideas submitted annually by amateur inventors. One that really impressed Ryan, and one that showed he wasn't always right, was a very special ball that could bounce higher than anything like it on the market. "I brought Elliot the Super Ball and I bounced it for him," recalled Ryan some years later, "and I was so excited, and I said, 'This guy has this terrific ball. Look at that thing bounce!' And Elliot looked at it and he said simply, 'They'll get lost.'" There was no doubt—Elliot Handler had a good take on what was and wasn't marketable.

■ ■ ■

From around the world Jack Ryan recruited the best and the brightest engineers and designers to blue sky and develop innovative, marketable, and highly profitable new toys for Mattel. But his recruiting techniques were considered bizarre, because he always combined conventional business with unconventional pleasure.

Denis Bosley, a 29-year-old chief engineer at a British company that was moving to "godforsaken Scotland," as he put it, had spotted a Mattel jobs ad offering a new life in sunny Southern California, a perk that would always draw talented people from dreary regions. He applied and was invited to appear for what he expected to be a typical job interview.

Instead, he and his wife, Loretta, a vivacious 24-year-old mother of three who had accompanied him to London from the North, found themselves part of an outrageous "Medieval" bacchanal that Jack had tossed in the Elizabethan Room of the posh Goring Hotel near Buckingham Palace—a Swinging London revel replete with buxom wenches, a roving band of colorful minstrels, vats of mead and other libations, and for the sybaritic feast, a giant roasted boar with an apple in its mouth. Seated around an enormous T-shaped table, ready to savor the sensual dinner, was a bevy of glamorous British movie stars, along with a gathering of roués, groupies, and sycophants.

"Jack Ryan, of course, sat at the head of the table and was the King, and he chose my wife as his Queen," says Bosley. It was a scene he and his mate have never forgotten, and one the couple discovered when they got to Mattel underscored the Father of Barbie's eccentric management approach and his flamboyant lifestyle.

"Jack didn't have a date, I was really cute, so he chose me as his Queen," recalls Loretta Bosley with delight, years later. "We were the royalty, and everybody thought we were husband and wife that night. When we sat down, Jack asked me to cut into the big boar's head. I looked at it, and I looked at Jack, and said, 'I can't cut into *that*,' and he said, 'You have to, nobody else can eat until you do,' and I said, 'Well, I can't,' and he said, 'Just take a sliver off his cheek.' Everybody was drunk out of their minds."

After gorging, Ryan dragged the Bosleys and a dozen other revelers to the Bag O' Nails, one of Soho's trendiest basement clubs, a hangout for rock stars and the place where Linda and Paul McCartney first met. "I'd never been to London, or to a nightclub before," says Loretta Bosley, "and here I was dancing with Jack Ryan, and I was like a green cucumber, and he probably thought it was amusing. He asked me, 'Are all English girls like you?'"

The frivolity ended at 3 A.M. Back at the hotel, Ryan assigned Mrs. Bosley to be his unofficial secretary "for the fricking morning," fielding mostly phone calls from actors and actresses who were at the party and who "wanted to meet Jack the next day because they thought he knew all the directors and could get them into something." She also had to make sure Ryan was sober enough to do what he had come to London to do—conduct recruitment interviews for Mattel.

Candidates such as Denis Bosley were required to take a battery of knowledge, personality, and psychological tests selected by Ryan, who had done research in personnel psychology at Yale and was a longtime group-therapy patient of a prominent Beverly Hills psychiatrist, Dr. Marvin Klemes, who also specialized in corporate human relations management. (When the working relationship between Ruth Handler and Ryan verged on the intolerable because of Ryan's perfectionism and Ruth Handler's push to get an idea into production, Klemes was consulted to help resolve their problems.)

The best candidates for Mattel were those who were aggressive, entrepreneurial, very bright, highly creative, somewhat eccentric and extremely confident leaders in their field. Among the tests selected by Ryan and given to potential Mattel designers and engineers was the Buss-Durkee Hostility Inventory, which measures an individual's aggression, hostility, and even guilt feelings.

"They were looking for people with the right aggressive personality," says Derek Gable.

> And everybody who worked there under Ryan had the same personal profile. Jack Ryan understood that he was basically taking a bunch of children and managing them to get the best out of them, without putting them in a rigid environment.

> Mattel was just full of these very entrepreneurial hotheads. Very, very talented people, but they really weren't made to work in a corporate structure. They were people designed to run their own businesses. So we had a whole company full of them, sort of running around making things happen, and bouncing off each other. The energy was something to none. To my mind it was those kinds of people with a sort of childlike drive and curiosity and ability to get down on their knees and make things happen that had a great deal to do with the early success of Mattel.

As a manager of people, Ryan was both admired and despised. A few, such as Marvin Barab, characterized his style as excessive, even sadistic. "Jack as a person—I don't think anybody liked," Barab asserts years later.

> He was a brilliant guy, but from a personal point of view he was a bastard. And Ruth and Elliot put up with it because they couldn't afford to do otherwise. If given their druthers, he'd have been out of there on his ass within the first year. They felt they were paying him too much, and he had that wild lifestyle. They did *not* like him as a person, but that was not what they hired him for, so they put up with him as long as they felt they had no choice and it was to their advantage.

Looking back, Barab believes that the one personality trait that Jack and Ruth shared in common were Goodyear Blimp–size egos.

"Ruth's," he observes, "was less diseased. Her obnoxiousness was in an acceptable form, and Jack's wasn't. But they both were pretty obnoxious."

Ruth Handler's unpleasant behavior often surfaced in meetings with her design and engineering underlings. "She was not a very nice person," claims Janos Beny.

> I did a lot of Jack's very preliminary models and we'd just stick them together with tape and if they broke or didn't work very well she'd shout, "What the fuck am I paying you guys for?"

> She didn't pay deference to people who really made the place move along. I was a high producer, designer, and inventor. I was intimately involved in the Hot Wheels design, but she would look right through me in meetings, and ignore me when I was making a presentation to her. Times that I had to deal with her I'd walk away feeling, what is she all about? But Elliot was different. He'd stop by and talk and see what I was doing, and listen very carefully. He treated you like somebody, unlike Ruth.

Years later, Elliot Handler says his personal philosophy in running Mattel was, "I wanted most people to be content, happy, and enjoy their work."

Ryan's "psychotic" treatment of Barab, meanwhile, stayed with him for decades. As Barab saw it, Ryan "took pleasure in making people as uncomfortable as possible."

For Barab it started at one of the many parties at The Castle. Barab and his wife were sitting by the pool when Jack suggested that they race from one end to the other. Barab hadn't brought swimming trunks, but Jack told him he didn't need them. "He says, 'You're going in the way you are.' I was in a suit. I said, 'Jack, forget it.' But the implication was, if you want to keep your job, Buddy, you're going to jump into the pool, so I jumped in the pool. What do you do if an eight-hundred-pound gorilla asks you to dance? It was his pleasure in creating discomfort for other people once he could find their weakness."

The precipitating incident that caused Barab to quit Mattel occurred at a product planning committee meeting at which he was to present superior, but less costly, packaging for Barbie—a goal set by "the powers that be—Ruth, Elliot, and Jack."

"We worked our tails off on the project because Barbie was about 75 percent of Mattel's business, and therefore got 85 percent of the attention, which it deserved," says Barab. "The Handlers were constantly looking for ways of keeping ahead of the competition, whether it be packaging, the product itself, or costuming."

Barab's team got close to the established price point, but failed to hit the number. In the middle of his presentation, with Mattel's top executives seated around the conference table, Jack stood up and lit into Barab. "You were given directions to bring it in at a certain cost, and you did not do it. You're not doing your job!"

A few days later, the embarrassed and humiliated executive turned in his resignation.

While Barab had his problems with Jack, Janos Beny notes that the Father of Barbie "only responded to people who were creative, and whoever was creative and produced was very well treated by Jack and very well regarded, too."

# Chapter 5

# Real-Life Barbie Dolls

The Father of Barbie adhered to a libertine philosophy in his personal life at The Castle and in his professional life at Mattel, where he hired young, pretty women because he believed his designers and engineers would be more creative and thrive if there were gorgeous females in view, all of which raised eyebrows with the Handlers.

"Jack would say, 'Why do you think airplanes have such pretty stewardesses? It makes people relax, takes their minds off of fear of flying.' He just felt that men are the best they can be if there's a pretty female in their midst," relates Nancy Hudson, who was a perky 29-year-old suntanned, platinum blonde divorcee who favored micro-miniskirts and high heels when she was hired to work for Ryan as a secretary.

Jack had to find women who knew how to look good all by themselves and all the time. A woman who could really type and take shorthand wasn't what he cared about. He liked somebody who was more sparky.

Mattel wanted to keep Jack happy. He operated pretty independently, so whatever arrangement worked for him was okay. The Handlers looked upon Jack as creative and inventive and a genius and they weren't going to enforce a corporate culture on him. Whoever Jack wanted to hire was fine with them.

At the same time, Ryan had enormous respect for the intelligence of women. "Women's work isn't given the proper value, and, as a result, they get angry," he espoused. "More than that, they try to become amateur men. The thinking process of women is quite different from men, and we should recognize that—and also recognize its probable superiority."

Jack adored Hudson, though she points out they were never romantically involved. They became "close buddies" during her seven-year tenure at Mattel and after, when she began helping out at The Castle, where Ryan had established his own private R&D think tank, called the Jack Ryan Group. For one of Hudson's birthdays, Jack threw a little celebration at Mattel and presented her with a three-quarter-length white mink coat. He also paid for her group-therapy sessions with his psychiatrist, Dr. Marvin Klemes, and Ryan took Hudson, Annie Constantinesco, and another beauty named Charlie on an all-expenses-paid vacation in Acapulco.

"Jack was an extremely generous man," notes Hudson.

Gwen Florea, the first Voice of Barbie, was another example of Ryan's philosophy of hiring the best and most beautiful.

She was an aspiring actress and part owner of a rowdy Santa Monica bar called the Oar House when the Father of Barbie's brother, Jim, spotted the statuesque redhead bumping and grinding barefoot to the music of "The Stripper" atop the bar—barely clad in what she later described as "hip-hugging blue jeans that are almost a G-string, and a red halter top barely covering her jiggling breasts . . . like a Barbie doll come to life." Jack came to see her in action and immediately ordered Jim, who was married and a known womanizer himself, to recruit Florea for a job in Mattel's recording studio and acoustics lab, which Jim headed.

The Ryans wanted her at Mattel not only for her looks, but because she had conceived an amazing sound system in the Oar House with a tape of eclectic music and booming sound effects, ranging from a roaring steam engine to a flushing toilet. "How much are you making?" Jim Ryan asked her. Before she could answer, he told her, "We'll double it."

Many years later, Florea clearly remembers the goggle-eyed look on the faces of Mattel's designers and engineers when she sashayed in for her first day on the job. "The guys looked at me and went—*Aha!* Look at this babe! And everybody assumed right away that I was there because the Ryans wanted to get in my pants."

■ ■ ■

On the desks of the engineers and designers in Ryan's department Barbie dolls were perched in erotic poses. "Some of the guys put black stockings and black gloves on Barbie like the *Playboy* cartoon characters," recalls Fred Adickes. "Your head would turn every time you walked by one of those things."

On Ryan's birthday, the crew would give him off-color gifts, which he sometimes savored, like the year they stuffed his office with a giant weather balloon filled with confetti and a scantily clad buxom young lady. Another year, he wasn't so happy when they gave him a one-off doll called "Pooping Polly" that had a diaper filled with a mixture that looked and smelled like diarrhea. Ryan watched in horror as the concoction made in Mattel's chemistry lab for the occasion dripped down his suit jacket.

Every so often, the designers and engineers had races with custom floats in the parking lot. The women who worked in the Barbie fashion department, for instance, entered the race with a four-poster bed on wheels into which they climbed wearing provocative nightgowns; from under the sheets they discarded intimate apparel along the course.

Nancy Hudson had been hired to assist Ryan's executive secretary, Linda Henson, a Mormon, who was in her early twenties and was the devoted and obedient mistress of the Father of Barbie. Henson had become romantically involved with Ryan when she began working at Mattel in her late teens and he was nearly twice her age.

With all of the creative types and attractive women in the personnel mix, affairs were rampant in the highly competitive culture of Mattel. "There was always stuff going on," recalls Derek Gable. "It was a little bit like the Playboy Club. The people there were all outrageously creative and outgoing." One of the many long-remembered affairs involved a married secretary in Ryan's R&D and a married R&D executive. When her husband found out, he physically assaulted the executive and was fired, and the lovers later married. To deal with the competition, stress, and sexually charged atmosphere, employees would gather after work on the beaches near the House of Barbie's Hawthorne headquarters for pot, wine, and sex parties.

Some compared the scene at Mattel to the 1970s sybaritic ethos portrayed in films like *Boogie Nights* or *Bob & Carol and Ted & Alice.*

"That's what it was like at Mattel—free love before AIDS," maintains Derek Gable. "People hooked up. It was outrageous for me coming from stuffy old England and seeing all this going on. It was a swap meet and Mattel was in the thick of it. That's why Jack was having all those parties. His tree house was full of chicks in their underwear. It was considered the thing to do. If you weren't doing it you weren't in the in-crowd. That was the feeling."

■ ■ ■

While the Father of Barbie was having his affair with Linda Henson, he was still married to his first wife, Barbara, the mother of his two children, who were still living at The Castle. It would take a scorecard to keep track of Ryan's many dalliances and four subsequent marriages. After his divorce from Barbara Ryan, his second wife was Zsa Zsa Gabor, his third was Henson, his fourth was a one-time actress named Gary Hardy Lansing, and his fifth and last was an émigré from Poland—but more on these relationships later.

Linda Henson was an extraordinary beauty, says Nancy Hudson, who became Henson's close friend and confidante and a trusted friend of Ryan's.

"She was the image of Snow White—skin as white as snow, hair as black as ebony, eyes as blue as the sky. She was taller than Jack and had a very hourglass figure."

Still, she wasn't quite perfect enough for Ryan, who had certain criteria for his women. One of them was that they have long, shapely legs like Barbie. Henson's legs were long, but not shapely enough, so Ryan decided to have them molded to suit his fantasy. "It was a *huge* issue with Jack," says Hudson. He ordered Henson to attend sessions with a trainer to the stars who gave her exercises to develop her calf muscles.

"Linda would get up early in the morning three times a week and travel over to the San Fernando Valley and do those exercises and, of course, her calves never did develop," says Hudson. "But it showed that she would do *anything* for Jack."

Eventually she would die trying to win his love.

■ ■ ■

As with designing real-looking toy dolls, the Father of Barbie had an obsession with remaking real-life women if they didn't meet his high, albeit twisted, standards. Henson wasn't the only one who came under his mesmeric influence.

Ryan introduced a friend, James Miner, who was in the geothermal energy business, to a certain girlfriend whom Ryan had had cosmetically enhanced from head to toe according to his specifications, which included facial reconstruction, breast augmentation, and vaginaplasty. At the same time, Ryan had redesigned the passenger seat of a Rolls-Royce so that it swiveled 180 degrees, specifically so he could, according to Miner, proudly exhibit his newly sculpted flesh-and-blood Barbie—all of her—to select friends riding in the backseat as he cruised through Beverly Hills.

"He acted as if he was routinely presenting a new doll design to the Handlers," asserts Miner. "It was pretty kinky."

Ryan's daughter, Diana, thought the story sounded too far-fetched and bizarre, even for her father, but she was aware that he had arranged for his compliant fifth and last wife, Magda, to have some facial surgery.

Diana Ryan adds still another twist to her father's extreme fascination with female transformation. She says that one of his "pastimes" was sitting at a Beverly Hills café closely examining the faces and bodies of glamorous female passersby. "Dad was quite a people watcher," she notes, "so he would try to guess the name of the plastic surgeon who had done work on different women who walked by. Each surgeon had sort of a signature look, and Dad got to know the look, and he would ask women, 'Was it doctor so-and-so who did your nose?' "

Jack liked the women around him to be thin, as unrealistically skinny as Barbie, so at Mattel he suggested they start taking diet pills, which became trendy, and kept the Father of Barbie happy. Svengali-like, his mantra was, "Be as thin as you can be." A famous British super-model named Twiggy had the skinny Barbie look. "It was the Twiggy era," notes Nancy Hudson. "We were all trying for that body. I took diet pills; Linda took them."

An ingredient of the pills was amphetamine, an addictive drug. "I wouldn't eat that whole day after I took one, and I kind of liked the way it made me feel—wired. I got a lot of work done," recalls Hudson. "When Jack got uncomfortable in his clothes he would take diet pills, too, to stop eating so he'd lose weight. Many, *many* people at Mattel were doing that."

Through the years, the Barbie doll has been criticized for giving young girls false expectations about their bodies, and about keeping thin. Linda Henson's tragic trajectory, directed and controlled by the Father of Barbie, underscored those views.

At Ryan's behest, Henson was popping diet pills to stay thin in order to remain his real-life Barbie, even while knowing that he was constantly cheating on her. Eventually, he married her and she became the third of his five wives. Despite their long relationship, the marriage quickly turned sour. Never satisfied with one woman, Ryan had become involved with his future fourth wife, Gary Hardy Lansing, a blonde-bombshell former actress once billed at MGM as the "new Ann-Margret." She was 22 years Ryan's junior, and had been married to the actor Robert Lansing, with whom she had a daughter. Devastated, Henson began drinking heavily, put on weight, and lost her gorgeous figure.

"I was embarrassed for her," says Nancy Hudson. "It was like you don't want to look at a wreck."

Henson sought psychiatric help from Dr. Klemes, who also had as patients Hudson and Ryan and others in his circle.

Disgusted with Henson's body, Ryan divorced her after a relatively short, roller-coaster marriage. Still desperately in love with him, and trying to win him back by losing weight, she stopped eating altogether, even stopped drinking water, became fatally anorexic, and died in her bed watching TV of an apparent heart attack. She was in her thirties.

"My Dad found her body. He was devastated," says Diana Ryan, who remembers going into Mattel as a child on Saturday mornings with her father and sitting on Henson's lap and playing with the keys on her typewriter. Nancy Hudson, Henson's friend, also was grief-stricken. "I thought, what a sad, sad thing. I always wondered how Jack felt, and whether he took any responsibility for the ruination of this beautiful woman."

■ ■ ■

Even during his early marriages, The Father of Barbie had a coterie of gorgeous "social secretaries" who arranged his busy dating schedule, planned his many parties at The Castle, acted as hostesses, or just looked beautiful and mixed with Ryan's glamorous guests, many of them Hollywood celebrities, who were enchanted by him and his home.

Annie Constantinesco was one of his secretaries, and more, while he was still married to his first wife. The multilingual Fulbright scholar, daughter of a fashion designer and a United Nations official, had met Ryan in Paris where she operated an upscale tour guide service, and he had retained her to show him around. He had arrived in the City of Light from Germany with a fraulein he had met while touring the Neuschwanstein Castle built by the so-called Fairy Tale King Ludwig II. Jack had visited the enchanted location because he was always seeking design and architectural ideas for his own castle, which he was constantly and obsessively redoing, but never finishing.

By the time Linda Henson had arrived in Paris at his request to continue his castle tour, he'd already fallen for Constantinesco.

"Jack was totally in love at first sight with me, and it was like, 'We gotta do this! You have to come to California,'" she says.

In order to be alone with her, he sent Henson off on a trip around the world, and bade *auf wiedersehen* to his German conquest. Before heading back to Mattel and his wife and two daughters, he gave Constantinesco a one-way, first-class airline ticket to Los Angeles. "Jack really knew how to do it up right," she observes. "He wooed me and offered me a job, a chance to stay on his estate, and a car." It was too good of an offer to refuse, since she'd recently been divorced and was looking for a new life.

On her arrival at The Castle, where Ryan's first wife and children were still in residence, Constantinesco "became his right arm. I was involved with every aspect of his life. He kept saying I was *the* woman in his life. But there were many."

Gun Sundberg, the glamorous Swedish beauty-pageant winner, who was a veteran Ryan social secretary when Constantinesco joined the stable, sometimes accompanied him to parties in his obsessive quest for more playmates.

"I learned his patterns in life," she says. "When we would go out, I could guess whom he would like. If he saw a woman who was very provocative and had a great body he would say to me, 'What do you think?' And I'd say, 'We can get to know her, and then you can see if you like her.' I would introduce myself, and say, 'I work for Jack Ryan. Would you like to come up to the house? We're having a little cocktail party.' We got to know an awful lot of women in Hollywood, and a lot of women wanted to go out with him. There was a certain mystique about Jack. He took them to the best places and he knew everybody."

Sundberg continues,

Barbie was Jack's fantasy woman because we always looked for that type in Hollywood. There were a few around—long legs, tiny waist, big boobs, and fluffy hair. They just came and went. Jack was a perpetual hunter. He got to know one woman but that manic quality in his personality never left him happy for too long. He had to go on to the next one. He would date many women at the same time. On occasion, they came to the same party—women who thought they were exclusive with him, and he would get a little chuckle out of their jealousy. It was a *game* to him.

Not long after Ryan bought The Castle with his enormous royalty payments from Mattel and began transforming it into his own version of a combination of San Simeon and the Playboy Mansion, he and Barbara Ryan separated. She was disgusted by his hedonistic lifestyle, sickened by his many women, and revolted by the constant round of parties, both wild and tame.

"Barbara was very East Coast, very reserved, very dignified, very classy, and withdrawn," observes Constantinesco. "She did not want to be exposed to any of Jack's shenanigans. She did not like what was going on at The Castle—all those UCLA students running around, all those parties. She was the exact opposite of Jack—a loner. She was very private. Jack told me that she would lock herself in the bathroom for hours to escape. She hated the whole thing."

Rather than see Barbara and his daughters move out during their so-called separation, Ryan reconfigured The Castle so that she and the girls had their own living quarters, which were off limits to all of the merrymakers; a sign outside her part of the house read, PRIVATE— Do Not Enter. Ryan also installed a one-way door between his suite of rooms and what was called the "family side," which allowed him to visit them, but kept his decidedly decadent side virtually impenetrable. In order to feed his private demon of loneliness, Ryan also had installed his parents in a suite of rooms of their own, and his father helped supervise the unending castle renovations.

"My dad needed constant activity around him, and in that way he and my mother were so different," observes Diana Ryan, years later. "My mother coped mostly by creating a smaller, quieter life for herself within that environment [of The Castle]." Diana Ryan says as a child she never questioned the family's curious way of living, and claims she was unaware of her father's promiscuity because "when you're a child, it's just the way it is. It was just the way we lived. When you're growing up what you see in front of you is normal and you don't know anything else. I missed some family closeness."

Ryan waited until after his Catholic father died in 1971 to begin divorce proceedings with Barbara. They reached a no-fault settlement under which he bought her a house in Bel-Air and a Volvo, and gave her money for a vacation place on Cape Cod.

■ ■ ■

Notwithstanding all of the beautiful and intelligent women in his life, Jack's sexual compulsion drove him to prostitutes, ranging from high-class

call girls to streetwalkers. At Mattel, Nancy Hudson recalls Jack getting calls from a madam. When he got off the phone with her, he'd tell
Hudson, "She's got a woman for me."

He also became involved with a waiflike young prostitute whom
he had met at a party. "She was very needy, like an urchin, very thin and
childlike, and he sort of adopted her," says Hudson. "She was a hooker,
but she wasn't flamboyant. She didn't wear makeup and she had big
eyes and looked like something a man like Jack might want to adopt."

The Father of Barbie somehow rationalized that he was the only
man in her life—until he was diagnosed with a sexually transmitted
disease, gonorrhea.

"He was so angry that he wanted to see if she was with other men,"
says Hudson. "Somehow when he was at her house he found her diary
with codes in it about other men, and information about him. He told
me it was the first time he ever caught anything. He must have learned
some kind of lesson."

■ ■ ■

Back at Mattel, the Handlers, a close-knit, very private and conservative Jewish family, were infuriated with the father of Barbie's wild lifestyle. Practically every week Ruth Handler saw another colorful item
in the gossip columns about Mattel's "flamboyant creator-inventor"
being seen around town with different women, or about his endless
parties. She felt he was giving her toy company a bad name, and personally embarrassing the Handler name, which was becoming the biggest in the toy industry.

"In the beginning, Jack would invite Ruth and Elliot to some of
his parties, which were really pretty fabulous," observes Nancy Hudson.
Ryan was a platinum member of the star-studded Thalians, a Hollywood organization devoted to raising funds for those with mental and
psychological problems, an A-list crowd that included such icons as
Frank Sinatra, Bob Hope, Lucille Ball, and Debbie Reynolds. Ryan
often threw open The Castle for Thalian balls and other festivities.

"Jack would tell me that Ruth and Elliot loved to meet these
famous people, and he liked to give them an opportunity to step on

the wild side, so to speak," says Hudson. "They enjoyed his celebrity and his energy *in the beginning* because it brought Mattel a lot of publicity. Any article about Jack usually mentioned he worked at Mattel and he named the Mattel toys. But then he went overboard. He was just going off the deep end, and the Handlers thought it was no way to run a business. He was just getting too kookie."

One of his more uninhibited parties, a bash to which the Handlers weren't invited—but some 500 other revelers were—included Mickey Dolenz of the popular rock group The Monkees, who arrived at The Castle "giggling to himself intermittently," accompanied by "two skanky, tall girls" known as the "the Gemini Twins" from the Mexico City production of *Hair*. Along with Linda Henson were two of Ryan's future wives, Zsa Zsa Gabor, in a skin-tight orange-and-white gown, and Gary Hardy, who was described as "eye-catching" and "peroxided" and who wore "a backless white mini-dress with navel-deep neckline plunge."

At some parties, he installed a large phallus-shaped dial over the entrance with numbers from 1 to 10. When a woman entered the room, he had a cohort pull a cord that moved the dial up, stopping at a certain number that indicated how sexy she was, a 10 being *va-va-voom*. He called it the "Peter Meter."

Because of the sometimes-bawdy goings-on at The Castle, Charlotte Johnson, an unmarried loner, who headed Barbie fashion design, demanded that her female workers leave any Ryan party no later than 9 o'clock, lest they get caught up in any unsavory activity.

A close Ryan pal was stockbroker-turned-actor Kem Dibbs, who played interplanetary space hero Buck Rogers in the 1950s TV series, among other film and television roles. But he was best known to Jack for supplying his parties with beautiful women. "Kem was an interesting rascal, a handsome bachelor in the Omar Sharif style, who was always bringing girls around," says Annie Constantinesco. "Kem had a lot of style, was clever, and could put a party together with lots of women very quickly. That appealed to Jack, who didn't like people who had two left feet." There are some in Ryan's circle who thought Dibbs, who died in 1996, might have acted as procurer for the Father of Barbie.

Hungry to be known as a bon vivant, and with a hugely inflated view of himself that was equal to, if not surpassing, Ruth Handler's,

Ryan had hired a prominent Hollywood publicist, Russell Birdwell, who had handled film campaigns for the likes of Howard Hughes and David O. Selznick, to generate as much press as possible. The coverage ranged from Ryan's appearances on Merv Griffin's talk show to an embarrassingly candid profile in *Esquire* magazine's first issue of the Swinging Seventies decade, ironically entitled, "Class in Our Time."

The story made Ruth Handler seethe, because she and Elliot were briefly mentioned mostly as "The Couple," and the story further noted that Ryan, not the "The Couple," was the one who had "visualized a doll that was like a young woman . . . a merchandiser's dream . . . a mixture of precocious sex and instant affluence."

Moreover, Ryan's carousing and adultery sickened Ruth. "We knew how he lived, but there was nothing we could do about it," Elliot Handler acknowledges, years later. "Ruth was upset. She was not happy with his lifestyle and the fact that he had a wife—and he acted like he *didn't* have one."

■ ■ ■

Unlike the Father of Barbie, the founders of Mattel lived conservatively and relatively modestly for all of the tens of millions of dollars they were accumulating; Mattel was their be-all and end-all.

But like anyone coming from poor circumstances who suddenly hit the jackpot, they did splurge. Elliot went from driving a simple American sedan to work to a spectacular Aston Martin—the James Bond model—and then to a Rolls Royce. At one point, the Handlers, moving on up like television's *The Jeffersons* or *The Beverly Hillbillies*, bought the Beverly Hills estate of one-time movie cowboy star Tom Mix, on which they planned to build a new home, recalls Marvin Barab.

"Ruth and Elliot were very much into playing tennis, and the unique thing about their plans for the house was that the tennis court was going to be on the roof," he says. "The neighbors raised all kinds of hell. The Handlers were getting the plans approved and said they could probably win the battle, but they'd create enmity in the neighborhood, so they sold the property."

The sudden riches from the Mattel toys bought them a mansion in exclusive Holmby Hills; a beach house they purchased from the singer

Frankie Lane in the exclusive, celebrity-studded Malibu Colony for 30 percent less than he was asking, as Ruth boasted in her book; and a luxurious, 28th-floor custom penthouse in Century City with spectacular views. Led by Elliot, they invested in art—Impressionist and Post-Impressionist paintings by Monet, Pissarro, Leger, Derain, and Renoir, among others, lined their walls.

But Ruth publicly played down all of that luxe. "We are very simple people living a very simple personal life," she told a *New York Times* writer. "Our travel and entertaining is related to business." And in an apparent veiled reference to the Father of Barbie, she added, "We're just not swingers."

Fred Adickes had a somewhat different take. "I'm sure they were jealous of Jack's lifestyle," he asserts. "The Handlers were *dull*. You wouldn't want them at a party. All Ruth could think about was business and Elliot was a very introverted artist."

If anything turned on Ruth Handler more than seeing the money roll in, it was rolling into work every morning in her Cadillac El Dorado and taking in her empire. "The thing that gets me is coming to the plant and seeing this sea of cars—then I am overcome by the reality of what we have wrought. It *is* a little unbelievable."

To Ruth Handler, Jack Ryan's lifestyle was immoral. But his carousing and philandering had no adverse impact on Mattel. However, her actions would eventually wreak havoc on the company and almost destroy what she and Elliot had worked so hard to build.

# Chapter 6

# Horrific Scandal, Controversy, and Indictments

As the Watergate scandal was tightening a noose around Richard Nixon's neck in 1973, little notice was given to a White House announcement by the beleaguered commander-in-chief appointing another president, Mattel's Ruth Handler, to a prestigious committee dealing with the economic role of women in America.

If anyone at Woodward and Bernstein–besieged 1600 Pennsylvania Avenue had bothered to vet Handler before the appointment, they would have unearthed a minefield of questionable—soon-to-be-criminal—activities that would all but bring Mattel to its corporate knees.

As with Nixon, who that same year famously declared, "I am not a crook" and soon resigned, Handler, too, was caught in wrongdoing—illegal acts that would lead to her own scandalous ouster and worse. The two presidents had much in common: ego and arrogance. She admired Nixon, who she later stated "was so much warmer and smarter and [more] insightful than I'd ever imagined." She described one of the stiffest presidents in history as "relaxed and sincere." Unlike the Mother of Barbie, the Father of Barbie detested Nixon. A political liberal, he threw campaign fundraising parties at The Castle for the likes of George McGovern and Jerry Brown, and had Jane Fonda as a guest when she was being vilified as "Hanoi Jane" because of her opposition to the Vietnam War.

Ruth Handler's fall from power could be blamed in part on Hot Wheels, Mattel's monster boys' toy, and the indisputable fact that its phenomenal sales had suddenly and unexpectedly screeched to a halt two years after its introduction.

Mattel, which the Handlers had taken public in 1960, had long been Wall Street's wonder child, promising and recording record profits through most of the 1960s. This was mostly due to Barbie, but sometimes even more to Hot Wheels, which was considered the ultimate in die-cast toy cars, a plaything that was to boys what Barbie was to girls. When President Kennedy was assassinated in 1963, Mattel was met with a wave of parental and political resentment toward toy guns and rifles, a major profit center in its boys' toys product line. With the gun sales precipitously falling, the Handlers needed another big revenue generator.

Noting the success of toy cars such as the Matchbox line, Elliot thought it wise to get into the game, but Mattel's marketing people were skeptical, contending that the toy car market was oversaturated. Nevertheless, Handler instructed Jack Ryan to get his Preliminary Design group started on what he hoped would be a revolutionary product based on a conventional boys' toy, a little car. It was a top-secret project that would consume about a year of intense work.

"Elliot was kind of a frustrated automotive designer," says Fred Adickes, who became one of the lead players in the cast that designed, marketed, and produced Hot Wheels. "He did a couple of toy cars years before at Mattel, but they were a failure."

At Ryan's behest, Adickes went to Detroit and hired an automotive designer named Harry Bradley, who knew styling and had an eye for the "California Car" hotrod look. Ryan and Handler were heavily involved in the project. Ryan, for example, spent about $20,000 on a steering mechanism that he had in mind, but failed to make it work.

Adickes hated the idea of using the Matchbox product as a model. "Matchbox was not a good representation of a car," he says years later. "If you dragged it on a desk the wheels wouldn't roll and they'd just scratch the desk. To me a car was something that had springs and rubber tires and rolled and was fast. All the toys that Mattel had succeeded with were replicas of real life—whether a doll or a rifle—and that's what I wanted in the toy car."

He sketched a design, had one of the model makers make a quick prototype, and tested the little car on a 20-foot-long rubber gasket from a garage door. "I put that thing on it and—*zoom!* I had to go look for it and by the time I came back to my office, Elliot, Jack, Ruth, and the marketing director were there. I demonstrated the car again and Elliot said, 'Okay, that's what we're going to do,' and that was the end of the development. It probably cost Mattel $150, but so many people contributed so much to make it successful."

With the New York Toy Fair looming, the Handlers held a sneak preview of Hot Wheels for Kmart, one of Mattel's biggest buyers in the late 1960s. Ken Sanger, the boys' toys buyer for the discount store chain, watched the demonstration, which lasted less than a minute. The Handlers' jaws dropped when he told them he would initially order a mind-boggling "fifty million cars," and declared, "You'll sell every one you can make."

The first candy-colored Hot Wheels, representing most of America's most popular cars, or custom versions thereof, hit the market around Christmas 1968, along with race tracks and other never-before-seen accessories, in order to destroy the Matchbox brand. As with Barbie, it was the *Gillette razor theory* in action: Give away the car, and sell the other stuff to make it more fun and generate bigger profits.

It was celebration time at Mattel. Hot Wheels was a smash. Through 1968 and 1969, sales were in the stratosphere. But then the money machine ground to a halt and Mattel ran into a series of problems that brought about its first loss and opened a window into company corruption.

■ ■ ■

Christmas 1969 was no holiday at Mattel. In fact, it was an utter disaster when a fire gutted the company's warehouse on the Mexican border. The structure was underinsured, and there was one fatality, but even worse, the Handlers were unable to ship about 30 percent of Mattel's holiday orders. Next came a strike by dockworkers that impacted much-needed supplies for toys for Christmas 1970.

With the big holiday on the horizon, there was virtual panic along Mahogany Row, the name given to Mattel's fancy executive suite of offices, which looked out onto the 405, the crowded and polluted San Diego Freeway. Hot Wheels had dominated the market a bit too much, and store shelves were now sagging under their weight. The cars weren't moving; Hot Wheels appeared to be out of gas. Sizzler, a version of the little cars with a tiny motor in it, also had bombed with kids.

To make matters worse, Wall Street analysts had been promised another year of record Mattel profits. Panicked, the Handlers and their top executives held a crisis summit meeting to deal with the potentially catastrophic situation. The top item on the agenda had a big question mark: How do we increase sales to meet Wall Street expectations based on our promises?

The answer was a simple business concept known as *bill and hold*. Mattel's sales force would be turned loose to snag huge orders from their customers, and the long-trusted toy company with the catchy slogan—"If It's Mattel, It's Swell"—would simply hold the products in its warehouses for delivery sometime down the road.

Under normal circumstances, bill and hold is on the up-and-up *if* the orders are genuine and *if* the sold products are actually put aside for the customer.

As it turned out, however, Mattel was running a scam, according to a 500-page special report by independent lawyers and accountants who conducted a probe as part of a Mattel settlement with the Securities and Exchange Commission (SEC), which had accused the company of releasing false earnings reports.

The report, which Ruth later claimed "was riddled with half-truths," charged that Mattel's sales force was secretly telling the customers they could cancel the orders, which were already on the books. According to the report, one order that was documented at $615,000 later shipped at the actual selling price of $185,000. In another instance, an order for almost $5 million was counted twice, and inventor royalties were understated by several million dollars.

In total, the crash sales program and other finagling allowed Mattel to have another fiscal year of record earnings; Wall Street and the stockholders were delighted. Mattel was still the whiz kid—or so it seemed.

In 1972, despite all of the manipulations, Wall Street awoke to the shocker that Mattel, the leader of the toy industry, and promising still more profits, had a $31.2 million after-tax loss on sales of $206.4 million. Before taxes, the loss was $59 million. The Handlers soon were placed in the humiliating position of restating announced future profit projections by issuing a press release for another major loss for the first quarter of 1973. The banks Mattel dealt with quickly lost confidence in the company. Ruth later called it "a horrifying mess. . . . For years, people had been making millions of dollars on our stock. . . . Now it plummeted. . . ."

And plummet it did. The scandal was like a pin bursting a balloon. Everyone who owned the stock took a bath. Once over the $100-a-share mark, by September of 1974, it sold on the New York Exchange at $2 a share, and traded over-the-counter at little more than $3. Longtime dedicated employees, such as the first Voice of Barbie, Gwen Florea, were devastated.

"I was being paid in stock options, not salary increases, and my stock went through the floor," she says. "It went down to pennies. They lost a bundle—an absolute big bundle of money. I left Mattel just before the shit hit the fan, but I kept my stock because I loved the company. I asked the stock people if I could have the actual Mattel stock certificates because I wanted to wallpaper my bathroom. It was that bad. Oh God, yes."

The special investigation determined that the bill-and-hold sales spree failed to meet "any minimal legal or accounting standards," and revealed that 80 percent of the orders were canceled within a few months. The SEC accused Mattel of issuing false earnings reports, and the investigative report, documenting blatant falsification of profit and sales figures during the fiscal years 1971 and 1972, placed most of the blame on Ruth and Elliot Handler, and on Seymour Rosenberg, a former executive vice president for finance and administration, who had been forced out. Rosenberg had been recruited in the late 1960s to spearhead penetration into the international market and forge acquisition of new businesses, which was his forte and a major goal of the Handlers, who felt they needed to expand beyond toys to keep Wall Street happy.

Mattel, according to the investigators, had shipped five million Hot Wheels cars near the close of fiscal 1972 at a loss of $400,000, but it wasn't until the next fiscal year that the loss was reported.

Beyond the bill-and-hold scheme, the investigators discovered numerous other abuses because of top management's pressure for profits. The investigative report charged that Mattel's expenses were purposely understated by $6.6 million; that accountants were pressured by top management to generate numbers that would impress the financial analysts who covered Mattel because "a few members of management had a preeminent concern over Mattel's Wall Street image"; and that profits were increased further because Mattel side-stepped contributing to the employees' profit-sharing plan in 1971, the company's best year at that point, and the year when accounting manipulation started. According to the report, Mattel reported pretax profits of $34 million, but an auditor's investigation revealed that as much as $20 million resulted from questionable and improper accounting methods.

Because of the bogus earnings reports, Mattel stockholders had filed five class action suits against the company, resulting in a $30 million settlement, the largest in a securities case at that point, and one in which the Handlers had to make a big contribution—more than two million shares of stock and $112,000 in legal fees that had been paid by Mattel on the founders' behalf.

In a front-page headline, the *Los Angeles Times* called the case "The Mattel Debacle."

Once cocky, Ruth Handler said of the scandal, "We are deeply, deeply distressed and I don't know how else to say it." Elliot Handler was quoted as saying, "It's a very sad feeling but life has to go on."

In the biggest shocker of all, the pioneer founders of one of America's great companies were forced to resign from the Mattel board on October 17, 1975, ending all ties to the world's largest toy maker, which they had started on a shoestring three decades earlier.

"I packed up my belongings and walked out of Mattel's doors for good," Ruth later stated.

Before she left, though, Ruth threw all of her support behind a bizarre doll project that she thought might even surpass Barbie in popularity and sales. However, what "Growing Up Skipper" ignited was an enormous controversy for Mattel. If Barbie's predecessor, Bild-Lilli, was considered a plaything for bawdy adults, this latest version of Skipper, who since the late 1960s had been billed as Barbie's younger sister, was thought of as virtually pornographic, a 9-inch plastic children's version of an inflatable life-size doll sold in stores frequented by dirty old men.

By a crank of her left arm, platinum blonde Skipper sprouted little plastic breasts, her waist became slimmer, and she gained three-quarters of an inch in height. Mattel billed her as "Two Dolls in One," and the packaging promised she'd "grow slim and tall and curvy."

"That idea was far out there, pretty risqué," observes Derek Gable. "It was debated and laughed at by some at Mattel, and others were saying, 'God, are we really going to do that?' The thing is Ruth was very out there. Ruth was adventuresome, way ahead of her time."

Many parents and feminists were outraged. Right after the doll's introduction at the New York Toy Fair, the National Organization for Women (NOW) denounced Mattel's emphasis on breasts over brains, and asked in a letter for a male doll with a penis that grew when *his* arm was cranked. Projecting sales of 1.5 million, Mattel's public relations director's response was, "How can you take someone seriously when they make a suggestion like that?"

On February 16, 1978, the bomb dropped on Ruth Handler.

■ ■ ■

At 61 years of age, and a grandmother, the Mother of Barbie, along with three other former officers and a current employee, was indicted by a federal grand jury in Los Angeles on charges of conspiracy, mail fraud, and making false financial statements to the SEC.

The 10-count indictment alleged that Ruth and 54-year-old Seymour Rosenberg influenced the market price of Mattel stock by falsifying company records regarding sales and earnings for the three-year period 1971–1973. Falsified records also allegedly were used to acquire assets in other companies with overvalued Mattel stock, borrow money from the Bank of America, and sell the stock for personal gain.

The indictment charged that Handler and Rosenberg directed another employee to keep false records from being discovered by Mattel's auditors, Arthur Andersen & Co., and the following month Ruth signed a letter to Andersen claiming that the auditor had received all financial and accounting records. Handler also was accused of directing an employee not to correct a $4.8 million error overstating sales to the dime-store chain S.S. Kresge Co. The indictment noted that with Mattel stock up, Ruth sold 16,600 shares as a trustee for her children, Barbie and Ken, for $383,000.

The indictment also alleged that Handler and Rosenberg had hidden questionable financial statements from outside auditors. "The marketing guys who had done most of the 'dirty work' were not indicted," Ruth later asserted.

Elliot Handler was not indicted, a decision made by the grand jury, and "based not on titles but on what the evidence showed," stated the prosecutor, assistant U.S. Attorney A. Howard Matz. Mainly, Elliot was not prosecuted because he was involved in the creative end, while Ruth oversaw business affairs.

If convicted, she and the others faced stiff sentences—two to five years in prison and a fine of up to $10,000 on each of the counts.

Declaring that she was "deeply offended" by the charges, Ruth Handler stated, "I am not guilty. My integrity is on the line. I am coming out fighting and will exert every ounce of strength at my disposal to prove my innocence."

The day of the indictment, she was taken to the basement of the courthouse, where she was fingerprinted, photographed, and ordered by a stern matron to take off her gold jewelry, diamond wedding ring, and belt. She was then led to the hellish women's lockup. Gripped by panic and fear, she broke free of the guard, screaming for Elliot, who was nearby with her lawyers, and they arranged it so she wouldn't be placed in the cell.

"I wanted to die of shame," she noted years later in *Dream Doll*. "I had always prided myself on being fair and honest, and always valued my business reputation."

Ten days later, she pleaded innocent to the charges, and a trial was scheduled for June.

But seven months after the indictment, on September 5, 1978, the white-haired Mother of Barbie dropped her vehement claim of innocence and pleaded "no contest"—equal to a guilty plea—on the charges under an "agreement" that guaranteed she would *not* have to serve a prison sentence ranging from 20 to 50 years. The next day, the headline in the *Los Angeles Times* blared, "Ruth Handler Changes Plea: Won't Be Jailed."

Asked in court by U.S. District Judge Robert Takasugi whether she understood that her plea of nolo contendere would be treated in the records as a guilty plea, Ruth declared: "I believe that I am innocent of any criminal wrongdoing. But I decided, with my attorney's concurrence, to plead nolo." She said she was aware that the plea would be treated as guilty on all the charges, and that her plea would be entered as a conviction on charges of conspiracy, mail fraud, filing false reports and registration statements with the Securities and Exchange Commission, and making a false statement to a federally insured bank.

U.S. Attorney Andrea Ordin was furious about Ruth's statement, reiterating her innocence. "We believe the public interest requires a final, public and unambiguous resolution," the prosecutor said. "Although the law makes it clear that the plea is the equivalent of a plea of guilty . . . such a plea has apparently allowed a defendant [Handler] to make the claims being made here. Giving credence to such claims calls into question the integrity of the system and is therefore deeply unfortunate."

The Mother of Barbie, whose routine boast in the prescandal, boom days of Mattel was "We'll cry all the way to the bank," charged that the prosecutors were out to get her and see her imprisoned because she was a woman. "Bring down a woman, a famous woman, an uppity woman who had the nerve to climb to the top. . . ." She figured in her book that that's what the white hats were thinking as a way to make their reputations—a common theme among female white-collar criminals; domestic diva Martha Stewart and hotel queen Leona Helmsley would make similar assertions years later, before and after they were sent up.

And like other white-collar criminals who had become extremely successful, Ruth Handler felt a sense of entitlement, felt she could do no wrong because of her enormous success. Conceivably, she even felt above the law. This woman, who rose from near poverty to the heights of co-founding an international behemoth, saw herself as a superwoman.

On December 11, 1978, as the big Christmas toy-buying season was in full swing, with Mattel releasing SuperStar Barbie and Fashion Photo Barbie, the woman who helped start it all was sentenced to five years' probation by Judge Takasugi, and ordered to concurrently perform a total of 2,500 hours of community service—the largest community service sentence ever handed down at that point—and to pay a fine of $57,000.

■ ■ ■

As happened when the stock plummeted, Ruth's no-contest plea floored many longtime employees. "Nobody could believe that they would do anything criminal, because they'd always been decent to the employees," says Derek Gable years later. "You couldn't believe that those guys would be crooks. Everything was going along and then all of a sudden it was sort of—*No, it can't be!* It didn't make any sense. A lot of it was guilt by letting things happen. She may have known they were happening, but I don't think she said, 'Hey, let's go in and cook the books.'"

In *Dream Doll*, published almost two decades after the scandal, Ruth pinned the wrongful acts that resulted in her no-contest plea on other company executives whom she did not name in the book, referring to one of them only as a newly hired "executive vice president" and "an acquisitions expert."

At a meeting to discuss acquisitions early in Rosenberg's tenure, she claimed, he put her down, declaring, "You're Jewish. . . . [Y]our style is all wrong. If you were to deal with the investment community you wouldn't create the right impression." Ruth was furious, telling Elliot, "I'm going to fire that son of a bitch." He talked her out of it because the hiring of Rosenberg, who had a good reputation on Wall Street, had caused a big spurt in Mattel's stock. Nevertheless, she despised him. "In one stroke," she stated, "a man had gained power over me in my own company by putting me down." Later distancing herself from the charges against herself and Rosenberg, she asserted, "I steered clear of and left him to operate more or less on his own"; this was an assertion hard for many at Mattel to swallow, since she was known as a control freak who had her finger on all aspects of the business end of Mattel.

Yet in news accounts after Rosenberg was hired away from Litton Industries, Inc. he was highly praised by the Handlers and given the green light to speak for the company. A *Los Angeles Times* story, for instance, quoted Ruth as saying that Mattel in the mid-to-late 1960s was weak in financial managerial abilities and long-range financial planning, and that was one of the reasons Rosenberg "was enticed aboard." She said Mattel, with Rosenberg on the team, was ready to "go big," with a five-year plan to achieve $500 million in sales and reach 15 percent of the U.S. toy market and 5 percent internationally. There was no indication, as she later maintained, that friction existed between her and Rosenberg, or that she had left him to his own devices to run things.

In the late 1960s, with Mattel's enormous and hugely profitable growth slowing somewhat, the ambitious and hungry Handlers felt they needed to expand beyond toys in order to keep their stockholders and Wall Street happy.

With Rosenberg in charge of acquisitions, the company had what Ruth called "diversification fever," and went on a wild corporate shopping binge, scooping up a variety of companies: the pet supply business, Metaframe; the playground equipment company, Turco Manufacturing; the toy model company, Monogram; the tape cassette company, Audio Magnetics Corporation; the country's largest children's book company, Western Publishing; and last but not least, Mattel's most precarious high-wire acquisition, the Ringling Bros. and Barnum & Bailey Circus, which the Handlers saw as "a virtual money machine" and a way for Mattel to get into family entertainment.

In *Dream Doll*, Ruth claimed the deal happened because one of the owners, a Walt Disney wannabe, needed an infusion of cash—$25 million to $30 million—to build a theme park called Circus World near Disney World in Florida.

But another story also circulated. According to Rita Rao, a former Mattel executive vice president, "I did hear that Ruth couldn't get a ticket to take a child, a niece or something, to the circus, so

Ruth said she'd buy it so they could always get in. By that point in time, she had enough ego to do that. The Handlers were out of their element with those acquisitions and that really contributed greatly to their downfall."

Mattel management had even manipulated the ticket sales and other revenue generated from the circus subsidiary, according to that special investigative report, which charged that profits were shown as being lower to give the appearance of a bigger jump the following year.

Later, as Mattel sank deeper into scandal, all of the purchases were sold off, mostly as losses. Ruth later acknowledged that "things are never quite as they look on the surface."

Derek Gable, who years later said he never for a minute believed that Ruth consciously committed criminal acts, put it another way: "Most of it went down the toilet."

■ ■ ■

Ruth also implied in *Dream Doll* that the crimes might not have occurred if she had been in good emotional and physical health. Sadly, in June 1970, she was diagnosed with breast cancer and lost her left breast. She was devastated, and felt her power as a woman had been stolen. "After the mastectomy," she maintained, "I never was able to grab hold of things at Mattel and regain control. . . . I didn't seem to have the self-confidence required to take charge and take over leadership."

She once revealed to a reporter for the *Los Angeles Times*, "[M]y anger took on such statements as 'I'd like to chop off parts of the doctor.' Things like that."

Whatever her emotions, she actually was stable enough, even through the discovery of the financial manipulations and the related emotional stress, to start another new and very successful business. Like the bosomy Barbie doll that made her rich, her new venture also had to do with breasts; the idea came to her as a result of her mastectomy.

Even before she was indicted, but after being ousted from Mattel, she founded a company called Nearly Me, which manufactured and sold a new form of breast prosthesis for others like herself who were unhappy with the "commercial breasts" that were on the market.

On leaving court after making her plea of no contest, she told the news media that she took that step because she didn't want "many years of seemingly endless investigations and litigation and the personal commitment demanded by a lengthy trial" to interfere with her new money-making venture. In sentencing Ruth, the judge said she could pick any form of community service—but not anything that would involve or promote Nearly Me. At one point, she had suggested giving away the prostheses to women in need as the way to do her community service, but the judge, Handler asserted, saw that as a way for her to get "free advertising." Later, she complained about the length of her community service—one week a month—"not easy to do when you're tending a fledgling new business," which she said demanded long hours and extensive travel.

In the end, because of her work with a youth program, her probation was terminated 18 months early by the court. Her "legal nightmare," as she termed it, was finally over.

Once again, Ruth and Elliot had gone to Sears for the necessary power tools needed for her Nearly Me startup, just like they had done decades earlier when Mattel was in its infancy. They recruited a few of their former employees, and designed a breast made of material used in some Mattel dolls—polyurethane as the outer skin, over silicone gel. "Nobody was making rights and lefts then. We were the first to do that," she boasted to the *Los Angeles Times*, one of a number of national publications that profiled the ex-con's new venture.

In a lengthy piece about Ruth and Nearly Me in the *New York Times*, Robert Lindsey wrote:

> There's the same feisty sense of self-confidence, the same buoyant forecast of future growth, the same aggressive, sometimes brash approach to marketing. Ruth Handler, who made a fortune in the toy business, and then lost most of it in a spectacular episode of alleged corporate shenanigans, is back in business . . . on her way to making another fortune. . . . [S]he has defined a need and filled it. . . . [D]emonstrating her old skill as a promoter, she spends much time these days discussing her new breast prosthesis with reporters and frequently opens her blouse during interviews and asks a reporter or photographer to feel her breasts to determine which one is real.

He quoted her as saying, "I'm a marketing genius—I know it."

Ruth made the rounds of the nighttime TV talk shows aggressively promoting her latest product, and got a hearty laugh out of Merv Griffin when she asked him to squeeze her breasts and tell her which one was hers, and which was Nearly Me.

In *Dream Doll*, Ruth Handler declared: "When I conceived Barbie, I believed it was important for little girls' self-esteem to play with a doll that has breasts. Now I find it even more important to return that self-esteem to women who have lost theirs."

In the early 1990s, after almost two decades of self-imposed exile from Mattel, she was brought back into the House of Barbie. In 1994, at the time of Barbie's 35th anniversary, Ruth was asked to participate in the celebration, and help publicize the event. Overjoyed, she was mobbed by Barbie fans in Germany, and signed autographs in New York and Chicago. She also agreed to be interviewed for *Barbie Nation*, an unauthorized documentary about Mattel and the Barbie phenomenon and obsession.

"At the time that I interviewed her she was going through this comeback," says filmmaker Susan Stern in an interview with the author.

She was being embraced as the Mother of Barbie. All of a sudden she was achieving stardom all these years later, being invited by Mattel to Barbie conventions after being estranged from Mattel, and then being lionized by all these Barbie collectors. She told me about this one woman who came up to her at one of the conventions and just devoted herself to her, packing her luggage and becoming her little assistant. She loved the adulation. She was like a movie star in her last years.

The early 1990s were a time of immense joy and terrible unhappiness for Ruth and Elliot Handler. The joy was attributable to her Mattel resurrection. The unhappiness involved their son Ken.

A talented musician who was passionate about film and architecture, Ken Handler was far more academic and intellectual than his parents and his sister, Barbara—Ruth considered him "cerebral," and later observed that he "was a difficult sort of child" who "lived in a world of his own."

All of that was no surprise since Ken grew up embarrassed and humiliated by having an anatomically incorrect boy doll named after him; unlike Barbie who had breasts, Ken had no hint of genitalia. As he grew older, real-life Ken also was self-conscious about the fame and riches the Barbie and Ken dolls had brought to the family, and he was particularly disturbed about the negative impact Barbie had on some young girls—so much so that he refused as an adult to have the dolls in his home, or to allow his two daughters and son to play with them.

To all those who knew him, Ken Handler was a wonderful father, a loving husband to his wife Suzie, his childhood sweetheart; a bright and sensitive man who, with his various endeavors such as writing, direct-ing and producing a small film in the mid-1980s—a bizarre comedy about prostitutes, sculptors and one-time Nazis holding pizza delivery boys hostage on the night they were to participate in a break dancing contest—made his parents proud.

But there was another side to Ken, and in 1990 he was formally diagnosed with AIDS. His parents and wife were shocked, but Ruth overcame whatever feelings she had about his hidden life and took charge of her son's treatment, seeking the best and latest for him. For months he had been traveling back and forth to Ecuador seeking "nat-ural" treatment that he hoped would cure him, according to his then Washington, D.C. oncologist, Dr. Pamela Harris, a noted AIDS expert, who says she prescribed for Handler the drug AZT, which was making headway in extending the lives of some AIDS patients.

But Ken, who had done extensive research on his own, wanted only homeopathic remedies, says Dr. Harris. Besides, he was soon too far gone for *anything* to help; he had developed the skin lesions Carposi Sarcoma, and was experiencing dementia. "When he had to undergo an emergency appendectomy," recalls Harris, "it was difficult to find a surgeon because they were all afraid of the disease."

In June 1994, a day before his daughter, Stacey, was to be mar-ried, and with his entire family sitting vigil, Ken Handler died in the bedroom of his family's stately townhouse in New York's Greenwich Village. He was 50 years old.

While Ruth mentioned his tragic passing in *Dream Doll*, calling his death "untimely," she kept the cause secret to shield the family. The Handlers' remaining friends at Mattel had heard various accounts—that Ken had picked up a virus while traveling in South America, that he had suffered a brain tumor, or encephalitis. "I don't think any one of us knew what the truth was," notes Derek Gable. "Ruth and Elliot never talked about it." In Handler's obituaries there was no mention of what was still called "the gay plague."

In an odd coincidence in the year before he died, Mattel released an updated version of the Ken doll, one of the doll's most controversial iterations over the years. This one was called Earring Magic Ken, a plastic figure with blond highlights in his hair, and sporting a purple shirt, lavender vest, a charm necklace and a diamond earring in his left ear, giving him the look and feel of one of the Village People. The doll sold well—mostly to gay men who saw it as a campy reflection of themselves. Like other Mattel toys that sparked controversy, Earring Magic Ken came under attack for its stereotyped gay look—mostly criticized by heterosexual parents, church groups and the like, and Mattel was forced to take it off the shelves in the same year real-life Ken was buried.

After Ruth Handler died in 2002 at the age of 85 from complications following colon surgery—she was interred next to Ken in the Hillside Memorial Park Cemetery, in Culver City, California, Mattel management commissioned one of its premier Barbie artists, Aldo Favilli, to sculpt a three-by-three-foot bronze high relief of Ruth and Elliot, which is on the wall of the second floor lobby of Mattel's El Segundo, California, headquarters. It depicts the founders seated at a table, with Ruth holding a Barbie doll, and an unclothed Barbie resting on the table with Barbie garments in front of her.

"It took so many years to heal the old resentment," observes Favilli, who spent three decades at Mattel. "The company had a beautiful party when the sculpture was unveiled. I was very honored to do it because I felt those two people were the reason Mattel existed."

Even in death, Ruth Handler sparked controversy. When in 2004 California's First Lady Maria Shriver Schwarzenegger put her power behind a museum exhibition called "California's Remarkable Women" that included the Mother of Barbie and Elizabeth Taylor, three museum board members resigned in angry protest. "That's why we have wax museums and Ripley's," one of them declared, referring to Handler and Taylor.

# Chapter 7

# A Civil War and a Hollywood Romance

Even before the financial mischief started, Ruth and Elliot Handler decided that the Father of Barbie had served his purpose, that there was no more that Jack Ryan could offer in exchange for the huge royalties he was generating on a deal that was almost two decades old.

The first salvo came when Elliot Handler instituted a second preliminary design group.

"It was set up deliberately to create competition—and to keep Ryan on his toes because the Handlers were paying him a lot of money," says Derek Gable.

Placed in charge of the competition was a Mattel executive named Jack Barcus, who was the exact opposite of Ryan in looks and style. "It was fascinating to watch," recalls Gable, "because on the one hand you had Ryan, who looked like a gnome, a total sideshow, and on the other hand was Barcus, who was a giant with big muscles and a crew cut, who had sort of a Gestapo look to him."

However, when product presentations were made, or discussions evolved between the two groups, Ryan was the Goliath who always won the points over Barcus.

Between the two groups a high wall was erected, like the one that separated East from West Germany during the Cold War, and that same combative atmosphere prevailed between Ryan's team and the new Barcus group. "It was a crazy idea," says Denis Bosley, who was assigned to co-manage Ryan's group and subsequently took it over. "Eventually, Jack got less and less involved. He would come in occasionally and stick his finger into certain projects to which he took a fancy."

Nancy Hudson watched her boss become increasingly depressed with the deteriorating situation with the Handlers. "They made it so unpleasant for him to work there," she says. "He was very unhappy, didn't like the competition, and some of the people who he always worked with were now working for Barcus. Jack was drinking more, taking Valium."

Mattel's next and final attack on Ryan was stopping his royalty payments when his contract with the company was due to be renewed in the early 1970s, according to close Ryan friend and business associate Roger Coyro.

"For a number of years prior to the end of the contract, Jack was feeling that he was being short-changed by Mattel in their accounting," asserts Coyro, who would manage Ryan's eventual lawsuit against Mattel.

As this competition between the Handlers and Jack developed, they formed that separate R&D group and Jack didn't participate under his contract in any of the royalties on products developed by that group. They were really trying to screw him, but in a legal way. They had the right do it. But you don't do that sort of thing when you've got a good relationship and you want people to continue to do the same good work as has been done in the past.

The group the Handlers set up to compete with Jack's didn't foster team spirit. People were in turf battles and it didn't make sense. Things were pretty bitter, and there were some real hard feelings between the design groups fostered by the Handlers, who were working every way they could to ace Jack out of opportunities, or even the best design pool. The Handlers brought in some real corporate operators to maximize profits, please the banks, and try to find more money for Mattel wherever they could, and that's why there was such a vigorous battle put up to stop paying Jack.

Ryan was shocked and devastated by the Handlers' treatment because he had always liked and respected them. He had been happy helping to create great toys and see Mattel grow, and see himself grow rich in the process, according to intimates.

"He never really said anything negative about Ruth or Elliot," notes Annie Constantinesco, one of his closest confidantes, who was married to Coyro.

He was pretty much complimentary when he spoke about them. Jack had quite a lot of respect for Elliot's artistic nature and commented on that quite often. I think he was always looking for their approval, or their recognition. Jack was *always* hungry for recognition, for glory. So the way the Handlers began treating him by setting up the second preliminary design group, and then chopping his royalty payments, destroyed him.

One of the big problems was that they were envious of him. He was enjoying his life and his money and they weren't. They absolutely didn't approve of his lifestyle. One needs to place Jack's lifestyle in the context of the times—the 1960s and 1970s—when everybody was having a grand time, and Jack was having a grander time than anybody else, and he didn't think it should stop. He was having *such* a good time, and he was working hard, and he couldn't understand why he would have to stop, or change because people tried to tell him to put a lid on it. Some of the designers said, "Cool it, Jack." I know that I did. I used to say, "You don't have to be so much in everybody's face. You don't have to press your point," and he would just laugh. Too much was never too much for him. If he had to choose between not enough and too much, Jack would go for too much.

When the royalty payments petered out around the time of the financial manipulations by Ruth Handler and the others, Ryan severed his once-lucrative and friendly ties with Mattel in 1974, after almost two decades. He established the Jack Ryan Group, about a dozen engineers and designers—some former and present Mattel people—who worked out of offices at The Castle. After he left Mattel the preliminary design group set up to compete with him was folded back into Ryan's original operation, and eventually was disbanded altogether by the Mattel management that took over after the Handlers were ousted.

As with the Mother of Barbie, who got caught playing fast and loose with Mattel's financials, the Father of Barbie's life became equally hellish while he was fighting Mattel for money that was owed him. He became obsessed with going through years of royalty statements, and finally quietly sued Mattel, charging that the company had understated royalty payments to him—by almost $25 million—and demanding an accurate accounting of the amounts and a detailed statement of all products involved.

"More and more, Jack would see sales continuing to climb for Mattel, and yet his royalty income was going down and down," states Coyro.

> He knew something was up in terms of accounting, so at some point he had to pull the trigger and sue them. He was not gaining anything through discussions. There were some products later in Jack's cycle at Mattel where, instead of getting straight royalties, Mattel kept trying to figure out ways to reduce payments to Jack and they kept coming up with, "Well, we'll give you royalties, but only after a product breaks even," so there were complex formulas developed to determine when a product had broken even and recouped its development and manufacturing costs—not unlike what the movie industry does.
>
> Jack was really personally hurt that it came to having to file a lawsuit after spending so many productive years with Mattel. He told me, "I gave my heart to Mattel."

■ ■ ■

During that time, the Father of Barbie was acutely depressed, drowning his sorrows in alcohol. He was prescribed lithium for his bipolar disorder, but he often stopped taking the medication, sparking his manic phase, and then there would be more parties, more sex, and still more unnecessary and mostly unfinished renovations on The Castle.

It was during that frenzied period that he decided to remarry. The Father of Barbie chose as the second Mrs. Ryan a flamboyant mate—the famous-for-being-famous, and for being married, Hungarian spitfire Zsa Zsa Gabor, who lived up the block from him in a gracious home she bought after her divorce from the second of her nine husbands, the hotel baron Conrad Hilton. Like all of Ryan's marriages (and seemingly Gabor's), this one came out of the blue, and mainly for one reason: "My dad did not like being alone, and his decisions to get married from Zsa Zsa on [through his fifth and last wife] seemed to happen quite quickly," says Diana Ryan.

Others say Gabor jumped into marriage with Ryan because she thought he was very rich from the way he lived, though not quite on par with her previous beau, the elderly, ultrawealthy oilman J. Paul Getty. "Instead of opting for Getty, and gathering a multitude of diamonds while I could," she said later, she "fell for" the Father of Barbie because he was "a genius," besides living the high life.

Gabor and Ryan had been friends and neighbors for a number of years. She sometimes complained to him (and the Bel-Air Patrol, the private police force owned by Howard Hughes) about the loud noise emanating from The Castle grounds when he had one of his blowout bashes, especially ones to which she hadn't been invited. When she was invited she was very demanding—for instance, asking for filet mignon to take home to her lapdog. Ryan later stated that he married her to "shut her up," but the two had an amicable relationship, although no one in Ryan's sphere ever imagined that he'd take her for his wife.

Jack loved her glamour, flamboyance, and celebrity as an occasional actress and, more frequently, as an outrageous guest on TV talk shows; plus he apparently was on one of his bipolar highs when he decided to marry her. Before they tied the knot, and some two decades after Gabor starred in the John Huston film *Moulin Rouge*, Ryan did one of his off-the-medication renovation projects. He decided that Zsa Zsa needed a third floor on her home, so he had workmen construct a replica of the Moulin Rouge itself, at what Zsa Zsa later claimed was a cost of $1 million. When guests pulled up to Zsa Zsa's home, a stone lion welcomed them—he had placed in it an electric-eye sensor that triggered the audio greeting.

"I was thoroughly beguiled by him," she said.

Diana Ryan was in her freshman year at college and had come home for Thanksgiving break in 1974. At dinner with her father and Zsa Zsa, "it became clear to me that they were dating, and I said something to my father like, 'Why are you seeing *her?*' And he said, 'Well, if you're going to date somebody, you might as well date somebody who speaks five languages.'"

Within days of returning to school, Diana got a call from Caesar's Palace on The Strip in Las Vegas. "We're about to be married and I thought I'd like to let you know," Ryan cheerfully informed his youngest. "We're here. We're doing it."

Ryan had given his beloved a $12,000 ring from Van Cleef & Arpels, and she took the vows wearing a white gown designed by Bob Mackie (who some years later would design for Mattel a special holiday Barbie Collector gown.)

Nancy Hudson, Ryan's longtime gal pal and secretary, who had followed him when he left Mattel to help out with the parties and the Ryan Group at The Castle, also got a celebratory call. "He told me that Zsa Zsa thought he was the most fantastic lover of all her husbands—and he believed it," she recalls, chuckling at the moment, since Gabor similarly raved about all of her husbands. "Even though she was older than him, Jack told me how great she looked from her toes to the top of her head. Knowing Jack as I did, I'm sure he just married her because of bragging rights. It was a big feather in his cap to be hooked up with her because she was a celebrity. I don't think he really loved her. I could never see him settling down with any woman. He loved them all—for a little bit."

No less a chronicler of world events than *Time* magazine dutifully reported the nuptials in its February 3, 1975, issue:

> Married. Zsa Zsa Gabor, 55, sometime actress and talk-show queen; and Jack Ryan, 48, Los Angeles millionaire who, as head of Mattel Inc.'s research division, supervised the development of the Barbie doll. The couple wed in a civil ceremony at Caesar's Palace, Las Vegas; he for the second time, she for the

sixth. Said the white-gowned Mrs. Ryan: "If this doesn't work, I shoot myself."

In Gabor's 1991 autobiography, *One Lifetime Is Not Enough*, Zsa Zsa noted that some of the press had quipped at the time of their nuptials that he "had married his very own Barbie doll. . . . I was now Mrs. Jack Ryan and I felt wonderful."

That ebullience, however, seems to have lasted as long as it took for the newlyweds to settle into their Tokyo honeymoon suite. Ryan was seething over an event that happened at the airport upon their arrival, an incident that suggested to him that marriage to Zsa Zsa might have been a big mistake.

Because of Gabor's fame, they were welcomed at the gate by a top airline executive. Zsa Zsa had her little dog with her and, being the diva she was, said to the airline official, "Dahling, *you* carry the dog." Jack later told friends he was mortified that she was giving such orders and embarrassing him.

Besides honeymooning, Ryan also had business to conduct in Japan. After leaving Mattel, starting the Jack Ryan Group, and filing the lawsuit, he began designing toys on a royalty basis for a Mattel competitor, the Ideal Toy Company, inventors of the Teddy Bear and the Betsy Wetsy Doll, among many other iconic playthings.

On the newlyweds' second day in Tokyo, Ryan told his bride he had to go to a business meeting and that she would be escorted around the city by a guide, who took her to a fancy lunch and then brought her back to the hotel. She claimed in her book she was horrified when he informed her, "Miss Gabor, your husband has paid me to go to bed with you."

After they returned home from Japan, Gabor said she "discovered that, far from building a life with me, with one woman, Jack had every intention of continuing his swinging lifestyle. . . . We did have fun together, though, because Jack really was a very bright and witty man."

One example of his playfulness with her occurred when Gabor and Eva—one of Zsa Zsa's glamorous sisters—starred in a Chicago performance of *Arsenic and Old Lace*. In one scene, the sisters hide a body in a window seat. When Zsa Zsa opened it she became hysterical with laughter because Ryan, who had snuck backstage and onto the set, was curled up inside.

Most of the time, though, they fought because she claimed he never gave up his mistresses, and she and Ryan only occasionally lived together in the same house. "I just couldn't cope," she said in her book. "There was also the matter of Jack's dungeon, a torture chamber painted a sinister black and decorated with black fox fur. All in all, Jack's sex life would have made the average *Penthouse* reader blanch with shock."

Annie Constantinesco says Ryan never had a dungeon and asserted there were no ex-wives or mistresses living at the Castle at the time he married Zsa Zsa. She says that much in Gabor's book about the Father of Barbie was highly exaggerated, if not untrue.

Moreover, Constantinesco paints Zsa Zsa during her brief marriage to Jack as a jealous shrew. "The thing with Mattel was crushing to him, and that's one of the reasons he married Zsa Zsa," she maintains. "Jack just felt so down, so betrayed by the Handlers and depressed that marrying a celebrity like Zsa Zsa got him excited and out of his depression for a minute. He was flattered by her interest in him, and by her name. He didn't have anything going at the time, so it sounded like a good idea to marry her."

Zsa Zsa kept a tight watch on her groom. She was especially worried about Constantinesco. "Zsa Zsa probably knew that I had dated him, so she thought I should be expendable," says Constantinesco.

Zsa Zsa's paranoia about her husband became so intense that, according to Ryan, she had put Constantinesco under surveillance. "Jack used to say that she had Hilton security people bug my phone to make sure if Jack called me that it wasn't a romantic call. He said she had me followed, but I never paid much attention to it."

At one point, as the marriage was going downhill, Ryan offered to turn Zsa Zsa's Rolls Royce into a stretch limo. But after he had the expensive car sliced in two, they separated, so he never bothered to complete the customization, and left her with the two halves, according to friends. Zsa Zsa was furious, and nailed him in the divorce settlement.

He later told Virginia Smith-Rader, his secretary at the Ryan Group, "That marriage cost me $400,000 a bang."

# Chapter 8

# A Bloody Tragic Ending

Zsa Zsa Gabor was Carol Brady compared to the next woman in Jack Ryan's life.

In the late 1960s, the Father of Barbie had told Nancy Hudson that he wouldn't smoke marijuana, which was in vogue at Mattel as it was everywhere else in that era of sex, drugs, and rock 'n' roll, because he was afraid of losing control and because it was illegal. But in the mid-1970s, with his new lover, Barbara Kerr (15 years his junior), he sank into a black hole of drug abuse—mostly cocaine.

The two had met at a dinner party in Chicago around 1975, and she moved in with him at The Castle. Dark-haired and sensual looking— one of the few in Ryan's harem not in the Barbie mold—Kerr was a journalist with an office in the Playboy Tower who had been involved with the women's liberation movement from its beginning, and worked in George McGovern's 1972 presidential campaign.

She had gone to San Francisco in the hippie era of the mid-1960s and lived in the Haight-Ashbury section, where she researched women who were using drugs and then turned to drugs herself. Around the time she met Ryan, her book, *Strong at the Broken Places: Women Who Have Survived Drugs*, had recently been published and received a blurb on the jacket from Chicago novelist Nelson Algren (best known for *The Man with the Golden Arm*, about a heroin addict). She dedicated the book to her young son, Scott, whom she had from a college marriage—one of two failed marriages.

Besides the sex and drugs, Ryan was attracted to Kerr because of her extraordinary intellect and her friends in Hollywood, the closest of whom was Gail Fisher, the first black actress to win an Emmy Award for her role as the secretary Peggy Fair, in the hit show *Mannix*. She also was into drugs and often partied at The Castle with Ryan and Kerr. Around that time, Fisher was arrested for possession of cocaine.

"Barbara was an interesting, tall, skinny intellectual, not a bimbo, but her whole life she was involved with drugs," says Annie Constantinesco.

> She lived with Jack and they did drugs together—cocaine—and drank together. She was a bad influence. It was easy for Jack to fall into any kind of excess. The combination of coke and alcohol on a tormented brain like his was lethal. But there was nothing any of us could say to him. He became totally erratic, was inclined to be angry and mean and suspicious of everything. Something was missing from the house, which later turned up, but she told him I was involved, and he turned on me, he accused me, which was absolutely unheard of in our relationship. Because they were both nuts on drugs, she accused several people at the same time. It wasn't a pretty picture.

Ryan seemed to be in love with Kerr, or maybe it was the drugs that gave that impression. In any case, he thought enough of her to accompany her to her hometown in Indiana to meet her mother, Grace Tracy Bessire, and her brother, William "Jed" Bessire. Kerr's mother reciprocated by visiting Jack and Barbara at The Castle.

Physically, the cocaine had a visibly terrible effect on Ryan. "His face was skinny, and he had kind of caved-in cheeks," Jed Bessire recalls. "My sister brought him to meet Mom and he was here for one night. The difference in ages didn't bother my mother, because she was pretty much a free thinker."

Bessire said his impression of Ryan was that of "a wild genius. There are touches of madness in anybody that's that far ahead in their thought as he was." During Ryan's brief visit, Bessire mentioned an interest in CB radios, which were a craze at the time, and Ryan offered him a layman's explanation about how radio waves work.

He also recalls his sister telling him that Zsa Zsa Gabor had referred to her as "that bitch from Chicago," apparently after learning that Ryan was involved with Kerr before their divorce was final. "It's possible that my sister was the straw that broke the camel's back, but I do know that Zsa Zsa and Jack were not living together when my sister was with him."

Somehow, Ryan pulled himself out of his drug haze, and he and Kerr had a falling out. She moved into the pool house, and then drifted away, moving back to the Chicago area where she continued writing. She died of cancer at the age of 59 in 2000, the same year her friend Gail Fisher died of kidney failure.

With Kerr out of his life, and clean of drugs, the Father of Barbie faced the stark reality of his lawsuit against Mattel and financial ruin.

■ ■ ■

With his high-living style, and the lawyers' fees, the Father of Barbie had run through the millions he had made in royalties. As Virginia Smith-Rader, who had lived through the Mattel case with Ryan, and had been called to New York to give a deposition, noted: "One person going up against Mattel is a fearsome situation. Jack just went through all his money. But he never gave up. He went into bankruptcy and called upon all his friends for help and eventually got himself out of bankruptcy, but also paid them dollar for dollar for their help."

Worst of all, around 1976, he was forced to sell his most prized possession, The Castle, which he had purchased in 1962 mostly with Barbie royalties. The property was listed with a prominent broker, but other than tire kickers intrigued by the curious-looking mansion, there were no serious buyers.

Finally, a developer who got a tip from a Mattel source who said Ryan was desperate to sell at a fire-sale price, showed up and made an offer for everything—what now looked like an amusement park funhouse, all of its contents, and the very valuable Bel-Air land that The Castle sat on. Ryan let it all go for "just nothing"—under $2 million, according to Constantinesco. "It was a terrible deal for Jack. It should not have been made. It destroyed him to lose his house. He was in such a funk, such a depression during that whole time. It was just awful. He saw the sale of his home as a big failure on his part."

(The property was later purchased by the royal family of Saudi Arabia, who erected a controversial monstrosity of a palace, removed all of the imported trees and plantings, and covered most of the vast expanses of lawn with marble and concrete. The Saudis left the country after 9/11, and the dated and ugly house, considered a teardown by agents, was on the market for $40 million in early 2008.)

The stress and anxiety was mounting for Ryan, especially with the lawsuit against Mattel taking over his life. He went through several lawyers in the legal battle—a complex accounting case and high-stakes saga that played out largely behind closed doors, and one that would drag on for close to a decade. Ryan's contract with Mattel was, according to a Mattel attorney involved in the case, "arguably ambiguous, but there was a contractual entitlement for him to get a certain percentage royalty on products, no question." Mattel contended that Ryan had to be personally involved with a product in order to be compensated. The litigation involved virtually every Mattel toy from before Barbie to Hot Wheels, and, overall, some two decades of Mattel's product history.

"Mattel fought him every step of the way," says Roger Coyro. "There were a few times when Jack was slow in answering some depositions and interrogatories and Mattel would move to either have the lawsuit dismissed, or sanction Jack because of his slowness in responding. It was just a matter of pure paper, and they would just flood Jack with paper. It was the typical corporate philosophy of keeping the ball in the air as long as they can."

One of Mattel's attorneys defending the lawsuit, who requested anonymity, on the eve of Barbie's 50th anniversary still proudly displayed a framed check from Jack Ryan in the amount of $25,000—a sanction award ordered by a judge because Ryan "failed and refused" to respond to discovery in the case.

"There were perhaps 200 products that were at issue that Ryan was claiming he was entitled to royalties on," says the attorney.

I prepared a set of written questions asking a half a dozen or so questions as to each product, which were designed to go into the role he played in it and the basis for his royalty claim. For almost two years, we never got a response from him, or we got responses that weren't sufficient, and we kept after him. Ultimately, we took the matter to court and got an order requiring him to provide answers, and sanctioning him for $25,000 for not properly responding. The check was paid on April 11, 1979. It would be worth three or four times that today. Ultimately, we got the responses from him.

It was during the period of constant depositions—more than 200 days of sworn questioning over a two-to-three-year period—that Ryan suffered an almost-fatal heart attack, which caused a six-month delay in the case. The lawyer, who says he personally liked Ryan, believes the physical and emotional strain of fighting Mattel was too debilitating for the Father of Barbie. "As I understand it, literally all his vital signs had stopped, but they were able to revive him. He in one sense died." Coyro says Mattel "deposed Jack to death," but the Mattel attorney looked at it differently. "I kind of viewed it as Ryan's stalling to death."

Ryan had to undergo life-saving quintuple heart-bypass surgery at Cedars Sinai Hospital. "The lawsuit was hard on him," says his daughter, Diana Ryan. When he recuperated, the depositions in the lawsuit continued. "It was like Lazarus coming back to battle Mattel," observes the former Mattel lawyer. Roger Coyro says Ryan never considered giving up. "Jack was as determined as they were, though not as strong. He didn't have the corporate wherewithal that Mattel did." After dropping his first two lawyers, he retained the legendary California trial attorney Joseph A. Ball, who had been a senior counsel to the Warren Commission, which investigated the assassination of President Kennedy. "He was very tenacious and effective reviewing the Mattel accounting, and analyzing the underpayments and understatements to Jack," says Coyro.

Just prior to the trial date, both sides dropped the attitude and got serious about discussing a settlement. Over the course of about a month, a so-called courthouse-steps confidential agreement was reached in early 1980 that called for payments to Jack over a 10-year period. "He got a fraction [less than half] of what they really owed him, and that's the game Mattel played," says Coyro. "It was a decent sum in those days, between $10 million and $15 million—before legal expenses."

Ryan later told a gathering of inventors, "Ruth and Elliot Handler owed me $24 million in royalties and unfortunately our relationship ended when I sued them for $24 million, and I had to settle for $10.1 million. Mattel earned millions of dollars of interest on the money they didn't pay me, so they invested $1 million a year in harassing me for eight years where I had to prove that I was a real inventor even though I had over a thousand patents at that time."

The former Mattel lawyer says he viewed the settlement

> . . . more as splitting the baby. But, looking at the case objectively, Mattel certainly had delayed for a lengthy period of time paying him. And, as is true in any settlement, they paid him less than the demand. From a financial viewpoint, Mattel certainly paid a lot of attorney fees. But ultimately they certainly paid less. The net to them was both a substantial delay in payment, a lesser sum, and, as I recall, capping the amount owed to Ryan because he might have been entitled under his contract to being paid infinitum. I liked Jack. He had his idiosyncrasies. But I would never dispute that Jack was important in building the Mattel institution and the creativity in toys that that company had. He was an adversary, but I certainly had respect for him.

After the case was settled, an embittered Ryan came to despise lawyers, declaring, "Unfortunately, the lawyers are taking over the country, and taking over the world, and like any disease I hope it kills itself."

At times, throughout the ordeal, he was emotionally and physically spent from his efforts of trying to get what was due him.

"He was pouring so much energy into negative work—the lawsuit and dealing with Mattel—that should have been going into productive, creative work that he thrived on," notes Coyro.

Jack was a strong character, but he also was someone who always liked approval and appreciation from people for what he was doing for them. He really felt betrayed by the Handlers.

Mattel was his home for some 20 years, developing one of the great toy companies of the world, and yet they were just fucking with him every chance they could get, and thinking up new ways to do it. In the meantime, Ruth and the others were fucking Mattel by misstating financial statements just to keep Wall Street happy. These were the types of people he was dealing with.

■ ■ ■

After the settlement, and in the wake of his heart surgery, Ryan hit the brakes somewhat on his manic sybaritic lifestyle—he didn't have the financial wherewithal, or the energy, sexual or otherwise, to pursue the high life anymore. He began obsessing about his emotional and mental health, and in his research he discovered the work of Dr. Kay Redfield Jamison, who was director of the UCLA Affective Disorders Clinic. He contacted her and was knocked out by both her brains and her beauty. As with so many other women in his life, he instantly fell in love.

Before long, Ryan and the pretty psychiatrist had developed a close relationship. She was enamored by his charm and intelligence, but rejected his many proposals. One of the reasons was because the two shared a commonality that would make marriage difficult, and had "the potential for catastrophe," she observes years later. "We had the same illness. My field of research and clinical study is bipolar illness. He knew that, and somewhere along the line I told him about my illness. He was aware that he had manic-depressive illness and was interested in talking about it. He was particularly interested in the illness's relationship with creativity. He thought a lot of inventors had it, and he thought that the illness had been involved in his success. He had many of the characteristics that make highly creative people creative. He asked me about mania and depression and suicide from time to time and we talked about those things very openly."

In 1999, seven years after Ryan's death, Jamison's book *Night Falls Fast*, about understanding suicide, was published to critical acclaim. By then a professor of psychiatry at the Johns Hopkins School of Medicine, she wrote in the prologue about her relationship with Ryan, and a curious pact that they had made one evening at their favorite restaurant, the chic Bistro Gardens, in Beverly Hills.

> We were talking about suicide and making a blood oath: if either of us again became deeply suicidal, we agreed, we would meet at Jack's [first wife's] home on Cape Cod. Once there, the nonsuicidal one of us would have a week to persuade the other not to commit suicide . . . a week to cajole the other into a hospital . . . to impress upon the other the pain and damage to our families that suicide would inevitably bring.

With Jamison, Ryan "repeatedly" talked about the most important and meaningful part of his life—his relationship with the Handlers and Mattel, and how it all ended so depressingly for him. "He was devastated," she says. "He felt betrayed. He felt like he didn't get the recognition, the intellectual credit, the inventing credit, the financial credit. All ways around he felt he had been treated badly."

Eventually, Ryan and Jamison moved on with their lives—she to further her career, and he to promote his latest inventions. One of these was a "top secret" doll that he told associates would far surpass the success of "my Barbie"; the other was called "The Magic Cup," which instantly cooled hot coffee or tea to a drinkable temperature and kept it there for almost a half hour.

■ ■ ■

Always needy and desperate for companionship, Jack Ryan married his fifth and final wife, Magda, a Polish émigré, in August 1984. He literally swept her off her feet, seemingly without her knowing what was happening, she says.

When he met her, she was working as a companion for a wealthy but elderly and sickly Polish woman who lived in Beverly Hills. Magda spoke little if any English. She had been in the United States only six months, coming from Poland, where she had studied law and had been married and divorced. To impress her, Ryan took her to the best restaurants. "He had accounts at the Polo Lounge at the Beverly Hills Hotel, where he always had the same table. He took me to the Bel-Air Hotel, the Bistro Gardens. The son of the woman I was working for was telling me to 'be careful, don't get involved, he wants to use you.'" Ryan was suddenly calling her, telling her he loved her. "I thought he was crazy. How can you love somebody you don't even know?"

The next thing she knew, they were at the courthouse in Santa Monica getting a marriage license. "The clerk said, 'Congratulations,' and I asked, 'Are we married?' She said, 'No, you have to go to the minister.'" Ryan called his brother, Jim, from one of the first cellular phones in existence and he immediately arranged for a minister to conduct the service that same day. "I wasn't exactly ready to get married," she says. "Jack always put me in that situation with no time to think."

Magda was a quarter-century younger than Ryan when they tied the knot, and her birthday, by odd chance, was the same day Barbie was introduced to the world at the New York International Toy Fair.

She wasn't as glamorous as most of the women in Ryan's life, according to Ryan pals, so the Father of Barbie got busy transforming her. "She was basically kind of a plain, nice gal—and he had her teeth done, a brow lift, and some facial reconstruction," asserts Virginia Smith-Rader, Ryan's trusted administrative assistant at the Jack Ryan Group, who was associated with him for at least a dozen years. "Magda was young and willing, and while she was with him she blossomed and became very pretty."

However, Magda claims that all she had had done was "a nose job—and not because Jack forced me to do it. I wanted to do it. Jack had this idea that he kind of liked me to wear high heels and dress sexy. I had long hair and my natural boobs were kind of okay, so I didn't have to do anything else to please him in how I looked. Jack was a very young man in an old body. He didn't look very good. But his mind was so young, his spirit was so young, and he treated me like a princess. I felt good with him."

With his new bride, Ryan rented a house whose previous tenants had included Liza Minnelli and John Belushi. Not long after they married, the calls started coming from old girlfriends. "One was like a porno star," recounts Magda Ryan. "One was like a James Bond girl. Sometimes he had a conversation in front of me with them on the phone saying, 'Look, I have my wife here. I am so in love with her. I cannot meet you.'"

But she says she spotted him with another woman on at least one occasion, and knew there were others, one of them demanding money from him.

> I was so angry. I wasn't jealous, but I felt stupid. I considered leaving him, but then he had serious health problems with his heart and diabetes, and I couldn't leave. He used to tell me that his mother loved to talk, talk, talk, and when she had a stroke she couldn't speak anymore, she couldn't function. He said, "Maggie, it was so awful. I never would want to live like that if the same thing happened to me."

In 1989, it happened.

The Father of Barbie suffered a serious stroke and lost his ability to speak, couldn't swallow properly, and the entire right side of his body was paralyzed. "I became his nurse," Magda says. "I was never sure how much he could understand. He was very emotional. He cried a lot. He was very depressed, wouldn't go out, wouldn't see anyone. I bought a wheelchair, but he would never sit in it. He couldn't do anything by himself. He knew he would never recover. He knew his life was over."

The most the stricken Ryan could do, or wanted to do, was lie in bed isolated from the world and watch television. One of the last programs he saw was an interview with Ruth Handler, who would outlive him by a decade, taking credit for the Barbie doll. "She never mentioned anything about Jack," Magda Ryan recalls in an interview with the author. "It was so upsetting for Jack because only he would make a doll like that with the boobs and the legs."

■ ■ ■

It was Tuesday, August 13, 1991. Magda Ryan fed Jack breakfast—she had to feed him or otherwise he could choke because of the stroke's effect on his ability to swallow. Once he was settled, she went out to run some errands. When she returned home, the first thing she did, as always, was open the door to the bedroom to see how he was doing. This time, he wasn't there. "I could not see him. I said 'Jack, Jack, where are you?' I was running around the place [they had moved into a simple two-bedroom condo] and I couldn't find him."

Then she looked in the bedroom again and spotted his crumpled body in a pool of blood on the floor beside the bed. Lying next to him was the .45 caliber pistol he used to fire one bullet into his mouth. Ambidextrous, he had used the trigger-finger of his working left hand to end his life. Before he fired the fatal shot, he used Magda's lipstick to write on a mirror, "I love you," along with a few affectionate words in Polish. He was three months away from turning 65.

Says his widow years later, "I believe he had this plan to kill himself. It was his last project."

■ ■ ■

Because of the manner of his death, the funeral services were kept private.

Several of his close friends offered eulogies. One of them was Dr. Irene Kassorla, a psychotherapist who wrote a big bestseller in 1981 that was right down the Father of Barbie's dark alley. It was called *Nice Girls Do*, which *Time* called "the hot-selling sex manual." One of the concepts she espoused was called "The Maxi Orgasm," described as an "untamable" orgasm within the reach of most women. Kassorla was a frequent guest at Ryan's parties at The Castle. "At dinners I always sat right next to him," she boasts years later. "On the other side, he'd have his little cutesy of the moment. He was largesse and generous. Everything flowed—champagne, food. He was a heavenly host. Everything was loose back then. What today would be called promiscuity then was called normalcy. Jack was of that era. He wasn't a pastor." When *Nice Girls Do* became a *New York Times* bestseller, she says, "Jack was very proud of me. He showed me off like an intellectual Barbie doll." (A year after Ryan's death, Kassorla made international headlines as the shrink for another highly sexed persona, the White House intern Monica Lewinsky, whom Kassorla counseled throughout her affair with President Clinton.)

A friend told the gathering that Ryan ended his life as he lived it—on his own terms.

Among the many mourners at St. Paul The Apostle Catholic Church in the Westwood section of Los Angeles were Ruth and Elliot Handler, who sat alone and offered no eulogy. Roger Coyro had made a special effort to invite them. For years after his death, members of Ryan's close circle privately blamed the Handlers' and Mattel's treatment of him for his declining health and suicide.

Another in attendance was ex-wife number two, Zsa Zsa Gabor, who never could resist a crowd. Only one publication reported at the time that Ryan had committed suicide—the *National Enquirer*—because Gabor, who loved publicity, directly or indirectly leaked the story to the supermarket tabloid and gave an interview. "The reporter for the *Enquirer* was out on the sidewalk at the funeral," says Diana Ryan. "They were taking Zsa Zsa's picture, and they interviewed her about her relationship with my father."

The glaring headline on the story dated September 10, 1991, read: Zsa Zsa in Tears as Husband Number Six Commits Suicide.

The tabloid noted that Ryan "took his life" just three months after Zsa Zsa's fifth husband, a "Texas oil tycoon," died of cancer. Of Ryan, Zsa Zsa, "choking back tears," declared:

Jack was a genius but he was very eccentric. All the while we were married he maintained young mistresses. I knew all about them but I put up with the situation because I loved Jack very much. I also recognized that I had married a brilliant man who did not lead the same life as ordinary men. He used to get up in the middle of the night, go up on our roof, and sit for hours listening to police messages on a short wave radio.

Yes, Jack was unfaithful to me but he was an exciting man. After we divorced we remained friends. In fact, just before I married my current husband, Jack asked me to marry him again. I was shocked and heartbroken by the news of his death, but I wasn't at all surprised. Jack had always been a man of enormous energy and drive. After such an active, productive life he couldn't bear being an invalid.

A caption under a photo of Ryan and Gabor said, "In happier times. He invented the Barbie doll."

Ryan's death received major coverage around the world. "It was his toy inventions that put his engineering genius into households across the country," the *Los Angeles Times* obituary noted.

> Ryan designed some 35 of the country's best-selling toys, including the Chatty Cathy doll, Hot Wheels and many electronic toys. But his best-known product was Barbie, the tall, slender young adult doll. . . . Never mind that critics said the doll with the torpedo breasts, tiny waist and disproportionately long legs gave little girls a false and unachievable ideal of the adult female figure. Just about every girl wanted one anyway, complete with clothes and accessories.

In London, the highly respected *Independent* newspaper carried a remembrance of Ryan by Billy Boy, a Barbie doll expert and designer and owner of the world's largest Barbie collection. Billy Boy had written a colorful history called *Barbie: Her Life & Times*, which included special outfits for the doll designed by the likes of Yves Saint Laurent and Bill Blass. Mattel, which he called "Barbie's parents," supported the project, and Mattel France had commissioned him to organize a Barbie fashion retrospective.

"Jack Ryan, inventor and designer, was an unsung hero largely unknown to the millions of the baby boom generation who came in contact with his genius," Boy wrote.

> Yet he was responsible to some extent for the forming of their life attitudes, their farthest reaching ambitions and fantasies, and perhaps also their greatest fears and anxieties. Most important of all, he was the developer of the Barbie doll. . . . It was Ryan's overseeing the directional design of the doll that allowed Barbie to have pointy breasts, to be clothed at first in quasi-haute couture then high school dress and when the time came, psychedelic garb and one hundred percent synthetic sports regalia. He realized the vision of the ultimate female with the new generation, which the new generation would idolize.

# Part Two

# A DRAMA PRINCESS AND THE BARAD ERA

# Chapter 9

# "Miss Italian America"

Next to the driven and avaricious Ruth Handler, and the brilliant and troubled Jack Ryan, Jill Barad was the most flamboyant and ambitious of Mattel's leaders. Like Handler, Barad had come a long way to reach the pinnacle of the corporate ladder.

If somewhere along the road she hadn't fallen by chance into the business world as a cosmetics company trainee, she might have had a career in show business. And at Mattel she instantly became known as a flashy performer in her personal style and executive capacity. She had the same kind of pizzazz and brass as another middle-class Jewish Baby Boomer who was also born in Brooklyn, her idol Barbra Streisand. Other than Barad's having a better nose and being raised on Long Island, both had star quality.

Born in 1951, nine years before the debut of Barbie, on which Barad would make her mark at Mattel, Jill was the younger of two daughters of Brooklynites Larry Elikann and Corinne "Corky" Schuman Elikann. If show biz was in Jill's genes, it was because of her father, who got into television in its golden age and rose from cameraman to become an Emmy Award–winning TV director and producer. The son of Harry Elikann, a New York City costume bead importer, and the former Sadye Trause, Jill's father had served as a staff sergeant during World War II in the Army Signal Corps, where he was a radioman behind enemy lines in the Philippines.

In 1947, after he was discharged, the 24-year-old veteran married flashy, attractive, and creative 18-year-old budding artist Corinne, daughter of Essie and Irving Schuman. Seeing that television was the future, Larry Elikann attended a technical school in New York, where he learned that the fledgling NBC television network was hiring technicians. He took the test and was hired as a $50-a-week cameraman on the *Philco Television Playhouse*, which featured live anthology dramas.

He remained at NBC as a technical director until the early 1960s, and then directed TV commercials for a time. In the mid-1970s, Jill's parents moved from Beechurst, in Queens, to Hollywood, where he began directing and producing major network specials and episodes of popular glitzy programs such as *Dallas, Falcon Crest*, and *Knots Landing* that featured glamorous characters much like his daughter.

"Because of Larry, Jill was always around show business and knew TV and movie stars, and the glamour and the power and especially the diva persona rubbed off on her," says a longtime family friend.

> Jill was seeking stardom from the time she was a little girl, but we all thought it would be in TV or movies because of her dad, and her own vivacious and gregarious personality—and her stunning looks. No one ever thought she'd wind up running a worldwide corporation. But the girl always had smarts. She would have been successful anywhere. Her father had ambition and drive and she inherited those attributes, too.

As a precocious child, she often kept her sister Jo-Anne, older by three years, awake at night while she jumped up and down on her bed belting out show tunes from *Oklahoma!* and *The Sound of Music*. Barad said she grew up in a "creative" home with much intellectual stimulation and with a parental message that she could be anything she wanted to be, as long as she was good at it. Her father once told her his key to success, which was, "Put your mind to it, learn what you need to, and go for it."

She followed Daddy's golden rules to the letter. One of her first jobs was working behind the counter at her grandparents' pharmacy. During the hippy summer of 1967, after having a Sweet Sixteen party, she modeled bell-bottoms for a small family-run firm called Happylegs. "She couldn't wait to try on the clothes, to learn how to meet customers, how to sell, how to talk," recalled one of the owners.

She spent three years at Jerry Seinfeld's alma mater, Queens College, in New York, and later became a big fan of his show along with *X-Files*. But an opportunity came up that caused her to drop out—an $18,000-a-year job selling Fresh Lemon bath products for Love Cosmetics, which introduced the lemon-smell craze to the American consumer. After a year hawking the products, Jill returned to Queens and earned a BA in 1973, having studied English, psychology, and drama, but never a business course.

With a show-business career in mind, she snagged a bit part with the help of her director father in the 1974 film, *Crazy Joe*, based on the rise and fall of murdered New York mafia hoodlum "Crazy" Joe Gallo, starring Peter Boyle, and featuring Henry Winkler ("Fonzie" from TV's *Happy Days*) and Herve Villechaize ("Tattoo" of *Fantasy Island* fame).

The future chairman of the board and CEO of Mattel had the uncredited, nonspeaking role of "Miss Italian America," or, according to the script, the "girl in sequin gown." That was her last acting role, at least in the entertainment world. She also worked as a production assistant for the film's producer, Dino DeLaurentiis.

Later, when she became the boss at Mattel, with 52 Barbie dolls in her plush office and Andy Warhol's rendition of Barbie as her favorite piece of art on the wall of her executive suite, she called her attempt at movie stardom in *Crazy Joe* the worst job she ever had, and described her father's Hollywood as "so superficial, so silly." Yet she was "Hollywood" personified in her style and executive persona, so much so that she avidly followed astrology. As a Gemini, she once revealed, "I am off the ground. I am definitely an air person. I am not calm. I am pretty stable, but I am out there, thinking all different things."

It was in 1974, after Elikann's shot as an actress failed to materialize more roles that, on a lark, she took a sales-trainee job at Coty Cosmetics, because she had no clue what she wanted to do with her life. As she once acknowledged, "I just saw jobs as fun. I had no goals." It was during her tenure at Coty that she began to display her talent as an innovative marketer. On the road as a cosmetician-trainer, she noted that her company's products weren't getting the kind of visibility they deserved, so she took it upon herself to design a new display, and sent it off to her boss. The company was still using her concept some two decades later. Within three years, she was named brand manager for the company's entire line.

With her parents ensconced in La-La Land, Jill was spending more time there, socializing and lunching at the chicest places, like the trendy Polo Lounge in the famous Beverly Hills Hotel, known as the "pink palace," *the* place to see and be seen.

"If Jill were fictional, she'd be the protagonist in a chick-lit novel, or a character in *Sex in the City*," a friend from those days observes. "Jill was that kind of chic, sharp, glib, trendy Jewish girl."

One evening at the Polo Lounge, while the impeccably turned out Coty girl was having drinks with a friend, she fixed her eyes on a man sitting with an older couple. In her mid-twenties, Jill was ready for a husband. "I look over and here's this really nice-looking guy with his mom and dad. I said to my friend, 'See that guy over there? I'm going to marry him and move to L.A.' "

Jill always got what she wanted, which years down the road would lead her to a scandalous fall from power at Mattel. But in 1977, the 26-year-old cosmetics girl set out to win Thomas K. Barad, also 26, a budding independent movie producer. They dated, fell in love, and she quit Coty and moved to Los Angeles to be with her man. She immediately got a job with the hot advertising agency Wells Rich Greene, which handled the Max Factor cosmetics account to which Barad was assigned. Jill became Mrs. Thomas Barad in 1979; a few months later, she was pregnant with the first of their two sons. She left the agency, as she later said, to "put my energies into my new child."

After Alex came into the world, the new mother became depressed. "It wasn't the baby," she was later quoted as saying. "He slept all the time. It wasn't fair."

Always a fashionista, she spent afternoons wheeling her first-born up and down the aisles of a nearby May Company department store, eyeing the dresses and mentally critiquing them. It was clear after some

18 months as a stay-at-home mom that her boredom had become intolerable. She wanted more from life. Her husband perceived what he later called her "unspent energy" and told her to get a job.

Jill Barad wanted a job that would utilize her cosmetics and marketing experience, and she was aware that the company that marketed her favorite doll, Barbie, had a reputation for hiring women. She retained an executive headhunter to make the connection for her.

Enter Mattel.

■ ■ ■

An obscure department—the novelty-development section—had an opening, and Barad had the looks, the drive, and the ambition that Mattel was looking for, dating back to the profile established during the Father of Barbie's recruiting days. Barad was hired one week after her interview in 1981, as a product manager. At the time, Mattel was the nation's second largest toy company behind Hasbro. During her almost two decades there, it became number one.

She displayed her corporate grit and loyalty when her second son, Justin, was about to be born. In the hospital delivery room, about to undergo a Caesarean, Barad asked a nurse for a phone so she could make calls to her office about Mattel business. A little over a month later, she was back at work, winging her way to New York to hawk Mattel's latest products and Barbie updates.

Another Barad plus was that she had come from the world of makeup. "Mattel liked to recruit from the cosmetic industry," observes former Mattel vice president of Barbie design, Margo Moschel, who had also come from cosmetics. "Mattel, strong in girls' toys, favored cosmetics people because both toys and cosmetics are based on newness and product. Mattel was strongest in Barbie, and she was very cosmeticy, if you will, very fashiony, always built on newness every quarter."

Barad was on her way.

Her husband, who gave her the kick-start to get the job, later became known behind the couple's back as "Mr. Jill Barad" by the snipers at Mattel, because she had become more famous and powerful in corporate America than he had in the movie business. Jill Barad later acknowledged that her husband "played mom and dad" at home, which, when she reached the stratosphere at Mattel, was a spectacular mansion in movie-star-land on Sunset Boulevard in Bel-Air, a big move up the real estate ladder from the far simpler home the Barads first owned in swanky Pacific Palisades. Besides her husband taking care of the domestic end, there was a fulltime live-in nanny and housekeeper.

As a working mom and career woman with her eye always on the top job, sometimes putting in 12-hour days—not because she had to, but because she wanted to—Barad once acknowledged that the most painful moment in her life was when her first-born's third-grade teacher met her for the first time and blurted out, "Oh, Alex really does have a mom." Barad believed concessions have to be made in order to have it all. For important times in her children's lives, she made sure either she or her husband was on hand. Later, she took her sons on glamorous trips overseas while on Mattel business, and brought them to Mattel headquarters to test new toys.

Over the years prior to her fall from grace, Barad was heralded by the media as the poster girl for successful career women—she had beauty, brains, a powerful job, and a family to boot—and was praised by feminists and business leaders alike for her ability to balance it all.

The *Los Angeles Times*, in one of the first of what would be many glowing profiles of Barad as she rose to power, and before her fall, reported that

> . . . she doubled sales of the company's line of girls' toys by introducing female action dolls. . . . Mattel has seen an 82 percent sales increase in their girls' toys division. And all this while she's maintained . . . a marriage and reared sons. . . . That she has been able to do so is a testament to both Barad's talents and capacity for hard work. . . .
>
> If Barad's journey into the ranks of upper management has been unusually speedy, it has also been unconventional with detours for marriage, childbirth and a cross-country move. That hardly comes as a surprise from this striking ex–New Yorker, whose non-corporate approach to dressing for success also reflects her individualistic approach to her life and work.

In the not-too-distant future, she'd be named one of the world's 50 most beautiful people by *People* magazine; *Ladies Home Journal* bestowed upon her the honor of being one of America's 10 smartest women. How many corporate executives can make those claims?

One of her first bosses at Mattel was another tough, driven executive, Judy Shackelford. She had risen in three years during her decade at Mattel—1976 to 1986—from manager of preschool marketing to executive vice president of marketing and product development worldwide. She was then the highest-ranking woman in the toy industry—that is, before Barad skyrocketed up through the ranks. "Those were the days," Shackelford observes years later, "when people thought no man would work for a woman. It was just absurd. I was the pathfinder. I was the one that had the machete in my hand to beat a path."

Shackelford, who post-Mattel started her own successful toy company, does not have fond memories of Mattel, or of Barad. The same viciously competitive corporate culture populated by aggressive personalities that existed during the era of the Handlers and Jack Ryan was still operational. Shackelford put it bluntly, "Mattel was a place you had to watch your back. It has always been a place where people are pitted against each other. It was a shark pond. You throw people in and see if they can swim fast enough to stay alive. For Jill, it was a fit."

When Barad arrived, Shackelford had been credited with helping to resuscitate the Barbie line, which had become somewhat moribund in the wake of the Ruth Handler mess. In fact, virtually anyone who had risen to high executive status at Mattel in the post-Handler era later took credit for reviving Barbie and made her success a part of their executive resume. As Moschel notes, "There was a tremendous amount of self-merchandizing. People were constantly going on about themselves, making it known as to how great their performance was in order to get noticed. Even if you were taking credit for something you really didn't do all yourself, management noticed you, and you moved up."

Barad had her eye on being involved with Barbie from her first day on the job. One day, she pushed her way into the office of Thomas J. Kalinske, who became one of a long line of 1980s Mattel presidents and chief executives. Standing brashly in her high heels and elegant and sexy pinstriped business suit, she intoned, "What the fuck do I have to do to get a decent assignment around here?"

Her career-building philosophy was simple: "I always fought for my point of view." She got her way and became a product manager for the Barbie brand, and in 1982 was promoted to the post of Barbie marketing director.

By the 1988 Christmas toy season, Barad, at 37, was executive vice president of Marketing Worldwide Product Design and Development—at the time one of four Mattel executive vice presidents, having control over design and marketing, and directing the work of some 500 employees.

■ ■ ■

As with many women who rise to a position of corporate power, especially a gorgeous, vampy female like Barad, there is always lots of gossip about how they got to be on top, and there was such chatter about Barad.

A former Mattel president who worked closely with her and admired her "intelligence, drive, and great presence" also observes years later that "she certainly set the women's movement in business back substantially by being the embodiment of what a woman executive doesn't want to be, or shouldn't be. She was very, *very* flirtatious with members of the board of directors," he asserts. "I used to find it amusing, because Jill would go up to some of the elderly directors who were on the board and sweet talk them and put an arm on their shoulder and bat her eyelashes at them—and they would just swoon, which is one of the reasons why she got the big personal contracts she did."

Other Mattel executives, male and female, who worked closely with Barad agreed she had "a strong physical and sexual appeal to men," but believed that was all part and parcel of her confident and vivacious personality. Colleagues recall her "look" before she began wearing expensive executive designer clothing, and it was a captivating, sexy style that caught the attention of men—a very short purple skirt with purple cowboy boots was one outfit of note.

Veteran Mattel executive Margo Moschel, who ran marketing and design at different times during her vaunted career and worked closely with Barad, noted that one of her gifts was that "she knew how to merchandise herself. She had the long, dark hair, which is something she used a lot. She tossed it. She would just flick her hair back, and it was part of her communication. She looked great all the time, looked fabulous all the time, pulled together, fashionable, stunning, always wore high heels, always, always, always—the whole thing."

But beyond her appearance and allure, there was a brilliant business mind at work.

"Jill was so smart and so bold and so in touch with what it took to innovate, but there were all kinds of rumors about how she came into power when I joined Mattel in 1990," says Nancy Zwiers, former senior vice president of worldwide marketing for Barbie, who worked closely with Barad.

Barad once noted that in her years climbing the executive ladder she had never experienced any of the sexism or exploitation that many other women in business felt. But when she finally reached the top and began her sudden fall from grace she would invoke sexism in part as an excuse for her demise.

But all of that was far down the road. For now, she was highly respected.

"She was the best speaker, the most wonderful performer, just so charismatic, and had a great flair for everything," asserts former Mattel executive vice president of product design and senior vice president, Diana Troup, who was a Barad colleague and friend.

When she walked in a room she was just a total knockout, glamorous and beautiful, and wore the most beautiful clothes, starting with Escada and graduating to Dior and Chanel. She was more like a movie star, but still incredibly gifted in management. And the woman knew how to make money. She knew what the ideas were that would make *a lot of money*. And she knew how to promote them. She had the talent to sift through a whole bunch of ideas and say, that's the one!

One key to her success and one that often caused friction with other Mattel executives was that Barad never took no for an answer. When Troup, along with senior vice president of marketing and product development Rita Fire Rao, began pushing for a new doll design with very long hair, Mattel's engineering department said they couldn't implement the concept. "I showed it and Jill loved it, Rita loved it, but engineering said no," says Troup. "We kept going back and forth, and Jill finally said, 'We *will* make hair that long.' And it was done. If she thought something was good, she would press for the creativity to do it."

If the marketing team told Barad they couldn't afford to do a certain product because it wasn't hitting the cost product objective, she'd say, "Raise the price!"

"To a designer that was music to my ears," says Margo Moschel.

What I loved about her was anytime you thought you couldn't give one more ounce of creativity, or work—just when you thought you couldn't do it—she'd figure out a way to make you see you could do it. She really had a way of pulling things out of people. The problem was the minute that you didn't deliver was the minute that you were on her bad list. And once you got on her bad list, honey, it was just a matter of moments and you were out the door.

Troup and others maintain that Barad usually took all the credit—even if the ideas weren't completely hers—much like Ruth Handler did in her feud with Jack Ryan over the creation of Barbie.

Troup, for instance, had got the idea for a large doll that resembled a girl of five or six which, with a bit of chemical magic, made it appear that she was applying and wearing makeup. From mothers in marketing research groups, Troup had learned that little girls liked to play with makeup and fragrance, along with their dolls. As it turned out, Mattel had a color-change technology. Once cold water was applied to the doll Troup had in mind, which would be aptly marketed as Li'l Miss Makeup, she sprouted eyebrows, eyelids with mascara-like coloring, lips that turned red, colored fingernails—even a heart-shaped beauty mark. Troup projected that her concept would be a big seller for Mattel.

"It was all my idea, and I found the sculpted doll in the Mattel archives, and that's how we got it into the marketplace in record time and did $58 million the first year," she says in an interview with the author.

But Jill was not much in sharing the glory. She took all the credit. I didn't feel it was necessarily the right thing to do. She wouldn't credit me. She wouldn't say to the press, "Oh, Diana Troup created this doll," but that Jill Barad created it. I always wished that I had gotten more credit for what I did. But I got promotions. I got a wonderful salary. But you had to bring in the goods. If you didn't deliver, you wouldn't get your stuff.

Besides selling like gangbusters, the doll caused a bit of a stir. The *New York Times*, in a trend story about how companies like Mattel were marketing cosmetic items such as stick-on painted fingernails for little girls, noted that "Mothers, especially those that came of age in 1960s—when cosmetics were frowned upon—may be aghast at these young make-up aficionados." The article was headlined, BABES IN MAKEUP LAND.

■ ■ ■

One of Barad's biggest supporters on her meteoric rise was John W. Amerman, who had joined Mattel in the company's dark days in the wake of the Handler scandal, working on Mattel's international business and raising it to new heights. For some 15 years he had been in chewing gum and cosmetics, where he rose to president of the Warner-Lambert Company's American Chicle division. "She wouldn't have gotten ahead if she hadn't had special qualities," the handsome, dapper, 50-something Amerman said of Barad after he promoted her to executive vice president. "She just understands our business, marketing, and how to deal with people. You put that all together and it spells success."

Under Amerman, who became chairman and chief executive in 1987, Mattel had record profits for more than five years running, and posted net growth of 20 percent. He bought up more than a half-dozen toy companies, and was especially proud of acquiring the British firm that first marketed the magnetic toy, Polly Pockets, which he grew to more than $80 million internationally during his decade-long watch. (Polly Pockets would surface as a danger to children during the toy-terror scandal of 2007. But that was far down the road.)

Amerman was unsuccessful in one of his biggest endeavors—an aggressive drive to pull off a $5.2 billion merger with Mattel's chief rival, Hasbro.

During his watch, he moved the company from the rundown Handler-era Hawthorne headquarters to the futuristic El Segundo location with its enormous fitness and day-care centers and volleyball and tennis courts.

Of Mattel's iconic toys, Barbie was Amerman's favorite, and because Barad had shown pure genius in hawking the doll in innovative ways, Amerman played a key role in Barad's meteoric rise within the company.

Still, observers noted that the two were competitive and had an ongoing power struggle—much like Ruth Handler and Jack Ryan.

Barad was said to have gone ballistic when *Los Angeles* magazine gave the fit, well-tailored, white-haired, bespectacled, and egotistical Amerman the royal treatment in a profile headlined KING OF BARBIE, because the equally postured and self-important Barad felt he took credit for things she had done with the brand. One of the quotes from baritone-voiced Amerman that infuriated her was how he "gussied up America's favorite little girl [Barbie] and turned my struggling company into a megatoyopoly." Barad, who would always be credited with doing the gussying, received only one brief mention in the article.

Even though it was a foregone conclusion that Barad would ascend one day to the CEO and chair positions after Amerman retired, it appeared the two were quietly out for each other's jugular.

Both Barad and Amerman declined to be interviewed for this book. She never responded to repeated calls and e-mails to her Beverly Hills office. But in a letter to the author, Amerman boasted,

> The performance of Mattel during the ten years that I was Chairman and CEO of the company is something for which I am very proud. At the time I assumed responsibility for Mattel, the company had serious financial difficulties. . . . [My] record of achievement was matched by very few corporations over that period.

Despite their competitive relationship, Barad hopped, skipped, and jumped up the Mattel corporate ladder under Amerman. Her first promotion to an executive position was as marketing director when she was four months pregnant. Once that happened, she knew she could "have it all," that Mattel "was a place that was going to be supportive and nurturing in terms of talent." The promotions came fast and swift after that—vice president of marketing; senior vice president marketing, girls' toys, and preschool games; senior vice president of product development; vice president of product design and executive vice president of product design and development—and upward until she eventually was appointed to succeed Amerman, as chairwoman and chief executive.

But that final step to the top would take a while. In 1987, *Business-Week* had already placed Barad on a watch-list of 50 women executives as potential CEOs.

Besides Amerman, one of Barad's other important mentors who taught her a lot and who helped change the direction and corporate culture of Mattel was Robert Sansone, an ambitious young executive with an interesting history before he arrived for what would be an ill-fated stay as president.

A New Yorker with an MBA from the Columbia University Graduate School of Business, Sansone served as a White House Fellow in the first term of President Nixon, and then served as special assistant to Maurice Stans, Nixon's Secretary of Commerce, and master fund-raiser for the dethroned president in the Watergate scandal. (Stans was indicted along with former attorney general John Mitchell, eventually pleading guilty to five violations of campaign finance laws and paying a $5,000 fine.)

When Sansone was appointed president of Mattel USA in October 1987 by Amerman, he had spent almost a quarter-century at General Foods, where he was credited with revitalizing that company's foreign operations. At Mattel, Amerman gave him the job of restoring the company's troubled and money-losing domestic operation, which accounted for about 50 percent of Mattel's sales the previous year, and bringing it back to profitability.

Within a year, with Sansone aboard, Mattel had gone from a third-quarter loss of more than $14 million in 1987, just before he was hired, to a more than $21 million profit for the same period in 1988. Amerman was so cheered by the upturn that he and Sansone invited some 800 Mattel employees to the company's cafeteria. The two executives rolled up their sleeves and did a rap number: "We thought you'd

like to know that the third quarter's fine. . . . Mattel is startin' to shine."
Amerman and Sansone were backed up by a trio of secretaries who
called themselves the "Mattel Rappettes."

From Sansone, Barad learned about brand segmentation and brand
extension, and how to build Barbie, which was always her baby, into
lines of additional products—an entire new world of Barbie accessories
for Mattel's iconic bestseller. Learning from him, she built the Barbie
brand to record revenues.

For example, Barad hit a gusher, selling Barbie and Barbie accessories to both little girls and their mothers, who had played with the doll
in their own childhood. The timing was right. Nostalgia for all things
Barbie had suddenly kicked in. The Barbie Collector dolls, which
became a separate division because of the brand's success, were more
expensive than the run-of-the-mill Barbie. The first one, called Holiday
Barbie, shocked even Barad by selling 300,000 units virtually overnight.
The marketing, however, infuriated genuine collectors of rare, early
Barbies—some worth thousands of dollars—who saw their world being
flooded with Barbie dolls that Mattel was hawking as collectibles.

■ ■ ■

"In the eighties through the late nineties, Barbie drove everything. She was like 50 percent of the volume and 90 percent of the
profit," observes Rita Rao, former senior vice president of marketing
and product development. Rao had had a couple of previous stints
at Mattel, leaving once because she didn't get a promotion, but she
returned in 1987 when Sansone was aboard.

While Rao credits Barad with the shrewd marketing of Barbie, she
feels that much of that success was attributable to Sansone's management. "He's the guy who really deserves the credit, but never really got
it," she says years later.

He was really the genius who turned the company around. He
was very goal-oriented and very disciplined about the goal.
There were performance reviews every six months and people
were rated one to five. If you got rated as a two, you were

gone. If you agreed to reach a number then you had damn well better do it.

It was the first time Mattel really functioned as a team where we were all in it together. His strong suit was management and motivation.

Rao, who left Mattel in 1998, attributed her promotion to executive vice president to "Barbie performance primarily."

Seemingly out of the blue, the successful Sansone suddenly resigned, and Amerman swiftly appointed Barad as one of two presidents of Mattel USA to succeed Sansone in late October 1990. Barad desperately wanted the post of president, so much so that she warned she'd quit if she didn't get the promotion, according to an account in *BusinessWeek*. "She threatened to leave for a top job at Reebok International Ltd.," the magazine reported in a cover story headlined, THE RISE OF JILL BARAD. *BusinessWeek* noted that Barad's "politicking and flamboyance" had caused much friction within the company, and she was quoted as saying, "Many men hated me. I think it can be a tough thing for a man to lose to a woman."

Sansone had been running the domestic operation for just three years. He was said to have resigned to become a part-time senior advisor to the chairman. The *Wall Street Journal* quoted the always driven-to-succeed Sansone at the time as curiously saying he was leaving the company because "he wanted a better balance in his life between professional and personal growth."

In fact, Sansone had been under enormous stress to increase sales of Mattel's weak line of boys' toys. "The pressure on Bob was intense to bring up the numbers, to come up with new product," observes a veteran Mattel executive. "It was probably too much pressure."

Healthwise, it clearly was. During Sansone's relatively brief tenure at Mattel, he was stricken with cancer, one of a number of Mattel executives over the years who were so diagnosed, beginning with Ruth Handler. Nine months later, on July 15, 1991, he died at the age of 49, leaving a wife and three children from a former marriage.

But at Mattel, the show just went on—as always.

As president, the 39-year-old Barad was given responsibility for virtually all Barbie products, licensed products, other fashion dolls, and entertainment and marketing services.

At Lincoln Center in New York City the year Barad became president, Mattel celebrated Barbie's 30th birthday with what was billed as a "Pink Jubilee" party. Barad was heavily involved in producing the glitzy affair. Guests guzzled pink champagne, munched pink candy, and sported pink corsages and boutonnieres in the promenade of the New York State Theater, which was draped in—what else—pink, a true-blue Barbie color.

Celebrities such as the singer Melba Moore were on hand to toast the iconic doll. "Barbie is my inspiration," she told the gathering. "She has almost as many dresses as I do." The guests received a special-edition Pink Jubilee Barbie wearing a silver lamé gown.

With Barad running practically everything in the girls' toys line, the boys' toys division was handed over to Barad's co-president, a newcomer, David Mauer, who had been recruited from Tonka Corporation's U.S. Toy group, where he was president. The *Wall Street Journal* headlined the appointment, MATTEL SHUFFLES EXECUTIVES TO BOOST BOYS' TOY SALES. As one key financial analyst noted at the time about Mauer's role, "Boys' toys is the obvious void Mattel has. This company has been a girls' toy company."

As Derek Gable, director of Mattel preliminary design from the late 1960s through the mid-1980s, puts it:

> Barbie had a certain persona and she was treated with huge respect. Jill, who kind of came out of nowhere, broke those rules and it worked. She was an amazing marketer and she was a promoter and she promoted Mattel and Barbie, but she really promoted herself even more. She actually hired a PR company to give her an image. For a long time, Barbie was going gangbusters. But while Barad was building the girls' side of things, the boys' side of things was slipping down the toilet.

> It wasn't always that way.

# Chapter 10

# From "He-Man" to Home Depot

While Jill Barad was pushing the Barbie brand through the Milky Way during her platinum reign in the 1980s, a Mattel designer conceived a toy for boys that virtually overnight pummeled all the competition—at one point even eclipsing Barbie in sales—and generated enormous revenue and controversy for the company.

Even Hasbro's iconic and hugely selling G.I. Joe had to take cover in his foxhole. The bombshell new product was called He-Man, star of a new line branded "Masters of the Universe"—the brainchild of a one-time weakling by the name of Roger Sweet, although others at Mattel quickly claimed credit for what became a $1 billion gold rush.

In the mid-1970s, Raymond P. Wagner, one of a long line of Mattel presidents after Ruth Handler (they seemed to have been as interchangeable as Barbie's outfits), had made one of the all-time enormous flubs in toyland history. Prior to the release of the movie *Star Wars*, the film's writer-director, George Lucas, had offered Mattel the golden opportunity to get the license to produce *Star Wars* characters—Luke Skywalker, Darth Vader, and the whole incredible cast.

Conservative in his thinking, and not getting the concept, Wagner, still back in the Handler era mindset, thought Lucas's demand for an upfront fee of $750,000 was too high a price to pay for a still-as-yet unproven product, and he didn't think the proposed action figures could get out in time for the *Star Wars* premier. "I was in the meeting when Ray turned down *Star Wars*," says Derek Gable, who headed Mattel's action figure line. "Almost no movies at that time translated into successful toy lines. The problem was timing. *Star Wars* came out just before Christmas and product wouldn't be available until March."

But "The Force" was with one of Mattel's lesser competitors, Cincinnati-headquartered Kenner Products, which saw the future, scooped up the line when it was offered by Lucas, and made a megafortune from the Kenner Star Wars Collection of plastic action figures, games, and accessories throughout the entire *Star Wars* trilogy, from 1977 to 1985. Kenner had also been faced with the time difference between movie and toy release. "But Kenner took a huge risk that ended up paying off," notes Gable. "They had the audacity to give coupons for the product to the kids at Christmas that could be cashed in when the toys were ready."

With the *Star Wars* fiasco still haunting him, Wagner around 1980 demanded a unique boys' action figure, and Roger Sweet took it on virtually as his own personal project. Tall, skinny, intense, low-key, but very creative, Sweet had joined Mattel in 1972 when the company was in dire financial straits with the Handler financial scandal brewing and the war with the Father of Barbie growing more intense. With an MS degree in product design from the Institute of Design in Chicago, he had come aboard from Lockheed, where he had helped design the interior of the Boeing 747, and before that the packaging for a number of consumer products.

Derek Gable's charter from Wagner was "to get the next *Star Wars*, the next big hit in male action figures. So every week, every two weeks, every time there was a product conference," Gable brought in different male action figure ideas, "and every time we went in there, they were completely dumbfounded."

But out of the blue, Sweet came up with three prototypes around Christmas of 1980 at the direction Gable, in whose group Sweet worked.

Roger came to me one day and he said, "I've got this idea. It's a guy who's bigger than big, as wide as he is tall, with huge muscles." Roger was then into weightlifting and he said, "Look, all these male action figures on the market are wimpy. I want to do a really big action figure." He called it "He-Man," sort of a combination of space and medieval, a medieval guy with weapons.

Years later, Sweet says his main motivation for conceiving He-Man was because of how he looked as a kid. "I was a scrawny dude and I read about all these heroes through history—very physical guys like Genghis Khan, and warriors like Charlemagne. And then Schwarzenegger was very big in the 1970s, a powerful-looking guy who was in very powerful action roles in the movies."

Sweet showed his initial three figures in model form at a product conference, and they were the three that brought He-Man and consequently Masters of the Universe into existence. "Other ideas were presented at the conference, but Ray Wagner didn't know what to do with this idea," says Sweet. "He knew He-Man was a strong product, but he didn't know whether it was applicable to the toy business. Of everything that was on the table, though, he pointed to my He-Man figures and he said, 'Those have the power.'"

Sweet got together with Gable and at Sweet's urging they decided to have marketing research killed on the other ideas that had been presented, because they knew the He-Man concept was strong. They met with the marketing honchos and it was decided to move forward with He-Man.

Sweet recalls, "The first marketing projection for the line was $7 million, and the next one was $11 million because it was looking a little stronger. Then they upped it to the unheard-of, white-knuckled height of $19 million. The first year the line got out in the stores it sold $38 million worth, then $80 million, then $111 million—and kept going up—and this is all domestically, in the United States."

In return for his idea, Sweet was promoted to manager of the Masters line, and received a bonus totaling about $90,000 over three years—peanuts compared to the revenue being generated by Mattel. He also felt "a lot of jealousy and resentment" from competitive associates in the shark-infested corporate waters of Mattel. "Within the first two months, there was more than one person claiming credit for having originated and named He-Man and originating the Masters line," he asserts. "People within Mattel claimed I didn't do it, and this was fast after I came up with it. They took credit because it became successful so quickly."

Derek Gable maintains years later that

> Roger deserves a great deal of credit, but He-Man and Masters of the Universe were a combination of many things, and Roger did have a huge part in making it happen. There were certain people at the company who didn't know what Roger did, or didn't appreciate his side of it. They all thought *they* did it. It was a process that developed. None of it would have happened if it wasn't for Roger, none of it would have happened if it wasn't for me pushing it along. There're loads of people who are responsible for having it happen.

As with the controversy over who invented Barbie years earlier, the debate over who really conceived He-Man and Masters continued ad infinitum.

Mattel claimed it conducted more than a dozen studies to get He-Man right.

■ ■ ■

Management's belief was that if a boy had one He-Man doll he would become a collector, just like what happened for girls with Barbie and her many accessories under Barad.

Beginning with the first He-Man and Masters of the Universe (MOTU) production run in 1982, a whole fantasy world had been developed—known as the magic Kingdom of Eternia. The $5-to-$8, 5½-inch polychloride He-Man, with his enormous Schwarzenegger-like muscles and bottle-blond hair, lived in the Roger Sweet–invented Castle

Grayskull (cost about $28.00), and was one of what would become dozens of characters, play sets, and accessories in the ensuing toy seasons. For almost $50, parents could purchase their little He-Man fan the Palace of Evil, known as Snake Mountain, with a built-in microphone that turned a boy's voice into a frightening "voice of evil."

In 1983, the He-Man line grossed $736 million for Mattel. After five consecutive quarterly losses, the company reaped a whopping 51 percent gain in sales, most of it due to Roger Sweet's He-Man and MOTU. That same year, Mattel president Ray Wagner, who blew the *Star Wars* acquisition, but green-lighted He-Man, became "disgruntled" with the situation there and left Mattel after a 10-year reign to become a toy consultant. One of his clients was Mattel's main competitor, Hasbro. Less than two years later, he died of a heart attack at the age of 53 while attending the toy fair in New York, where the latest MOTU products were getting a royal reception.

In 1984, Mattel was projecting sales of 55 million He-Man characters, which now included a scantily clad doll, He-Man's partner, Teela, who was billed as a goddess-warrior. In comparison, it took more than two decades for Mattel to sell 200 million of its stars, Barbie and Ken. There were now some two-dozen Masters characters—not to mention almost 200 spinoff products, ranging from He-Man pants equipped with a plastic sword to He-Man lunchboxes to He-Man underwear to He-Man electric toothbrushes from which He-Man's voice instructed kids to regularly brush.

Helping to push sales through the stratosphere was the number-one Nielsen-rated daily 30-minute syndicated TV children's show, naturally called *Masters of the Universe*, with a kid audience in the millions, which aired on some 160 stations in the United States, and in some four-dozen other countries and in languages such as Swahili, Arabic, and Zulu.

In January 1985, *Time* magazine noted that when He-Man, the hero of the afterschool program, shouted, "By the power of Grayskull, I have the power!" it had proved "puissant enough to capture the attention of more little boys than any other show in America." In order to bring girls into the TV audience, Mattel came up with a new action figure called She-Ra, billed as He-Man's twin sister, the "Princess of Power."

The Mattel-conceived and heavily promoted cartoon program, produced by Filmation in Los Angeles, had its debut in 1983, and immediately sparked controversy. Glenn Hastings, another Mattel president at the time, told the news weekly, "We were trying to fill a hole in the marketplace. We looked at boys ages three to six and found that, unlike girls, they [liked] good vs. evil."

Parents began expressing concern about the effect of He-Man and Masters on their children's psyches, and about violence in such programming. At the same time, Masters (and similar programs) were considered by parents and TV watchdog groups as tools to sell more toys and reap bigger profits for the likes of Mattel.

One such high-visibility nonprofit organization, Action for Children's Television, was especially critical. "These shows are not thought up by people trying to create characters or a story," the group's very vocal and high-profile president, Peggy Charren, observed. She told the *New York Times* that shows like *Masters of the Universe* were nothing more than "program-length advertisements . . . created to sell things. Accessories in the toy line must be part of the program."

Legislation had even been proposed in Congress requiring TV stations to offer five hours a week of educational programming for children, and two hours on weekends. Senator Frank Lautenberg, a New Jersey Democrat, who introduced the Children's Television Act of 1985, declared, "These shows are a violation of good taste and good judgment, and the worst thing is that there is no choice." The powerful National Association of Broadcasters, which represented almost 900 local TV stations and what was then just three networks, ABC, CBS, and NBC, opposed the legislation.

Filmation's president, Lou Scheimer, defended his *Masters of the Universe* program, noting, "We try not to have He-Man hurt any living creature, and the good guys always win." A senior vice president of marketing at Mattel, Paul Cleveland, also deflected criticism, declaring: "Having good guys and bad guys didn't start with He-Man. Little boys played that way 1,000 years ago."

■ ■ ■

By Christmas 1985, Mattel was predicting that its dozens of Masters characters and spinoffs would reap a whopping $450 million universally, a sharp 30 percent spike from 1984. Mattel bragged that if the brand were an actual corporation, it would be in the Fortune 500. Mattel, however, appeared blinded by its success, and to what was happening at its biggest competitor, Hasbro, then the number-one toy manufacturer in the United States. Hasbro had introduced a boys' toys line originally from Japan, called Transformers, which generated $100 million in revenue in 1984 and about $300 million in 1985. One of the many unique things kids did with Transformers was to convert a robot into a microscope.

Meanwhile, Mattel was utilizing new technology to spice up He-Man. This included characters that walked. Another was a dragon that spit water rather than fire. A Mattel executive, David Capper, another head of marketing for boys' toys, said strategies were in place to annually "freshen the products and keep the play patterns exciting."

One of the new Masters accessories was called Slime, a goopy product that came in cans, and that kids placed in another Masters product known as the Slime Pit. During the first six months of 1986, Mattel had given away thousands of cans of the green gooey stuff, which had first been marketed as a novelty product by Mattel in the late 1970s, selling some 10 million cans.

After the 1986 giveaway, however, the only way kids could get Slime was by having their parents buy two new Masters characters, or another Slime Pit. Mattel was again using the Gillette razor-and-razorblade theory of marketing that had been so successful with Barbie.

Parents were furious with Mattel's marketing strategy. The *Los Angeles Times*, in a story headlined, MARKETING TO CHILDREN RAISES BIG QUESTIONS, quoted a marketing professor at USC as calling Mattel's technique "manipulative. You only need a can of Slime, and you have to buy two figures to get it." Mattel, naturally, defended its practice, declaring the promotion wasn't onerous, and was put in place "to build momentum on Masters figures."

As the school year of 1985 was about to begin, Mattel had a big promotion to generate more interest in He-Man and Masters, and bring in more buyers. The toy giant announced in the September 8

Sunday newspaper comic sections across the land a contest that was open to children under the age of 12. Mattel promised to offer the winner a $100,000 college scholarship and, best of all, the rules specifically promised: "The Winning Entry will be made into an actual Toy!!!" as part of the Masters of the Universe line. Mattel declared that its "Create-a-Character" contest was established to "foster imaginative play in children." A Mattel spokesman, Martin Kleinman, was quoted at the time in *Education Week*, a magazine for teachers, as saying the company expected half-a-million entries by October 10, 1985, the contest's closing date. He noted that the entries would be a "telling commentary" on "what's going on in the minds of American children."

In fact, there was a winner—of sorts. He was a cute blond eighth-grader—11-year-old Nathan Bitner, of Naperville, Illinois. His idea was called "Fearless Photog"—an action figure whose head was a futuristic camera that supposedly could take snapshots.

Mattel made the splashy, full-page announcement in another moneymaker and promotional item, the official *Masters of the Universe* magazine, which had a circulation of some 750,000. In the Spring 1986 issue, Mattel congratulated Bitner, whose photograph and that of his drawing of Fearless Photog appeared. In the magazine, Mattel noted that he "received over 40,000 votes from across the country, and beat out four tough competitors. Nathan was awarded a $100,000 scholarship. He also won a five-day trip to California where he will spend one day as honorary president of Mattel."

In a press release, Mattel reportedly stated that it would "produce Fearless Photog as part of the Masters toy line." But there was no mention as to when.

Interestingly enough, the product never was produced. This ignited a huge controversy and a swarm of conspiracy theories among the He-Man cognoscenti, who appeared angered with Mattel for misleading them. It was assumed that they wanted Fearless Photog for their MOTU collections.

As time passed, He-Man and Masters fans inundated related websites, criticizing Mattel for its failure to bring out the figure. Even in the new millennium, He-Man bloggers on such sites as X-Entertainment raised questions about Mattel, Fearless Photog, and Bitner himself.

As late as the early-to-mid-2000s, the controversy over Fearless Photog and Mattel continued to rage online. Finally, Nathan Bitner surfaced. He had been in the videogame business, but also had had a sad life reportedly rife with personal and financial problems, as reported on message boards such as Big Brother Strikes Back on the Force.Net, and Ron Schuler's Parlour Tricks blog. Bitner was last known to have been serving as a medic in the Army in Iraq.

On Big Brother, the writer noted that "Bitner's plight had become the stuff of legend in the action figure world. . . . Obviously, Mattel bought off Nathan Bitner with the promise of education, but depriving the world of the Fearless Photog. . . . you've got to wonder if his life would have turned out differently if his dreams of the Fearless Photog would have come to life."

■ ■ ■

Meanwhile, MOTU appeared to be reaching its zenith. By early summer 1986, Mattel boasted that He-Man, in one form or another, was in almost 70 percent of American homes with boys in the 4-to-10 age group.

But by the Spring of 1987, there was a major downturn. Mattel was now being described in the media as "embattled," "beleaguered," and "lackluster" after reporting a whopping $127.3 million drop in domestic sales, which was mostly blamed on the decline and fall of He-Man and the rest of the brand. It was a mindboggling turnaround from the heights. During its amazing run, He-Man and MOTU had sold more than $1 billion worth of product, and 1985 even eclipsed Barbie in sales, but now the entire line had taken a dive into the Slime Pit.

When He-Man took off, says Roger Sweet, "I was treated very well at Mattel, and was treated very well through 1986 when the line was doing great; and then in 1987, when it collapsed, I collapsed, so to speak."

There were a number of reasons for He-Man's sudden and unexpected death. One of them was that Mattel, as was the case with Hot Wheels back in the 1970s, had been too confident and too aggressive and too greedy in pushing the product to retailers to increase profits and impress Wall Street. "It was *way* oversold, and in 1987 it collapsed and sold just $7 million," says Sweet. "There was just too much product put in the stores for the amount of demand for it. It swamped the shelves."The other major reason for He-man's burial was competition from the likes of Hasbro's Transformers, and another action figure series called Teenage Mutant Ninja Turtles (TMNT) produced by a company called Playmate Toys. TMNT was a toy that originated with a hugely successful comic book, followed by an animated TV series, a movie, and more.

Mattel made a last-ditch, albeit curious, effort to save MOTU. It hired actors to play the roles of some of the brand's characters, and sent the show—"The Masters of the Universe Power Tour"—replete with acrobats, a roller derby, and simulated explosions, across the country. MATTEL TRIES TO STAGE A REVIVAL: FLOUNDERING HE-MAN BROUGHT TO LIFE AND TOLD TO HIT THE ROAD, trumpeted a headline in the *Los Angeles Times* in March 1987.

The 90-minute extravaganza featured as He-Man a hulking, blond-and-bronzed member of the Teamster's Union, 33-year-old Jack Wadsworth, who sported a 49-inch chest, 20-inch arms, and 28-inch thighs. She-Ra, He-Man's twin sister character, was portrayed by Wadsworth's wife, 28-year-old Leslie. They'd met on the Universal Studios tour when he was playing Conan the Barbarian, and she Red Sonja. The MOTU tour was a success—it sold out in most cities, and was blasted by parents and children's groups as a "program-length commercial"—but the patient died.

With Masters and He-Man now a flop, Roger Sweet's star fell. Because he was such a competent designer, though, Mattel held onto him for a little while. He was transferred into the Barbie accessories area under the talented Diana Troup, who had been promoted to executive vice president by her friend, Jill Barad. There, Sweet designed a number of innovative items, the most elaborate of which was Barbie's $350 electrified colonial-style Magic Mansion, which was part of the Barbie Collectible line. "Barbie had always had collectibles," notes Sweet, "but Jill had pushed it like crazy and just segmented the line like crazy and expanded it."

In April 1991, Sweet got his final walking papers, and he "suspects" that Barad was behind his dismissal "even though I was coming up with excellent product. They had me stop working at Mattel, and I worked with a Human Resources guy in severance negotiations. I had to come in when they called me. They just wanted me out."

Without a job, Sweet assumed that with his background and the name he had earned for He-Man he'd be snapped up by another toy company. But no one would have him.

If you ask Sweet, the "impression" he got was that he had been "blacklisted." "I tried to get a job at several other toy companies and couldn't—and I had one of the best track records in the history of the toy industry," he says.

> But there were a few key people talking heavily against me. There were people at Mattel who, as a result of my coming up with the He-Man line, had their fortunes turn very bad at Mattel. It had to be frustrating for a lot of people and there was a lot of resentment. When somebody comes up with something that's *way* better than what other people are doing— other people resent it. When people are on top, people want to knock them down.

> I sometimes think that if I would never have come up with He-Man and Masters I probably could have worked at Mattel until I retired. In relation to Mattel and the industry in general I was never given the credit for originating and naming He-Man, and originating the general concept of the Masters line.

Sweet was able to snag some freelance work after he left Mattel, but not enough to pay the bills. He hit his low point when he was forced to take an hourly job at Home Depot in hardware sales, in the Seattle area, wearing the eponymous orange-and-white apron and a hardhat and driving a forklift. With a sense of irony, the man who helped make more than $1 billion for Mattel says, "I got terrific at driving a forklift. It pleased me no end to be able to maneuver a piece of equipment weighing several thousand pounds in and out of tight spots in a heroic way."

Like others who had worked for Mattel, he was struck with cancer. During chemotherapy, he had "enough radiation in one dose to kill a person," he says. "For three days in that hospital room nobody could come in because I was radioactive."

Unlike He-Man, Roger Sweet was a survivor.

■ ■ ■

The fall of He-Man was a major financial calamity for Mattel. In 1986, the company lost $1 million. A year earlier, North American operating profits fell to $6.2 million from $96.7 million. Calling the company "struggling, heavy and bloated," chairman and chief executive John Amerman essentially cleaned house, slashed costs, laid off 500 at the company's headquarters, closed Mattel factories in the United States, the Philippines, Canada, and Taiwan, and went back to the company's core brands, such as Barbie, whose sales were still skyrocketing as a result of Barad's marketing skills.

When Hasbro introduced a new doll called Jem to compete against Barbie, Barad fought back.

"Jem was a very tarty, trailer park, trashy rock-chick doll, and I mean *trashy*," says Lynn Rosenblum, a former marketing director at Mattel from 1987 to 1995, who helped push the Barbie collector and special editions line of dolls, such as Mermaid Barbie and Rockettes Barbie. "Jill just made Barbie a rocker, called it Barbie and the Rockers with capes and songs, and just totally wiped out Jem." Of Mattel's revenues, Barbie's wholesale sales amounted to some 40 percent, with the remainder coming from other toys. Analysts kept a wary eye on the company. "Mattel has a remarkable propensity to get people excited and a remarkable propensity to disappoint," observed one.

Roger Sweet's boss on the He-Man project, Derek Gable, a 16-year Mattel veteran, and his supervisor, Denis Bosley, also were dismissed when the Preliminary Design group, where great toy ideas had been developed ever since it was established by Jack Ryan, was dissolved.

"They got rid of all the preliminary design management—and I was having my best year ever," says Gable. "I couldn't believe what they were doing, and they were trying to come up with all these reasons for letting us go, and they kept changing the reasons because they were trying to cover their ass because they didn't want to be sued.

Eventually, we all went. I could see the writing on the wall," he says on the eve of Barbie's 50th anniversary. "Mattel had become very political—people were sucking up to people; it became more about ass-covering, and being seen with the right people. It all became decision making, not for the best interests of the company, but just for people's careers."

He firmly believed that the new corporate culture at Mattel, as he saw it, was "absolutely" primed for the continued rise of Jill Barad.

# Chapter 11

# A Fearsome and Firing Diva and the Great Whistleblower Debacle

I n 1992, Jill Barad approached John Amerman with a demand. She was aware that sometime in the not-too-distant future he intended to retire as chairman and chief executive, and she wanted to be assured—in no uncertain terms—that she would ascend to the vaunted top spot in the company with his approval.

While he intended to be around for a while more—it turned out to be another five years—he demonstrated his confidence in her by promoting her to president and chief operating officer. Tougher and more in-charge than ever, she negotiated a contract that doubled her compensation to $2 million annually with incentives. Better still, she was guaranteed a full five years' compensation if she didn't get Amerman's post when he stepped down.

In her new position of power, Barad's management style was both peculiar and fearsome. In order to catch her eye and get on her good side—and sometimes even get promotions—one had to look marvelous, but still not be more marvelous-looking than she in terms of dress, makeup, and overall style. Executives under her, women and men alike, joked that she had the same philosophy of success as the Fernando Lamas character played by Billy Crystal on *Saturday Night Live*, whose comical catchphrase was, "You look *mah-velous* dahling. . . . It's better to look good than feel good!"

Barad believed that if you looked marvelous, you'd perform in your job marvelously—and those were the kind of executives with whom she wanted to be surrounded—attractive and glamorous-looking people—real-life Barbies in Escada and Kens in Armani. "Everybody had to dress up, had to look glamorous," maintains Diana Troup.

Margo Moschel, also an elegant dresser who caught Barad's approving eye, notes,

> Jill believed you are what you wear, and no way would she ever even have a conversation with someone within Mattel, within the Barbie brand, if they didn't look good. Her comment would be, "Well, what does she know? Look at what she wears. Look what she looks like." She judged people pretty harshly as far as their appearance was concerned.

> There were women in the company who didn't even get considered for any higher-up positions like becoming a director or a vice president. They didn't stand a chance until someone took them aside and said, "You've got one thing that you're missing because you've got the intelligence you just need to know how to bring your look up and polish it and make yourself look like a VP who would be working for Jill Barad." The minute the person did it, they got promoted.

At the same time, Barad was idolized by many within Mattel despite her curious management style and her rigid likes and dislikes. Diana Troup maintains,

> People really wanted Jill's love because when she showed you her appreciation and told you, "Oh, my God, that idea's fantastic"—it just felt so good coming from someone who

was so smart, so very strong, and knew this was a business and that we had to have all the right people in there. Jill was *the* star. I don't want to say she had a personality cult. I don't want to use the word *cult* because that sounds so evil. But her personality was *so* powerful that people quaked in their boots when she walked around—quaked in both fear and adoration.

Troup often traveled with Barad to Europe and the Far East on Mattel business, and everywhere they went there was, in fact, a feeling of a cult following. She was idolized and adored. Other people in the toy business responded to her as if she was a rock star.

"I was in Japan with her and she was sitting next to me and one of these little Japanese ladies in the toy business in marketing who wanted to meet her came in and was actually trembling and crying in her presence," Troup recalls. "Jill's reputation was international. She was really, really something—very ambitious, and driven. I hate to think of her as that because it was more than driven and ambitious. She really *loved* her work, and she liked *all* the glory."

■ ■ ■

There was also the *fear factor*.

"People who worked with Jill were afraid of her—afraid of disagreeing with her, afraid to say no to her," asserts Nancy Zwiers, who headed worldwide Barbie marketing through most of the 1990s, when Barad rose from president of girls' toys, to COO, to chief executive and chairwoman.

As gutsy as Barad and considered more knowledgeable about the toy business, Zwiers did something no one else under Barad ventured to do—she often disagreed with her on decisions affecting Mattel. "People tried to second guess Jill," Zwiers observes.

> But I figured out what I thought was right and so I had Jill's respect. One part of her didn't like people to disagree with her, but the other part of her respected the person who was an independent enough thinker to have a point of view and to be a forceful advocate for that point of view. And so my relationship with Jill was unusual in the company. People used to marvel at how I would go toe-to-toe with her for what I believed.

Ultimately, Zwiers decided to leave Mattel after nine years because there were things that she thought needed to happen regarding the direction to take Barbie, and couldn't get Barad to agree with them.

"There came a shift when I felt like I knew the business better than Jill, and I knew what was best for the business better than Jill—not because I was better than her, but I was just closer to it," Zwiers maintains. "Jill was very intuitive—and that was a huge strength of hers, and so she had a tendency to say, 'Don't confuse me with the facts. I know what I believe.' She was so set on trusting her intuition that she refused to pay attention to facts that were contrary to that intuition, and that ultimately led to her downfall."

The fear factor under Barad manifested itself in increased competitiveness, in pitting people against one another, in placing blame on others for her own mistakes, and what was perceived as pure mean-spiritedness that went above and beyond her being a tough and demanding boss who expected perfection.

A female senior vice president of the Barbie brand in the 1990s, is said to have suffered constant verbal abuse from Barad. "Jill would reduce her to tears," according to a former Mattel president who was an eyewitness. "They would have a meeting and Jill would be so abusive that the executive would just break into tears. She ran the brand and was very effective at what she did but ultimately got pushed out."

According to a former executive vice president, the executive, who left Mattel on her own, and went on to work for the Disney organization, became one of Barad's scapegoats. Says the former executive, "In order for Jill to deflect any blame from herself, she chose someone to put the blame on. Jill was very convincing, and everyone would go along with her—the board of directors, whomever. There was no one who was going to come up against her—long before she became chairman."

If Barad despised a Barbie design being shown to her—or if she was just determined to "get" the person making the presentation—she'd humiliate him or her in front of others.

Margo Moschel recalls getting both Barad's praise and criticism. "When I was a star, I could do no wrong with Jill," Moschel states.

> We'd be in a meeting with standing room only, with all the top executives, and somebody would be making a presentation, and I'd be sitting in the back, and Jill's in the front row. She'd have

this disdainful look on her face about the presentation, and she did *not* hide her disdain. Out of the corner of her eye, she noticed where I was sitting, turned around, gave a little flick of her hair, and said, "Well, let's ask Margo. She's the *only* one with any taste in this room," which was her way of putting *everyone else* down. "Margo, tell us what we should do with this. I hate it! But I don't know why I hate it."

It made me feel good and it didn't because I thought, "Oh, shit, she's doing it now—she's doing it to me. She's pitting people against people, and those other folks in the room are going to end up hating me." I was on the winning side of the comments but I would *cringe*. But then she used the very same tactic when she wanted me out of there. I knew, one day I was her superstar, but tomorrow I could be chopped liver. If she wanted to get rid of somebody she'd pick at little things. She had the ability to take the least significant thing and make it look like a crime—like you had committed a crime.

As an executive, Barad had developed a take-no-prisoners reputation for terminating executives on a whim. For honchos under her at Mattel it was like taking a dip in the waters off Amity Beach, with Barad playing the Great White. Her firings were analyzed by survivors and victims alike during her reign and it was determined that as soon as she assumed a new level of power she terminated the people beneath her whom she perceived to be competitors.

"It was basically an attempt on Jill's part to eliminate any form of competition," observes a veteran Mattel executive who was a victim.

Her habit of firing capriciously would eventually become well known in the business world and the media that covered it. For instance, the *Ivey Business Journal*, in an article undiplomatically entitled, "The Seven Habits of Spectacularly Unsuccessful Executives," reported that Barad "removed her senior lieutenants if she thought they harbored reservations about the way she was running things. . . . At Mattel, along with firing senior lieutenants on a moment's notice, Jill Barad during her reign as chairman and CEO drove six [executives] to resign for 'personal reasons.'"

■ ■ ■

Before Jim DeRose accepted the position of president of Mattel USA in the Spring of 1994, he had one final candid and soul-searching conversation with president and COO Barad.

The Mattel job was a fantastic opportunity for the 44-year-old DeRose, he believed at the time. Mattel was an iconic company and the job would give him enormous visibility in corporate America, with substantial opportunity for advancement. When and if Barad ascended to the top job, DeRose figured he'd be in line to succeed her as COO. As president of Mattel's domestic division, he would be responsible for all North American operations in addition to having global responsibility for the development and licensing of Barbie, Hot Wheels, and the soon-to-be acquired Cabbage Patch Kids.

DeRose had a reputation for cleaning up corporate messes, and Mattel at the time was experiencing some supply-and-demand problems with major retailers, so DeRose's positive relationship with the retail sector was a big plus. Barad's expectation, DeRose understood from her, was that he would hit the ground running and put Mattel's domestic house in order.

But the move to Mattel would also involve major professional and personal lifestyle changes. The highly esteemed DeRose had an excellent track record in his current position as president of the Hanes Division of the Sara Lee Corporation, and his family, including children just starting high school, had a comfortable life in Winston-Salem, North Carolina. But he concluded it was the right time to make a major career move, and go west to Mattel.

Of greater concern to DeRose, however, was Mattel's corporate culture. A self-described pragmatic businessman, he had done his due diligence, and what he had learned troubled him.

Before making his final decision to come aboard, DeRose met with Barad at the Westwood Marquis Hotel and Gardens, in Los Angeles. For some three hours he candidly gave her his opinions of Mattel, and what he perceived to be some of the problems that existed. He described his management style, his skill sets, even areas he wasn't good at, and offered his pledge that he would always be truthful and honest with her. He felt that by laying his cards on the table he'd avoid the untenable situation encountered by other Mattel executives who'd been eaten alive and spit out.

At the end of the meeting, Barad stood up on her stilettos, gave DeRose a warm hug—he already knew she had a reputation for being touchy-feely and flirtatious around powerful men—and exclaimed, "Oh, Jim, you are wonderful! You're exactly what I have been looking for to come to this company. We are going to march to the boardroom together."

DeRose felt good about Barad's seemingly enthusiastic support. He flew back to North Carolina, gave Sara Lee four weeks' notice, moved his brood to California, and was on board as president by May 1994, in time for a worldwide executive meeting for which Barad demanded his presence.

"Initially, I thought I was in heaven," he later told a confidant, who has requested to remain anonymous, but provided the author with DeRose's experience at Mattel.

Soon, though, DeRose discovered worrisome "stress signs" within Mattel. In order to keep Wall Street happy and make the projections the company had been promising, Mattel had asked major retailers in the quarter previous to DeRose's arrival to buy additional product—millions of dollars' worth—with a promise from Mattel that the retailers would later get special discounts and special programs to assist them in moving the extra inventory.

Mattel's salespeople expressed serious concerns about the practice of "inventory loading" to DeRose. They viewed it as a "time bomb" because they felt retailers like Toys 'R' Us could never unload the glut of goods. Their concerns appeared valid, because DeRose soon discovered that Mattel customers were still jammed with excessive inventory and he felt that forecasts put forth by the company were not achievable.

He told the confidant, "I began to ring the alarm bell to Jill. I suggested that it was early enough in the year that actions could be taken to protect the profitability by basically pulling in the reigns, such as reducing advertising for the year. I was saying that we had severe problems that needed to be addressed." In a memo to Barad, he stated that the company was short some $40 million to meet its projections for the year, and that Mattel should "determine collectively how to address the profit fallout."

As DeRose looked further into the matter, it became "very apparent" that Barad "was a major factor in the inventory loading effort, that ultimately all decisions were being made by Jill," he told the confidant. "It was all driven by a desire to make the numbers. Your stock rises and falls based on your ability to deliver your numbers. In any organization there is the old saying that as long as you are making your numbers, everything is fine, and Jill was making her numbers."

And with good numbers, Barad would receive bigger bonuses.

■ ■ ■

Like DeRose, another Mattel executive, Michelle Greenwald, a senior vice president for marketing who supervised its business with the Walt Disney Company, had similar concerns about what was going on.

Greenwald was subsequently fired in July 1995, and in October of that year accused Mattel in what the *Wall Street Journal* described as "a little-noticed whistle-blower lawsuit" of inflating its earnings with various gimmicks and questionable accounting practices.

Once the lawsuit became public, all hell broke loose for Mattel.

The *New York Times*, in a June 1997 story entitled "Truth or Consequences Hardly," which was about the decline and fall of corporate ethics at the time, noted that Greenwald's lawsuit "paints a disturbing picture of Mattel's corporate environment."

According to the article, Greenwald had alleged that there was constant pressure to keep earnings on an upward spiral—something DeRose had also noted—and that Barad and chairman and CEO Amerman received compensation that was linked closely to how well the company performed under an incentive plan, which, according to Greenwald's suit, permitted top executives "to reap perhaps $100 million in payments, substantially from" certain allegedly questionable accounting procedures. The suit further charged that Barad and Amerman had disguised the actual cost of doing business and misled the public. In addition, Greenwald claimed that a "crisis" mentality existed within the company.

Mattel adamantly denied her allegations, believing the case was absolutely without merit. One Mattel director told the *Times* that "Ms. Greenwald's lawsuit against the company was 'just another nuisance suit.' " And a second director "called the lawsuit 'totally fraudulent.' "

The company then began an independent investigation.

But questions were raised about how independent that probe actually was, when it was revealed in a *New York Times* story, titled

"Independent Investigation of Mattel Data Is Questioned," that the head of Mattel's inquiry, a former Securities and Exchange Commission enforcement official, had passed on to Amerman a confidential letter he had received from Greenwald's attorney outlining areas that should be probed. Mattel claimed the letter's forwarding "was entirely appropriate" because it was part of the ongoing probe.

Mattel also declared it intended to sue Greenwald.

"In light of this repeated slander of our company, we will now take action by exercising every available legal remedy to defend Mattel from these unwarranted and baseless public attacks and to recover damages from Ms. Greenwald and her counsel for the harm they have done to the company and our shareholders," Mattel's spokesman, Glenn Bozarth, told the *Los Angeles Times*.

In the wake of the controversy sparked by Greenwald's allegations, Mattel announced a rare flat quarter, which sent shares plummeting by more than 10 percent.

Greenwald's lawyer responded to Mattel's threat by declaring, "If they bring any legal action, based on what I presently know, it would be unwarranted and unfounded, and I would defend myself to the fullest extent of the law, and Ms. Greenwald as well."

■ ■ ■

It seemed the past was repeating itself at Mattel.

Back in the 1970s, Ruth Handler's efforts to keep Wall Street happy was one of the reasons for her downfall. It appeared that similar shenanigans were happening once again, raising concerns that Mattel's corporate culture had not really changed, according to analysts at the time. But whatever scandal Greenwald's lawsuit had sparked would have no effect on Barad's rise to the top of the world's biggest toy company.

Handler and Barad, the two highest-ranking women ever to run Mattel, first met at a meeting of a charitable group called "Women of Distinction," where Barad told the gathering, "I have my job only because such a woman as Ruth Handler existed before me and created the company I now work in." Handler, who felt the contemporary Barbie doll resembled the glitzy and glamorous Barad, was "touched" by Barad's remarks, and later noted that Mattel had made "an excellent choice" in promoting her to the most powerful positions in the company.

■ ■ ■

It wasn't long into Jim DeRose's tenure before he realized that his style of management and Barad's were miles apart. His was sleeves-rolled-up, down-in-the-trenches, collaborative; Barad's was summoning people up to her ivory tower office where she held court—the ultimate Barbie Executive Princess doll. Because of DeRose's down-to-earth management style, he quickly became popular among the troops and other executives, while Barad was often the subject of snarky gossip. As a result, she was becoming increasingly wary of him as competition.

She was the epitome of the corporate politician. Not only was she worried about competition from DeRose, she even appeared to distrust chairman Amerman, her biggest backer within the company. This was underscored when she gave Jim DeRose strict instructions never to talk to Amerman and, if by chance he had any conversations with the chairman, DeRose was to immediately contact her and let her know in detail what was said.

To Barad's apparent annoyance, both DeRose and Amerman were early risers who got into headquarters before seven o'clock, and it was not uncommon for Amerman to grab a cup of coffee and pop down to DeRose's office, put his feet up, and say, "Hey, what's going on?" To DeRose, this meant Amerman was fishing for company intelligence that Barad might have been withholding.

It was then incumbent on DeRose, entangled in Barad's conspiracy, to track her down wherever she might be in the world—Europe, Asia, or at her hairdresser—and tell her that he had just had a conversation with Amerman, and give her a verbatim account.

As DeRose later told the confidant, "Jill obviously didn't want to be blindsided by her boss. She needed to know everything he said or asked about."

Regardless, DeRose tried to skirt the politics and do his job, which wasn't easy with all of the intrigue and backstabbing that permeated Mattel's executive suites. Among his successes during his watch was securing the Cabbage Patch Kids line—and keeping it true to the original rather than allowing it to become, as he once observed, "another typical Mattel plastic play piece."

At Sara Lee, DeRose had found the management style collaborative and cooperative, and if there was an issue it was put on the table and dealt with. Mattel, in his view, was the exact opposite—issues were swept *under* the table, and few if any wanted to confront problems that existed. While he saw negatives he felt he could fix, he was faced with a "tremendous amount of resistance to change," and was frequently told that "things are just fine, you don't need to make changes."

Shortly thereafter, DeRose saw that his relationship with Barad was quickly fraying. She had begun distancing herself from him, and when they were together he sensed a degree of irritation on her part. The only time that they met socially after his hiring was at a bar mitzvah for another Mattel executive's son. Still, he was hearing that Barad was "delighted" with what he was doing.

But DeRose came to the realization that his number was probably up six months into his tenure. In November 1994, in preparation for a board meeting, he had submitted a report to Barad with his projections for the year—numbers in his view that were actually achievable. A few days later, one of Barad's finance and planning people returned DeRose's report, telling him Barad found it "unacceptable," and gave him different figures that "Jill wants you to present to the board of directors." When DeRose argued that her numbers were unrealistic, the Barad associate shot back: "When you are the COO of this company, you can present any numbers you want. Until then, you will present the numbers that Jill tells you to present."

Through the Thanksgiving 1994 holiday, DeRose prepared a restructuring plan for Mattel and presented it to Barad, who quickly rejected it. She also turned down a subsequent plan.

One of the clues that an executive was about to be given the axe by Barad during her reign was when Joseph McKay, Mattel's senior vice president of human relations, was waiting in the employee's office with his or her personnel file in hand.

That was how Jim DeRose was greeted at eight o'clock in the morning on a Friday, two weeks before Christmas 1994—a day after Barad rejected his second restructuring plan, and just seven months after he had joined the company, an apparent record for a high-ranking Mattel executive to be axed by Barad.

"Jill wants you out right now," McKay told DeRose. "She's just not happy with you here."

When DeRose pointed out that he had moved his family across country, that he had worked hard for the last half-year, that he had made progress and pushed the company in the right direction, that he had kids in school and a mortgage to pay, McKay's only response was, "Sorry, Jim, but Jill's just not happy with you. It's just not working for her."

DeRose pleaded with McKay to speak to Barad and/or Amerman, but was told neither would see him, that they were terminating him on the spot without giving him the courtesy of a meeting.

McKay put a document on DeRose's desk that Barad wanted him to sign. DeRose refused and was escorted out of the building. After much soul-searching, and with the severance part of his contract being honored by Mattel, he decided not to sue for wrongful termination because he feared he'd be treated as a pariah in corporate America and never get another executive job. In fact, he became quite successful.

"Following that ugly period in my life at Mattel," he later said, "I turned the page and moved on."

Meanwhile, DeRose's nemesis, Jill Barad, was getting closer to her coronation as boss of bosses.

# Chapter 12

# The Princess Diana Fiasco, Praying for Success, and Demi Plays Barad

On August 22, 1996, 45-year-old Jill Barad, decked out in shocking Barbie pink—her suit, her shoes, and her lipstick—finally reached the pinnacle she had been striving for since that first day she walked into Mattel headquarters and began moving up the corporate ladder, beginning as a lowly $38,000-a-year product manager.

Mattel had finally announced that, effective January 1, 1997, Barad would succeed her mentor, John Amerman, as chief executive and later that year take over the chairmanship. With her promotion, she became one of America's most powerful women executives, one of only two women at the time running a company in the *Fortune* 500.

When she was solely running the Barbie brand, she had come up with a slogan for the doll, which was, "We Girls Can Do Anything." Now, with her promotion, Barad had proved it.

Soon after, she began putting her stamp on Mattel from the top—beginning with acquisitions. The first on her watch, in March 1997, was Tyco Toys Inc., makers of Matchbox and radio-controlled cars. The purchase, though, came at a time when Tyco wasn't considered a major coup because its sales were sliding, and Mattel's purchase price of $881 million was considered steep—more than Tyco's sales a year earlier. As a result, Mattel was forced to record a $275 million pretax charge against operations.

As time would tell, acquisitions were not Barad's forte.

She also began putting her stamp on Mattel's corporate culture, initiating flexible working hours. Fridays became half-days, and employees were permitted to choose to take off four Fridays a year. Those workers who volunteered at a local school were given two days off every year, and employees at El Segundo headquarters received two weeks off at the end of the year following the Christmas toy-buying season. She and other executives used a makeshift stage in the Mattel cafeteria to make announcements, such as when they dressed in casual clothing, including bathrobes and leather jackets, to proclaim that every workday, not just Friday, would be casual dress. But she herself continued to be a fashion plate, and was considered among the cadre "casually challenged." She participated in skits for employees—she still loved acting—and her memorable Mattel roles in the months after her promotion included those of a *Star Trek* character and a beatnik.

"The best people are attracted to places that not only fulfill them on an intellectual level, but also take into consideration life-style issues," she declared.

She gave special consideration to gays in the company, and there were many. When one executive learned he had AIDS and thought he should leave Mattel, Barad kept him on board. With Barad's support, he started the Children Affected by AIDS Foundation, and Barad threw her support behind the organization's annual "Dream Halloween" fundraising event. It was also said that when she learned an employee had undergone a male-to-female sex-change operation, Barad had authorized a special restroom for her use. She also didn't mind when a group of employees, including a top female executive—all born-again Christians—held hands and prayed joyously for a new product's success.

Despite all the joy and glad tidings, Barad continued to hire and fire on a whim, and instructed executives under her "to be ruthless" when it came to cutting expenses.

■ ■ ■

One of the many starred items on Barad's to-do list involved two dolls that she had been dreaming about producing—collectibles of Diana, Princess of Wales, and Miss Elizabeth Taylor. As one Mattel executive involved in both projects observes, "Jill was practically obsessed with having those two icons, Di and Liz, become Mattel dolls. Jill felt it would give her and the company enormous prestige, because neither had ever given their authorization for an exclusive doll in their likeness."

For at least two years prior to 1997, Barad and her top marketing people had pushed unsuccessfully to get authorization from Diana herself, the beloved and controversial international icon, to grant Mattel permission to produce a beautiful doll in the Princess's image for the Barbie collector market. According to a knowledgeable source, "Diana had categorically refused to be associated with Barbie, or commercially exploited as a doll."

It was only when Diana tragically died in Paris on August 31, 1997, in a car accident with her lover, Dodi Al-Fayed, that Mattel considered producing an unauthorized Diana doll. However, there was swift competition when the Franklin Mint, known for hawking collectibles ranging from commemorative coins to celebrity tchotchkes, beat Mattel to the punch by rushing two unlicensed Diana dolls to the market—one made of porcelain that sold swiftly for $245—along with a Princess Diana Tribute Plate, among other Diana items.

The Diana, Princess of Wales Memorial Fund charity, in Great Britain, unsuccessfully sued the Franklin Mint, owned by a wealthy Beverly Hills couple, Stewart and Lynda Resnick. The lawsuit charged the company with exploiting the Princess's name, "like vultures feeding on the dead."

Seeking to avoid such legal entanglements, Barad and her lieutenants began waging a major campaign to get permission from the Memorial Fund—and the late Princess's older sister, Lady Elizabeth Sarah Lavinia McCorquodale—for Mattel to produce a beautiful doll that had the Fund's approval. Mattel executives viewed the Franklin Mint's product with what was described as "annoyance and derision"—so much so that when a Mattel executive bought one to scrutinize, she was turned down for expense reimbursement by her boss because the doll was "considered too ugly to keep." She was instructed to return it and get a refund.

In late March 1997, some five months before Di died, an illustrator of doll fashions from Great Britain, Anne Zielinski-Old, had applied for a job at Mattel. Zielinski-Old had come with an interesting resume. Besides doll fashions, she had done packaging illustration work for prestigious English firms such as the famed London department store Harrods, owned by Dodi Al-Fayed's father; the food purveyor Fortnum & Mason; and Garrads, the Crown Jewellers, all of which were businesses that carried the prestigious stamp of "Royal Appointment" from Buckingham Palace.

Zielinksi-Old had an enthusiastic meeting at Mattel headquarters with a few executives in the Barbie Collectible division—including Ruby Knauss, vice president of the division, and Ann Driskill, the division's director. Everyone there liked her portfolio. Because there was a hiring freeze at the time, she was given some freelance design work for Fashion Avenue Barbie. She left to return to England with high hopes that she'd eventually get a job offer from Mattel, move permanently to California, and become part of the prestigious Barbie design team. Flying home, she figured there was interest in her because, "Jill Barad wanted to English-up the products in that it was the era of Princess Diana."

At least, that's what she thought at the time.

Curiously, the full-time staff job offer didn't materialize until September 7, 1997, just a week after the Mercedes-Benz carrying Princess Diana and Al-Fayed slammed into an abutment in Paris's Pont de l'Alma road tunnel as they were being chased from Al-Fayed's father's Ritz Hotel by a pack of paparazzi.

Ruby Knauss, a sprightly Texan, then the head of Mattel's collectibles division, called Zielinksi-Old at her home in the village of Ditchling, some 50 miles from London, and gave her the good news that she was being hired as a "staff designer" at an annual salary of $70,018, plus a $10,000 signing bonus and full company benefits. Mattel would pay for business-class airfare for her and her husband and their daughter, and all other relocation expenses. Mattel employment papers were faxed to the country store in the village for the grateful new hire to sign. Knauss wanted Zielinksi-Old to start work as soon as possible, but first she was assigned to attend as Mattel's representative the runway shows in London, Milan, and Paris—and to make contact with the people from Gucci regarding licensing deals.

She finally arrived at Mattel's Design Center on November 3, 1997, to begin her new career, with the understanding that it would involve designing Barbie dolls, and with at least a year to learn the complexities of the Barbie line. Two days later, after she asked what her beginning duties would be, she was hit with a shocker. She was told, "We've chosen you to do Princess Diana."

Instead of Barbie, she was assigned to Jill Barad's priority project, which had never been discussed with Zielinksi-Old.

Years later she says in an interview with the author, "They had actually hired me to do *that* doll. My being there was the manifestation of Jill Barad's greed. She wanted to do the Princess Diana doll and they thought, 'Here's somebody who actually works for these people who have the royal warrants—let's get her in, let's get the approval on the doll.' Apparently they thought I had royal pedigree myself."

In fact, Anne Zielinksi-Old, with her very proper British accent, and very proper British education, had been born in the New York City borough of Queens, and was an American whose mother was British—all of which she found "quite amusing" when it was discovered at Mattel.

Nevertheless, she quickly found herself working with a Mattel sculptor "actually designing Diana's face, and keeping it within looking like a Barbie product." She also picked up negative vibes from those involved in speedily pulling together the likeness of the dead Princess.

"From the time I was given the Di project," she says years later,

I was made aware of the general sour feeling in the Design Center about creating this doll. It had everything to do with accelerating the project when the princess had died suddenly, and essentially exploiting her death for profit after she had said she did not want to be a Barbie doll.

Ruby Knauss acknowledges years later that "sure, there were people in my group" who were against the project for reasons of taste. "But it seemed logical making a Di doll because Princess Diana was beautiful and charismatic."

Knauss recalls that Barad kept a close watch on the doll's progress.

A lot of time had been spent on designing the dress and making sure Jill liked it, and if she had changes, they had to be done. Jill had the last say. If she wanted the sash turned a different way, we did it. If the hair needed to be coiffed differently in Jill's eyes, we did it. Jill might have been obsessed, but that's pushing it. A person of that status to have a doll by Mattel would have been a coup. It would have meant we did it. We all wanted it to happen, and Jill had a great desire to see it happen.

■ ■ ■

Zielinksi-Old had a number of meetings about the design with Barad and chief operating officer Bruce L. Stein—that's how important the Diana project was to those at the top—and she recalls being introduced at those meetings "with the fanfare and sparkle" of a celebrity.

"A lot of people said a lot of things to me about Jill," says Zielinksi-Old. "She was described to me as a Jewish American Princess. I was terrified to meet this woman. But I had to, because there were constant review meetings, which were very intimidating because she wouldn't say what she wanted, and she didn't know what she wanted."

At those meetings, the British designer got a better take on the slightly built powerhouse American CEO. "When she didn't feel happy about something, she'd screech, 'You gotta be kidding!' in a Queens accent, and she had the air of a spoiled little girl," recounts Zielinski-Old.

She'd always be surrounded by an entourage whenever she moved through the building. Her eyes were like black saucers that faded away at meetings when she wasn't stimulated. She'd wear these stilettos that seemed too large for her small feet so when she came into a meeting they made this clickety-clack sound, and it seemed to me at least that her breasts were growing and getting increasingly pointy. They were visible because she sometimes wore a transparent top that showed her bra.

During one of the early meetings, Zielinksi-Old brought in the first of what turned out to be eight Princess Diana designs that she did, and Barad and her marketing team studied it closely. Then Barad turned to the nervous designer and stated, "Couldn't you Mackie it up a bit?," which was a reference to the fashion designer Bob Mackie, known for his glitzy and glamorous gowns, who actually had designed some outfits for Barbie Collectible dolls.

"When Jill said that to me—'Mackie it up'—I knew what she wanted, and I did it. It was a very complicated process," continued Zielinksi-Old, "but in the end I came up with the doll that got Jill's approval."

In early February 1998, she presented to Barad what was billed as the Ultimate Princess Diana Gown Doll.

Jill's words to me were, "Oh! She's lovely!" And I said, "She sparkles when she turns." Jill—whom I found extremely stimulating, skilled as a marketer, who sparked people into action—just saw dollar signs.

Barad's vision of Mattel's coffers filling with dollars from what she was certain would be a Diana doll approved by the Diana Memorial Fund, however, turned to shock and fury a month later when she picked up the *Wall Street Journal* and saw the headline, OH, YOU DOLL: PRINCESS DIANA COULD BE IMMORTALIZED BY HASBRO. The story she read stated that her main competitor, Hasbro, was in talks with the Fund's trustees about creating a collectible Diana doll and other Diana collectibles.

The *Journal* story emphasized, "Both sides are eager not to appear to be capitalizing on the death of the princess," and the Fund's trustees stated they would be sensitive to the "public feelings and sentiments" about the dead Princess. "It is the duty of the trustees to ensure that the fund raises as much money as possible for the causes that the Princess held dear." However, they added that they "would be absolutely wrong not to consider a doll."

British politicians were repulsed by the news. One member of Parliament called the doll idea "absolutely appalling," and Prime Minister Tony Blair said through a spokesman that he was "concerned about overcommercialism." By then, financial analysts had estimated that sales of Diana memorabilia were in the tens of millions of dollars, and skyrocketing.

While Hasbro and the Franklin Mint had taken much of the heat, Mattel's efforts to get in on the Diana action had somehow stayed below the media radar, and had never before been disclosed.

But there would be no approval for the doll, because someone at Mattel screwed up—*royally.* As Zielinksi-Old observes years later, "A lack of Mattel etiquette killed the relationship with the Fund."

While a new vice president of marketing was winging his way to London for a meeting with the Fund people in hopes of finally securing the required and lucrative authorization for Mattel to begin production, someone at Mattel had sent Zielinski-Old's Diana doll that Jill Barad had approved to the Fund, without any prior notice, where it was opened by the dead Princess's sibling.

"Sarah opened the box and sees her sister," recounts Zielinski-Old. "It's the most beautiful Princess Diana doll, but she was horrified. She was shocked that something could be so close to her sister in miniature. The Mattel project was immediately killed. Mattel never managed to recover from that. They never got the approval. They did it the wrong way, and that was a shame."

As Ruby Knauss notes, "It would have been a coup for Mattel to be able to say, 'We have designed and produced the Diana doll.' I would have imagined every SKU would have been sold, a good sell-through worldwide."

Never one to give up, Barad persisted. She personally showed a copy of the original doll—only two were in existence—at Toy Fair to special customers behind closed doors, but told buyers the doll wouldn't be produced without the Diana Fund's permission.

Mattel executive David Haddad made another unsuccessful attempt in May 1998. Before he left for London, he asked Zielinksi-Old, "How would I bring them back into Mattel's court if they say no?"

Beyond not bringing the Fund back into the court, Haddad was told in London by a Fund official "the even more depressing news" that the Fund favored Hasbro, although in the end no Diana doll was ever authorized. Haddad would later quit.

After getting the negative report from Haddad, COO Bruce Stein sent an e-mail, subject "Diana Response," to Barad and other Mattel brass, pointing out the "disappointing news" and declaring how it "underscores how fiercely we must protect our category from the attempts by competitors to steal our business. . . . Even when we were told no before, you went after it. Thanks for your valiant, never-say-die efforts and let's dial up the pressure we put on the outside. We must get to these before anyone else so that we are not playing catch-up as we were in this situation." In a postscript, he added, "Any last hope here, or could Jill or I make a difference?"

A year later, Stein would leave the company.

■ ■ ■

With the Diana doll as dead as its subject, Barad pressed the design team to move forward to produce what she hoped would be her next big doll coup and moneymaker—a miniature collectible likeness of "Miss Elizabeth Taylor" that the star would approve, something Barad had been seeking for years, and one that she hoped, with the failure of the Di doll, would help Mattel's projected earnings.

Anne Zielinksi-Old got the assignment in mid-June 1998, and saw it as "a new start at Mattel following the Princess Diana Fiasco." She was instructed to come up with the perfect "one-of-a-kind" replica that would make Taylor happy because, as the designer maintains, "Taylor was acutely aware and protective of her image and had her own ideas about how she wanted to be portrayed." The plan was for one special doll that would be auctioned off at the annual Dream Halloween party, a charity event for AIDS in which Barad was heavily involved, to be followed by a more mass-produced La Liz doll.

Zielinksi-Old did extensive research on Taylor, and prepared presentation boards depicting the star in five of her most famous roles in the films *Cleopatra, National Velvet, Father of the Bride, Cat on a Hot Tim Roof,* and *A Place in the Sun.* The boards were to be shown at the first big meeting in Beverly Hills with Taylor and her people. As it turned out, the star never once made an appearance—until the actual auction—but was always represented by her personal assistant and her attorney.

At the meeting, the La Liz's assistant told the gathering, which included Zielinksi-Old and a group of Mattel executives, that Taylor wanted the doll to be based on her image in the 1968 film *Boom,* which also starred Richard Burton. It became clear during the presentation that the representative from Mattel marketing hadn't done his research on Taylor's past charitable work and had to fudge it, causing mistrust and consternation in Taylor's people.

As Zielinksi-Old recalls it, "It was uncomfortable and the room was quiet and people's mouths went dry. It was just terrible because it was such an important moment."

She went on to tell Taylor's representatives that she felt the actress's look in *Boom* wasn't her best, that it was during her "troubled-woman era" with Burton, to whom she was married twice, and that a cross between how the young Taylor looked in *Father of the Bride* and *Cat on a Hot Tin Roof*—"a time when her face was perfect"—would give the doll "a little bit of innocence and knowingness."

They seemed to approve.

Afterward, Zielinksi-Old was told by a high-ranking executive that the Taylor doll would be "the highest profile doll Mattel had ever made," and that there would be a lot of publicity for the person who did the final design, resulting in what he called "a lot of jealousies." It was decided that the design credit would not go to Zielinksi-Old, but rather to Mattel's lead designer, Robert Best.

As Zielinksi-Old later characterized the corporate culture at the time, "Behind the cake and the muffins and the pizza that got brought in, Mattel was very cutthroat."

She alleges that a new manager–vice president recruited from the Franklin Mint had "started making things very difficult for me, telling me the project was failing, falling behind in the timeline, when actually it was running on time and everything was running very smoothly." She asserts that the executive, a big fan of Taylor's, had "started getting greedy for her contacts and for the notoriety of doing the doll because he wanted Taylor to know that."

In any case, the doll was completed on time, and received Elizabeth Taylor's enthusiastic approval, much to Jill Barad's immense relief. Mattel then began to publicize the doll in advance of the charity auction.

A crew from the celebrity TV news show *Entertainment Tonight* arrived at the El Segundo headquarters in mid-October with hopes of interviewing the doll's designer and sculptor, which became a virtual public relations disaster. Before the camera was turned on, Zielinksi-Old says she was warned by the executive, "Do not say you were the designer!" The executive also asked her to write down everything she intended to say on camera, which he then edited, "rearranging and contradicting my words." She claims that before the crew got there the head designer, Robert Best, redid her illustration of the doll, and that was the one that was videotaped.

> I was actually interviewed in my little gray cubbyhole with the executive standing behind the camera saying, "Don't say you designed the doll," and they were interviewing me *as* the designer. On the video I think I looked absolutely crazed with—*what do I say? What do I do?* So, I just told the truth. And then the design group secretary went and found *my* illustration and put it in front of the guys from *Entertainment Tonight* and said, "This is the *real* drawing of the doll."

The secretary was soon dismissed. Zielinksi-Old was fired in November 1998, and was escorted out of the building by a security guard. Mattel claimed she hadn't produced enough dolls, that her interpersonal skills were lacking, that she had dared to suggest that Mattel produce a Playboy Bunny Barbie, "probably the most forbidden doll you could do," and a host of other reasons.

She sued Mattel and [the executive] in March 1999 in Los Angeles Superior Court for wrongful termination, defamation, promissory fraud, and other charges. "When you sue them, it's almost like waving a red flag," she asserts. "I was forced to go through hours and hours and hours of depositions. They wanted to know where I had applied for jobs and I'd tell them and of course I never got another job. I met with a very abrupt end."

Because the two sides failed to reach a resolution, the case went to a mediator, one that Zielinksi-Old says had been used in the past by Mattel. At the first session, she claims, the female mediator sat at a table in her office in Malibu and began "to treat the session like a séance. She closes her eyes, lays her hands on the table, and she becomes Barbie. In a high-pitched Barbie voice, she's saying to me, 'Anne, you made me cry. You tried to change me too much. I couldn't take it.'"

In the end, according to Zielinksi-Old, Mattel offered a settlement of a year's salary, about $70,000. But she says she refused to agree to it, and she returned to Great Britain. (Mattel does not comment on personnel matters.)

Says the designer on the eve of Barbie's golden anniversary: "I knew the value of everything I'd done. I was making millions for Mattel. What I designed is still being sold in the Fashion Model Barbie line."

■ ■ ■

The October 24, 1998, auction of the one-off authorized Elizabeth Taylor doll was an enormous success. In front of a glittering audience of hundreds—Hollywood celebrities, Mattel executives, other VIPs—a proud-as-a-peacock Jill Barad presented the doll to a glowing Liz with the words, "I couldn't be happier if I were God!"

The auction began and the winning bid—a whopping $25,000— was submitted by telephone from Paris. The victor was the actress Demi Moore, a noted doll collector and Barbie aficionado. In early 2000, Mattel began marketing an Elizabeth Taylor *Cleopatra* doll— "the first authorized portrait of the film star," Mattel boasted—and announced plans for a *Father of the Bride* reproduction, each priced at $75. They were essentially the same ones drawn and proposed by Anne Zielinksi-Old before she was axed. The launching of the Cleopatra doll received worldwide attention. In Great Britain, where the star is known as Dame Elizabeth, the BBC noted, "Particular attention is paid to her famous violet eyes, adorned with heavy kohl liner and glitter eye-shadow, as in the film."

Five months after the auction in Los Angeles, Mattel, which was beginning to have major financial problems in 1999 under Barad, made a record bid of $150,000 at a Christie's Park Avenue, New York, auction, for the dress Elizabeth Taylor wore to the Academy Awards in 1969. The proceeds went to the American Foundation for AIDS Research, a cause of Taylor's since the death of her friend Rock Hudson. It was the highest bid for a celebrity dress since someone had paid $222,500 for a dress that had once been worn by Princess Diana. A spokeswoman for Mattel said the company bought the Taylor dress "because we have a relationship with her."

Demi Moore's winning bid for the doll didn't come as a surprise to a number of Mattel executives. Moore was known to be a friend of Barad's, and had visited Mattel's Design Center a number of times, where the star and ex-wife of Bruce Willis was given the VIP treatment. There were a few Mattel higherups aware of the Barad-Moore ties who even suggested the auction might have been rigged in Moore's favor. Zielinksi-Old, for one, who saw Moore being treated at Mattel like visiting royalty, declares, "I have no doubt!"

Moore, through her agent, did not respond to requests by the author for an interview about her fascination with dolls, and winning the Liz replica.

One executive who was assigned by Barad to wine and dine Moore when she visited Mattel was Barbie design executive vice president Margo Moschel.

"Demi was a devotee, or however you say it, of Barbie—a *huge* collector of Barbie dolls," says Moschel. "Demi approached Mattel and that opened up the communication between her and Jill that I was aware of. I spent a day with Demi. We had lunch in Jill's office, the three of us, and I was told by Jill to take Demi on a tour of the Design Studio"—an area of high-security, normally off-bounds to visitors.

Moore's 1997 film, *G.I. Jane*, in which she played the first female to become part of an elite Navy Seal training squad, had just been released, and Barad was especially knocked out by how buff the actress was. Moore had had her head shaved and did extensive weight training for the box office hit, in which her character's most-quoted line was, "Suck my d★★k!" when she battled the sexism and machismo of the men in her unit.

"Demi had brought Polaroid outtakes that she was showing us at lunch," recalls Moschel, "and she had done that body-building thing for the role and her muscles were huge and I remember Jill saying to her, 'Oh, my God, how did you ever do this?' There was a friendship, or relationship, forged between Jill and Demi."

Ruby Knauss recalls one visit in particular by Moore, who arrived with a relative, possibly a sister-in-law.

> Jill brought her in and Demi was charming, not flamboyant. Her visit turned out to be a funny little joke on my part. Pictures were going to be taken, and one of them was of me handing a doll to Demi and her sister-in-law. But when the photo was distributed, all of me wasn't in it. I got great jollies out of sending that picture to friends and saying, "This is my hand with Demi Moore."

According to Mattel sources, Moore and Barad, who ran in Hollywood circles because of her own executive celebrity, her brief acting past, and her father's and husband's positions in TV and movies, are said to have known each other for a number of years. There even was speculation that Moore had actually modeled the sexy, corporate executive character she played in the 1994 thriller, *Disclosure* (opposite Michael Douglas), on Barad.

"I'd put my money on it that Jill was the one who coached Demi for that role," maintains a Mattel insider.

> Demi spent time with Jill—they both had the long dark hair, the stockings, the high heels. Their suits were almost identical. When I saw the movie I was dumbstruck and thought, "Wait a minute, where have I seen this character before?" Demi's playing Jill. When you watch *Disclosure*, it's like a no-brainer.

# Chapter 13

# Another Whistleblower in the Ranks, Toyland's Worst Acquisition, and the End of a Reign

A round the time Jill Barad was giving Jim DeRose her Manolo boot out of the company in 1994, a new hire had come aboard, someone at the time low enough in the Mattel ranks at head-quarters that the then–chief operating officer probably never heard of her—just another worker bee among thousands in her domain.

But by 1998, Christine Casey's name was ricocheting off Barad's executive suite walls like sniper bullets in Baghdad, casting a darken-ing cloud over her second year as chief executive. Just like Michelle Greenwald during Jim DeRose's Barad-aborted watch, Casey had surfaced as yet another whistleblower who believed she had gotten the goods on financial hanky-panky within the company.

The 32-year-old Casey, a recent MBA graduate from the University of Southern California, had been given a complex assignment as a newly hired financial analyst. Mattel required updated data on which of its toys should be made, at which of its globe-spanning factories, and in what timeframe. This meant Casey had to begin probing such esoteric areas as market demand, the costs of manufacturing, and plant capacity—a daunting task but one that she apparently relished.

What she uncovered, though, came as a surprise to her, but was not too different from the kind of funny business dating as far back as the Handler financial scandal and as recently as the Greenwald allegations. Casey found that sales orders and production numbers—demand in general for Mattel toys such as Barbie—were being overstated by the marketing division "in order to tie to figures expected by senior management," according to an internal memo offered into evidence when Casey eventually sued Mattel after being forced out.

Casey "had come to believe" that Mattel "was misleading its shareholders about its likely future sales performance" and that "sales forecasts were so high that managers, who were meant to use them to plan production, routinely ignored the numbers . . . some managers kept two sets of figures . . . others would ring around to find out what they should really tell their factories to produce," according to an account in *The Economist*.

Casey characterized what was going on as "a joke around the office," "an open secret," and "systematic" at Mattel.

Of all of the products Casey zeroed in on, Barbie seemed to be in particularly bad shape compared to what was being forecast. By late 1997, the end of Barad's first full year as CEO and chairwoman, the doll that had propelled her to the top as Barbie's supreme marketer was suddenly losing some of its appeal among its audience, and demand was dropping. By the time Barad was made CEO, she had been credited with making Barbie a $1.9 billion brand from the $200 million pauper the doll was when Barad embraced her in the early 1980s. But now, all of that was changing.

As Casey put it, Mattel's customers "are two feet tall, their tastes are hard to determine, and they don't have a lot of money."

Princess Di and Elizabeth Taylor doll designer Anne Zielinski-Old says that when she first came to Mattel, Barad acted like a cheerleader when speaking at employee meetings.

She would dance . . . whoop up her audience, but she wasn't at all like that in the executive approval meetings, where she was agitated and hard to please. It was now your turn to perform. One after another, designers would get up at the head of the conference table with their doll project—and make her laugh, make her smile, entertain her, and if you did you were hero for the day—and that's what made you strive as a designer.

But when Jill got up to speak at the 1998 employee update and tried her dance routine it didn't work. No one even clapped. The floor was deadpan. One of the reasons, as I understood it, was because she had canceled the holiday vacation period [as business grew worse]. She underestimated the intelligence and business acumen of her workforce. They saw her greed and hated her for it.

Nevertheless, the forecasts Mattel's shareholders and Wall Street were getting from the glamorous and driven CEO were as bright as the midday sun. No gloom and doom was emanating from the office of the chairwoman of the board. Barad's bullish optimism continued into much of 1999, when she was issuing statements of Barbie's sales growth of as much as 10 percent; in fact, sales were falling like duck pins.

Casey recalled thinking, "Where is she getting her information?" Casey had worked the numbers. She'd even designed charts documenting "routinely inflated" projections at the start of the year and showed how they actually deflated—sometimes by as much as 25 percent—as the quarters ended. She alleged that Barad was "misleading the investment community."

Feeling secure in what she had found, she took her case to Ned Mansour, newly promoted to president of Mattel, Inc. by Barad, who called him "an incredible executive" who has "played a principal role in every one of the mergers and acquisitions that have made us the great company we are today."

At first, according to Casey, Mansour, a lawyer, appeared to treat her issue seriously, and looked positively at a plan she offered to deal with the situation—a proposal that would adjust inflated projections and put Mattel on the straight and narrow when it came to forecasting profits. Under her plan, a new department of information would be set up with her running it.

As he was a platinum member of Barad's inner-circle executive club, it was no surprise that Mansour deep-sixed Casey's plan.

From that point on, her life at Mattel became hellish, she claimed. Another executive berated her and made it clear he wanted her out of the company. Since Casey joined Mattel, she'd always gotten positive performance reviews filled with praise. But her first review after the Mansour meeting was negative, and it went downhill from there to the point where she lost most of her job duties and was ordered to work in a packing-box-littered cubicle. Even Mattel's Human Resources department, which was there to help employees, reportedly took no notice of how she was being treated, and even harassed her, she alleged.

In a letter to Mattel chief financial officer Harry J. Pearce, Casey asserted that "misrepresentation of earnings projection has made the company vulnerable to shareholder litigation." But her missive seemed to have had little or no impact. Mattel eventually had to ante up a whopping $122 million to settle shareholder lawsuits for allegedly putting out misleading sales forecasts.

■ ■ ■

As the *Los Angeles Times* noted in a February 2003 story entitled, "Former Mattel Employee's Battle Shows Whistle-Blowers Walking a Fine Line," which was about Casey's plight, "When it came to the dissemination of discouraging facts, Mattel evidently followed a policy of 'don't ask, don't tell.'"

Pearce had joined Mattel from Tyco Toys in the merger in Barad's first year as CEO and was named by her as chief financial officer, the same position he held at Tyco. As Mattel under Barad became more financially troubled, Pearce left the company. *CFO* magazine, noting "it's no longer playtime at Mattel," called the 55-year-old Pearce's departure "sudden," asserted that it was "related" to Mattel's increasing losses, and quoted a top analyst at Bear Stearns as saying Pearce had done a good job at Mattel, but "has other goals he wants to achieve."

Mansour also resigned reportedly for health problems, and began caring for his friend, Joseph McKay—the executive who carried out Barad's order to fire Jim DeRose. McKay had left Mattel as senior vice president of human resources when he was diagnosed with terminal colon cancer. (Mansour declined requests to be interviewed for this book.)

Casey remained in Mattel purgatory until the company offered to come up with a money offer if she left and waived her legal rights. She refused to negotiate, reported what she claimed were Mattel's questionable projections to the Securities and Exchange Commission (SEC), resigned, and then sued the company, alleging wrongful dismissal and harassment.

During the trial, Mattel's outside bulldog attorney, John Quinn, who over the years successfully handled a number of the company's major cases, characterized Casey as a "grasping, self-interested career woman who would do anything to climb the corporate ladder," according to the *Los Angeles Times*. Quinn was quoted as telling the reporter, Michael Hiltzik, "She's a true believer and she's not troubled with the facts," accused Casey of "trying to hold Mattel up," and asserted she never really understood the systems she was assigned to look into.

Casey lost her case when the judge ruled that she hadn't been harassed enough, or as he put it, was not "unusually aggravated." He also made a determination that she made "proposals" to change what she found wrong, rather than registering actual "complaints" about Mattel's actions, and therefore was not protected by whistleblower laws, which had been enacted during her battle with Mattel.

Mattel adamantly denied that it ever inflated sales forecasts as charged by Casey, and asserted that any earnings guidance was based "upon management's best judgment of the market place at the time." The SEC apparently took no action regarding Casey's complaint. The only response was for her to contact the commission's Office of Investor Education.

Casey's case was noted in *Business Week*'s 2002 cover story, titled "Year of the Whistleblower," along with such legendary whistleblowers as Enron Corp.'s Sherron S. Watkin, who nailed CEO Kenneth Lay, and WorldCom Inc.'s Cynthia Cooper, who uncovered fraud valued in the billions.

Casey, however, had difficulty getting another job. To make matters worse, Mattel petitioned the court to recover the legal costs from her.

"If I had to do this again, I'd never do it. . . . [T]he best legal advice is to keep your mouth shut," she sadly concluded after her shootout with Mattel.

■ ■ ■

Jill Barad apparently felt that as CEO she could make her biggest mark on Mattel by consummating flashy acquisitions as the iconic toymaker neared the new millennium.

Tyco Toys and its Matchbox cars line was the first, which she asserted gave Mattel "$500 million in the wheels business" along with Hot Wheels, which was still going strong. She expected that genre of boys' toys to eventually reach $1 billion. Her expectations, it seemed, were always high.

She next forged a merger in 1998 with the Pleasant Company—this was during the period when Christine Casey was making noise about the goings-on at Mattel. The Pleasant Company, a mail-order business, manufactured the American Girl line of dolls and accessories, which down the road would become quite successful for Mattel.

At the time of the purchase, though, toy industry professionals felt Mattel's buy price was too high—$700 million for a company that was bringing in only a reported $300 million in annual sales. However, by making the merger, Barad had shrewdly brought into Mattel's portfolio a Barbie competitor at a time when the doll was on the decline and other revenues were sinking.

For the second time since she became CEO, Barad was being taken to task for paying too much for an acquisition.

It would only get worse. Barad's extravagance was part of her nature—even on the most basic levels, such as having meals on the company tab. She always did it large.

Diana Troup, then executive vice president of product design, says Barad "loved fashion and she loved fun and she loved food." When the two traveled together on business, Troup was amazed at the lavish restaurant dinners her boss ordered.

> I come from a very humble background; I don't like to overdo. I was sitting at breakfast with Jill and she said, "What do you want to have, Diana?" I said, "Well, I'm not really sure whether to get pancakes, or the eggs and bacon, or an omelet." And Jill says, "Get everything! Order everything! And then you can just eat what you want of it." That's the kind of person she was. She never looked at anything in a small way.

As Christmas 1998 neared, Barad was forced to lower earnings growth by almost half, and the company's stock, which had skyrocketed more than 50 percent—from less than $30 a share to more than $46—in the weeks following her promotion to CEO, had fallen back to where it had started. Financial analysts, however, were confident she would make things right. In fact, Barad had a gift-wrapped surprise for Wall Street under Mattel's Christmas tree and Hanukkah bush.

Or was it actually a time bomb waiting to detonate?

■ ■ ■

Ten days before the holidays, Mattel announced the $3.8 billion stock deal acquisition of the Learning Company. Next to Microsoft, on whose board Barad also served, the Learning Company was the largest producer in the world of software for the consumer market, and the biggest producer of educational software in the United States.

Mattel needed to be a part of that exploding home computer world market, Barad strongly believed. After all, at home, she observed, "My two sons prefer computer games."

After she became CEO, Mattel was one of four toy companies to underwrite the design of high-tech playthings at the Massachusetts Institute of Technology using microprocessors. Barad said of the "Toys of Tomorrow" project, "There is no question in my mind that going into the new millennium technology will fundamentally change the way children play."

The acquisition of the Learning Company was part of her grand plan. But the Learning Company was starting to run on hard times when she snapped it up. Two of its most popular products, Carmen Sandiego and Reader Rabbit, were losing popularity, and, worse still, the Learning Company had been in the red except for one year since the early 1990s. Nevertheless, Barad agreed to pay a whopping 4.5 times the company's sales at a time when its projected revenue for the year was only $850 million. This was at a time when the kids' software market had reached $1.8 billion and was rising.

With the acquisition announcement, Mattel warned that 1998 would show dismal results. The company's stock fell to a 52-week low, losing more than $8.00. The *New York Times*, in a story titled "Mattel's Mixed Day: A Deal and Falling Profits," reported that "shareholders typically cheer news that a company is broadening its product line and thinking ahead." But it quoted a key analyst for Credit Suisse First Boston as stating that Mattel's bleak financial outlook "is so disappointing that it is really hard to say what it means for the [Learning Company] deal."

Moreover, wholesale shipments of Barbie were down 14 percent, but Mattel claimed the dolls' retail sales had increased.

Mattel's financial status at the close of 1998 was dire enough for the usually upbeat Barad to issue a downbeat statement, declaring, "This situation is very painful and disappointing for us." The company said it had been hit with weak sales to major retailers like Toys 'R' Us, which cut by 50 percent its inventory of Mattel toys. Barad said the severe cuts by retailers had "negatively impacted our sales by approximately $250 million" in 1998. Moreover, Mattel had begun a new inventory program that had the effect of further reducing sales by another $150 million. Shocked analysts felt that that wouldn't have happened with proper management.

Barad predicted "1998 sales to be flat with last year."

■ ■ ■

While Mattel had a dismal 1998 under Barad, with the company stock freefalling by 37 percent, she had nothing to complain about in terms of her own rich compensation.

All told, she grossed $4.75 million, which included a salary of $1.26 million, along with a $500,000 bonus—all of which was 14 percent higher than 1997, her first year as Mattel's boss lady, according to SEC filings. Beyond salary and bonus, she was awarded another $2,991,756 in long-term incentive pay and other compensation. Not a bad take-home for the head of what had become a deeply financially troubled corporation during her watch.

Regarding her home, as part of her terms of her CEO contract, she had received a mortgage loan from Mattel of $3 million, the principal and all accrued unpaid interest of which would be forgiven, unless she was terminated for cause.

In terms of compensation, Barad had actually done far better in 1997 because of special options grants valued at a whopping $24 million. Combined with her salary, her compensation was $26.3 million.

An expert on compensation, Graef Crystal, editor of the *Crystal Report*, said, "If you threw her package on a scale, all the springs would have fallen out" in 1997. "It looks like they went on a pay Weight Watchers all during 1998."

Even so, Crystal estimated that Barad's base salary in 1998 was 60 percent higher than that of other CEOs running companies of a size similar to Mattel, and almost 30 percent above the market average.

(In 1996, her husband, Tom Barad, also cashed in. Mattel paid his company, the Electronic Catalogue Network, in which he held a 50 percent interest, $691,116 and royalties based on resulting product sales to produce a Barbie infomercial.)

■ ■ ■

The year 1999, when Barbie turned 40, began as gloomily as 1998 had ended for the world's largest toy company. Everyone from stockholders to Wall Street analysts to Mattel's thousands of employees were wondering, What happened to our superwoman, Jill Barad?

The year's first quarter showed a $17.9 million loss—a 2 percent drop in revenue—and the stock price was in the mid-$20 range. Barad needed to take action and that involved cost cutting, which meant heads would roll. When she swung the axe, some 3,000 employees were laid off and some factories and offices shuttered.

To toy industry watchers, struggling Mattel began to seem like the Army's 82nd Airborne, with top executives bailing out of a plummeting plane seemingly about to crash and burn—pulling their ripcords either forcibly or voluntarily in a major management shakeup. Among the first to go was Barad's top lieutenant, 44-year-old Bruce Stein, the chief operating officer, who had been hired less than three years earlier, and 52-year-old Gary Baughman, president of the Mattel subsidiary Fisher-Price, who was part of the Tyco merger just two years earlier.

There was speculation that Barad had tossed the blame for Mattel's problems on Stein. There also was speculation that Stein bailed because of battles with Barad, which both Stein and Mattel denied. Stein said he needed "a new challenge," and Barad said his leaving was "most painful for me." Few in the know, however, believed any of it. Stein was not replaced and his duties were dropped in Barad's lap.

Putting positive spin on the dire situation, Barad claimed she was transforming Mattel—quite suddenly, it appeared—from the kind of company it had been for years, which was a traditional toy company— to what she called a "children's products company," with four core brands, and with fewer executives.

Barad appointed flashy Adrienne Fontanella to run Barbie and girls' toys. She had previously been in charge of Barbie licensing, and was a favorite of Barad's because she had close ties to the New York fashion world and had run her own small fragrance company, all of which had impressed Barad. Matthew Bousquette, who had started in Mattel marketing as a vice president, was named to head boys' toys. The recently acquired Pleasant Company would be run by its founder, Pleasant Rowland, and 36-year-old David Haddad was given Mattel Media, the software end, which Barad saw as the future.

Eight months later, Haddad quit, just a week after Mattel's stock plummeted to the lowest level in five years. The others would eventually go, too—with generous golden parachutes.

By the spring of 1999, the word on The Street was that Barad didn't have the wherewithal to turn around the troubled $4.8 billion company. Her leadership and ability to hold onto talented executives, along with her financial skills, were being seriously questioned. All of the adoration that had been heaped upon her when she marketed Barbie like there was no tomorrow was fast evaporating as the stock continued to decline. One criticism was that she wasn't coming up with increased profits because she spent too much time trying to keep bankers and analysts from becoming bearish on Mattel.

One analyst who covered Mattel observed that most of the people who did business with Barad were "professional men, and their ability to critique her can't be taken out of the context of them being men. Jill brings a level of animation and feminization to the role that people find off-putting at times because they are not used to it."

Executives who worked with her thought of her as outspoken and demanding, controlling and temperamental, a micromanager and not a team player. This was the exact opposite of how she described her management style late in her first year as CEO to the magazine *The Chief Executive*, to wit:

I try to do things with humor and a sense of fun versus an iron fist. I don't believe in firing people for mistakes. I've made mistakes in my career and I'm still here. . . . The worst thing someone can do is clone themselves. If you want to screw up your business, that's the best way—to have all the same personality types with the same vision and the same expertise.

■ ■ ■

With the fall and winter 1999 holidays looming, Mattel—with Barad at the wheel of what appeared to be a sinking ship—faced its worst financial situation in years. Barbie's growth, for example, had "slowed to a crawl."

But worse, Barad's huge and much-touted (by her) acquisition, the Learning Company, was in serious trouble. She had expected a $50 million profit. Instead, the company faced a loss of as much as $100 million. In "Mattel Warns of Yet Another Profit Shortfall," the *New York Times* called it a "debacle . . . sprung on shareholders," who wasted no time selling off their stock. By the end of the day, Mattel stock plummeted to a 52-week low and had dropped by almost 50 percent for the year.

For the first time, Barad's future—or lack thereof—had become fodder for public discourse. One senior portfolio manager, whose firm owned 3.77 million shares of Mattel stock, was quoted in the *Times* article as saying, "Clearly, she is going to be under fire by the institutional shareholders and, as a result, by members of the board of directors. This is a black eye on all of Mattel management." Another stated, "The fact that they closed on the Learning Company in the second quarter and in the third quarter they are announcing a substantial after-tax loss is really disappointing. I'm trying to give the company the benefit of the doubt, but all these explanations and disappointments don't seem to add up."

The latest development sparked business media speculation that Barad, less than three years into her reign, was probably on her way out—or should be. Wall Street was flabbergasted that it was getting positive promises from Barad and seeing negative results.

"I think to have two huge misses within the same year despite assurances that everything is fine looks really bad," observed prominent analyst Sean McGowan with Gerard Klauer Mattison. He was the first to publicly state, "I have a hard time thinking there won't be further management changes." Everyone in the business knew whom he was thinking about.

Gretchen Morgenson, the highly respected financial columnist for the *New York Times*, noting that $13.5 billion in Mattel market value "has vaporized," wrote in early November 1999:

> A chief executive's ultimate test is how he or she copes in a crisis. Mattel . . . is definitely in a crisis. . . . But instead of going on the offensive, Jill E. Barad, the chief executive, has gone into hiding. Although she generally loves the spotlight and thrives when she is putting on a show, Ms. Barad abruptly cancelled plans to attend an influential industry conference. . . . Mattel has almost never missed a chance to make a presentation there. But the company was nowhere to be seen this year, even though Barad was said to be in New York a day later for a board meeting. . . . [I]ndustry insiders draw an image of a company severely damaged by Ms. Barad's management style. Most of these people asked for anonymity when they spoke, fearing reprisals from Mattel. . . .

The ill-fated era of 48-year-old Jill Barad—her amazing climb to the top by turning Barbie into a superbrand, and her spectacular fall as a failed corporate leader—ended on February 3, 2000, just 11 days before the beginning of the prime industry event, the Toy Fair, when she was forced by Mattel's board of directors to step down. She was essentially fired—a wretched and embarrassing end to a spectacular career.

"There is nothing I can say to gloss over how devastating the Learning Company results have been to Mattel's overall performance," Barad acknowledged in a press release. "Because there must be accountability, I and the board agree that I must resign today as chairman and chief executive and from the board."

Barad's finale came swiftly after a secret board meeting—a week before one that had been scheduled—with Mattel's directors in New York. Mattel insiders say that negotiations for her removal had been quietly underway for several months.

Barad had forever lost the confidence of Wall Street and the board of directors by making upbeat pronouncements that never panned out. "Each time, it was the last time, and it wasn't going to happen again," observed Credit Suisse First Boston analyst Martin Romm. "Unfortunately, Jill went to the well a couple of times too many."

■ ■ ■

Lauded for years as one of Mattel's and corporate America's most inventive and powerful female executives, a marketing genius, and a symbol for working mothers, Jill Barad was devastated at what she viewed as the shabby treatment she received from the board of directors, the same board that had unanimously approved her decision to acquire the troubled Learning Company, the key cause of her fall from power.

"Jill felt the board in asking for her resignation had overlooked all she had done for Mattel over almost two decades," says a Barad confidante.

Despite what she said publicly, she was convinced that the board had caved-in to Wall Street pressures and used her as a scapegoat. She felt she deserved the board's loyalty. She felt she deserved better. What's ironic is that Jill herself was always finding a scapegoat when things were going bad. I guess her dismissal was a genuine case of that old adage, "What goes around comes around."

Another knowledgeable Mattel source says Barad had put up a ferocious battle to try to convince the board to let her stay on, that she was confident that with a little more time she could turn things around. But the board members turned a deaf ear. They had had it with the drop in the stock value, with all the red ink, with the negative news, with her failed dog-and-pony shows.

Diana Troup, who had left Mattel after being diagnosed with breast cancer, but who continued working at Barad's insistence as a Mattel consultant, recalled how terrible the once-proud and cocky chief executive felt when she got the axe.

"She cried on the plane on her way home from New York," Troup says. "Here she was coming back by herself and her whole career was over. It has got to be a big blow to anybody. Jill was negotiating, and then it was all over for her."

Barad claimed at times that she'd been judged differently from male executives—at the time of her resignation she was one of just four women running a *Fortune* 500 company—but Wall Street faulted her not for being a woman, but rather for offering inflated expectations and extravagant optimism. *Fortune* magazine, in fact, had named Barad as one of five CEOs who were "in denial" about how financially ailing their companies had become. Specifically, the article "CEOs in Denial Reality" noted that neither Barad nor the other four were able to accurately forecast financial performance two years in advance, along with their failure to control the number of high-ranking executives abandoning the company.

As for all the male executives who had been fired or who had fled during her reign, she griped that Wall Street viewed her as being unable to work with men. "The fact is that I worked with a man, and that man is no longer here. Somehow it then gets said that I don't get along with men."

The *Los Angeles Business Journal,* which kept close watch on Barad's rise and fall because Mattel was one of the L.A. region's largest companies aside from the movie and TV industry, described her leadership technique as "highly feminine and highly aggressive at the same time" and noted that it "has become the stuff of legend." The magazine called her "a flamboyant executive . . . who can work a crowd and signs off by saying 'I love you all" during video presentations to employees." It quoted a friend of Barad's, an attorney with political ambitions, Lisa Specht, as observing that Barad was "synonymous with Mattel to the extent that [then–Disney CEO] Michael Eisner is with Disney. It's a mistake to condemn her too quickly. . . ."

The public and boardroom drama involving Barad, like so much of the history of Mattel and its curious cast of characters, could have been bankable at the box office, or at the least was juicy fodder for a television miniseries. It had all the drama and all the glitz.

There was even speculation in credible quarters that Barad might have been "set up for a fall" because she'd reached the pinnacle so swiftly, and had developed a number of enemies along the way in the very competitive bitch-eat-bitch world of Mattel.

But Barad's Mattel colleague and friend, Diana Troup, had trouble buying that theory.

"First of all, Jill's not someone who would *ever* get set up. She's too smart for that," Troup maintains years later. "What she saw in the Learning Company was what Mattel didn't have—a product, educational software, that was beginning to be popular in the marketplace. I firmly believe she was sold a bill of goods by the Learning Company."

Many wondered, however, how that could have happened. Hadn't Barad and the board of directors done the required due diligence? The answer, according to Troup, a veteran toy industry executive, was quite simple, if not altogether plausible.

> Through the years, a lot of people wouldn't tell Jill, "Oh, you can't do this. This isn't going to work," because 95 percent of the time she was right. In this particular case, many people told her this was *not* a good deal, but she didn't listen because she trusted her instincts and would generally be right. The board of directors respected her opinion. God, with Barbie she went from $200 million to $1.5 billion, and we were trying to get to $2 billion. How could she not be trusted to make another right decision?

Troup insists all of the criticism was sparked by jealousy of Barad. "People said she took the company down the drain. But there wouldn't have been a Mattel without her."

Troup essentially owed her life to Barad, whom she described as a loyal friend and boss.

As with a number of others at Mattel, Troup was diagnosed with cancer, breast cancer like Ruth Handler. Troup's diagnosis came in the late 1990s, when she was serving as general manager of Barbie, with marketing, design, and prior development reporting to her. She continued working while she underwent treatment, but when she revealed her circumstances, Barad was horrified and leaped into action to help her.

"I'd had surgery but the margin wasn't clean," Troup recounts. "I was driving home with Jill and I said, 'Well, I have this little thing left,' and she said, 'That's not good enough, Diana, for you, or for me. You need to get all of that out of there, and I'm going to call Susan Love.'"

Dr. Love, a leading authority, director of the prestigious UCLA Breast Center, and author of *Dr. Susan Love's Breast Book*, was not someone easily accessible. But she was part of Barad's platinum circle of influential friends, and took on Troup's case, and Troup became a survivor. "Jill was so kind to me," she says.

■ ■ ■

In the wake of Barad's dismissal, Mattel's board came in for criticism, too. It was described in the business media as "troubled" and "sleepy," and unprepared with anyone to immediately fill Barad's shoes. Two months after Barad's departure, the executive search still proved fruitless. Moreover, Mattel's stock hadn't moved much over $10 per share since she left.

A new board member, Ralph V. Whitworth, was brought on board. He had earned a sterling reputation as someone who could straighten out the kind of mess Barad had left behind. A holder of more than 4 million shares of Mattel stock, Whitworth believed the company needed an infusion of new blood and a major shakeup of the board.

But there was still more drama and controversy to come, when it was revealed in an SEC filing three months after Barad went down in flames that she had floated back to earth with quite a cushion to brake her descent—a mind-boggling $50 million golden parachute, one that would come under intense criticism and scrutiny, adding yet another dark cloud over already embattled Mattel.

"Yes Barbie, there is a Santa Claus for failed chief executives," wrote Graef Crystal, considered the nation's best-known expert on executive compensation. In a column for Bloomberg News, Crystal lambasted Barad for her "incompetent tenure" and criticized the directors for "sending her out the door with a severance package that is a monument to failure."

He added:

For someone who had never run a major company, she extracted extraordinarily generous terms from her board. But sadder than the millions of dollars paid to get out of that agreement is that the directors felt compelled to ladle millions more on top of that. You have to marvel at a board that could willfully inflict so much damage on its shareholders. It's as if having put a bullet in the heart of the collective shareholder body . . . the Mattel board dug up the corpse . . . and shot it all over again.

In her agreement, Barad received:

- Five years of salary and bonuses, amounting to $26.4 million. Had she actually remained as CEO, and with her bad performance, she most likely would not have received a copper penny in bonus money.
- A pension of almost $709,000 per year for her lifetime, even though she hadn't worked until the age of 60, but was fired while she still was in her 40s. In the end, Barad negotiated a deal to receive $1.2 million a year for the next decade—until 2010, Barbie's 51st year.
- Her $3 million home loan, given in 1993, was forgiven by the board, as was a $4.2 million loan granted in 1997. Also forgiven was more than $3 million in federal, state, and Medicare tax liabilities.
- A life insurance policy of $5 million for the remainder of her time on earth, an amount that presumably will go to one or all of her survivors. Along with the policy, she took away paid health insurance, outplacement and financial counseling services, and private club memberships.
- For the thrift-shop sum of a measly two dollars, she was permitted to purchase all of her stately office furniture along with the leased corporate car.
- Full vesting in 6.4 million stock options, worth millions.

Graef Crystal noted, however, that the board wasn't letting Barad off "scot-free." She was required to give 40 hours per month of consulting services for the rest of 2000. Usually, such a clause is boilerplate, but "with a board that has acted this dumbly," observed Crystal, "they just might decide to call her up."

Stuart Varney, the anchor of CNN's *Moneyline News Hour*, declared, "Jill Barad's path out of Mattel" was "paved with gold." He observed that her severance package "is leaving every failed executive in America salivating, and may leave shareholders foaming at the mouth." He called her deal "a going-away present so rich it's almost stunning. . . . Imagine what she might have received upon leaving if the company had done well."

One of those who had an actual vested, rather than media, interest in being outraged was H. Carl McCall, the New York State Comptroller. And McCall had every right to demand—unsuccessfully as it turned out—that the board reconsider Barad's going-away gift. New York State's Common Retirement Fund, of which McCall was the sole trustee, held 1.2 million shares of Mattel stock, which he declared had fallen in value more than 55 percent during Barad's brief tenure as CEO—a nosedive that occurred at a time when the Standard & Poor's 500 stock index had doubled.

In his angry letter to Mattel's acting chairman, William D. Rollnick, the retired CEO of a privately held company that rented electronics equipment, McCall wrote, "It is disturbing to hear that the board has elected to reward the person who presided over this precipitous decline. . . . I am particularly disturbed that the board decided to forgive a $3 million loan granted for the purchase of a home and to provide payments on a $5 million life insurance policy." And he expressed "outrage" over the board's decision to pay for such luxuries as club memberships.

The most critical and in-depth study of Barad's tenure as CEO and chairwoman emanated from the Tuck School of Business at Dartmouth University, where, ironically, Barad's mentor and "corporate rabbi," former Mattel CEO and chairman John Amerman, had earned his MBA.

The paper, entitled "Learning from Mattel," described how Barbie, with Barad doing the pushing, had "fueled" Mattel into "a global powerhouse." It documented bad decisions by Barad in "turning to mergers and acquisitions for growth," and how she expected and paid too much for the Learning Company. Moreover, it focused on how she allowed the company to "slip into disarray," while her tenure was marked by "a steady stream of executive departures," and as a "passive board of directors" gave her "great leeway and likely one too many chances as chief—in large part due to her successful pre-CEO track record with building the Barbie line."

■ ■ ■

In August 2006, *Forbes* ran an article titled, "The World's Most Powerful Women: Angels and Demons." The account dealt with women executives who were "increasingly being called on to clean up corporate scandals."

But the piece, written by Claire Miller, also noted that "women can be troublemakers, too." The article listed Barad among the A-listers of fallen corporate stars and included such women as Linda Wachner, who helped lead Warnaco into bankruptcy; Carly Fiorina, who was axed from Hewlett-Packard after the much-criticized acquisition of Compaq Computer, and lifestyle maven and convicted white-collar criminal Martha Stewart.

With Barad gone, a new era in the new millennium was about to begin at the world's largest, and most embattled, toy company as it headed toward the astonishing half-century mark of its mainstay, Barbie. Few would have been able to predict the complications and legal issues that would arise.

# Part Three

# TOY TERROR, THE BRATZ ATTACK, AND THE ECKERT ERA

# Chapter 14

# The Processed Cheese Savior

R obert A. Eckert, who was recruited out of the processed American cheese and Oscar Mayer hotdog world of Kraft Foods, was named the new chief executive and chairman of Mattel on May 17, 2000, three months after the ouster of Jill Barad.

If Barad was considered by some cynics to be the ultimate Beverly Hills Barbie Princess, then Bob Eckert was thought in some quarters to be the epitome of the white-bread Midwesterner, Ken. Glitz-and-drama-free, Eckert was in fact the anti–Barad.

Unlike the glamorous Barad, who was said to have been the model for a sexy movie character played by Demi Moore, the understated Eckert appeared more like the likeable Chevy Chase character, Clark Griswold, the food additives researcher and jovial suburban dad in *National Lampoon's Vacation.*

But unlike Griswold, Eckert was no buffoon. Married and the father of four children, the 45-year-old Eckert had spent half his life climbing the ladder at Kraft to become its CEO, typical of the company, whose parent was Philip Morris, grow at a reported quicker pace than most other food industry companies. But despite his years of loyalty to Kraft, when Eckert was quietly approached by an executive recruiting firm on Mattel's behalf, he readily agreed to a series of secret interviews over a two-month period.

Eckert had been with Kraft, located in the Chicago suburbs not far from where he grew up, since 1977, and had been CEO for just three years, the same as Barad's tenure. When he joined Kraft, it had been publicly described as "the sleeping giant of the food industry," which he saw as an opportunity, a place to move up in the ranks. Eventually, Kraft was considered *the* venerable supermarket leader in providing America with ready-to-eat processed cheeses, lunchmeats, and desserts sold in vacuum-sealed clear plastic packages. Eckert often called the company "the undisputed leader" in such edibles.

Before being named Kraft's CEO, he'd spent three years—from 1993 to 1996—as president of Kraft's Oscar Mayer Foods Corporation, at a time when the division was "searching for ways to stoke the American appetite for processed meat." Oscar Mayer's best-known product was the all-American hotdog, which was promoted with what became a pop culture icon—a hotdog-shaped vehicle called the Weinermobile, a version of which was designed by Harry Bradley, who was a key player in Mattel's Hot Wheels project during the Handler era.

Unlike Barad, who had lots of flash, charisma, and creativity, Eckert was a rather bland, monotone numbers-guy who had a reputation for cost-cutting, brand-building, and manager-development. "It's challenging to do those three things simultaneously," the self-styled multitasking executive once offered.

Asked by the *New York Times* at the time of his appointment to describe his management style, Eckert simply said, "I try to be just another person."

■ ■ ■

Eckert's accomplishments early on were quite impressive for a seemingly low-key, unpretentious guy who grew up in middle-class surroundings in the conservative Republican enclave of Elmhurst, Illinois, a mostly blue-collar Windy City bedroom community, and typical of the mythical Chicago suburb where the fictional Clark Griswold resided with his wife and two kids.

The striking similarities between Eckert and Griswold are surreal. In the film *Vacation*, the Griswolds take the ugly green-with-faux-wood-paneling "Wagon Queen Family Truckster" on a cross-country trip to a Southern California amusement park called "Walley World— America's Favorite Family Fun Park." In real life, Eckert and his family had what's known as the annual "RV Getaway," which entailed the entire Eckert clan—elderly relatives and all—renting recreational vehicles and camping at a favorite state park in Michigan, a family tradition that had happened in the summer for decades.

He and his family were so tied to their Midwestern roots that when he got the offer from Mattel, he had trepidations, mainly about leaving the heartland. "I had the stereotypical perception of anybody working in Los Angeles as being the 'Let's do lunch crowd,'" which he felt was in "stark contrast" to the "Let's get to work" crowd that he had worked with for years at the Northfield, Illinois, headquarters of Kraft Foods. He was equally afraid of telling his children that they had to move to Southern California. However, they quickly jumped into the L.A. vibe, from volleyball to surfing to outdoor photography.

The *Chicago Tribune*, describing Eckert's leadership not long after he took over Mattel, said he was "the picture of Midwestern sobriety."

■ ■ ■

Born on August 14, 1954—five years before Barbie came into the world—Eckert was the middle son of the former Pearl Rippy, and Elmer A. Eckert, who became one of Elmhurst's few dentists after serving in World War II. Eckert had a younger sister, Linda, and an older brother, Edward, whom friends remembered as a "James Dean type" who rode a motorcycle and was "more rambunctious" than Bob.

The Eckerts were the epitome of an all-American family living in an all-American town. Bob's mother was known for her baking, a real-life Betty Crocker. His father, known to friends as "Elm," was a regular, easy-going, religious guy who was a member of the Fraternal Order of Masons, helped develop the town's YMCA, drove a convertible, repaired antique clocks as a hobby, and liked to use the expression "high on the hog."

Ralph Will, who was Master of Elmhurst Masonic Lodge 941 in 1969, was a friend and fraternal brother of Dr. Eckert, and thought of him as a bit of an eccentric. "He was a maintenance guy for our building, and was on the committee for maintaining the building. The lodge met there early in the week, and he used to go in there on Saturday and sweep and mop and dust the place so everything was nice and clean for Sunday when a church met there. The lodge didn't hire a janitor. They tried to get by as cheap as possible."

Bob Eckert described his father and mother as classic "Greatest Generation" parents—those who served in uniform during WWII, and those who kept the home fires burning and the defense plants humming.

"Those were people who were very community and civic-minded. We used to talk about sharing your time, your talent and your treasures for the benefit of others," he said in an interview for *Kellogg World*, the alumni magazine of the Kellogg School of Management, at Northwestern University, where he earned his MBA in 1977. "I was raised with the belief that we are very fortunate. Not only were we born in America, but we were born, certainly, on the other side of being poverty stricken."

He used those comments as a jumping off point to boast about his "good fortune to work for two companies that share similar values"—Kraft and Mattel, which he asserted were "both very involved in their local communities and share a culture of giving back."

Elmer, 91, and Pearl, 88, died one day apart in May 2008 after 66 years of marriage. Besides their children, they were survived by eight grandchildren and two great-grandchildren.

■ ■ ■

Sixteen miles west of the Chicago Loop, Elmhurst's claim to fame while Eckert was growing up was that it was home to the largest Chevrolet dealer in the country, and was corporate headquarters for the Keebler Company, the cookie maker. A commuter suburb, Elmhurst during the 1920s had been the largest city in Dupage County, long a powerful Republican stronghold.

In the sixties, while Eckert—known as "Bobby" to his pals—was coming into his teens, Elmhurst, all 10 square miles of it, had a population of almost 37,000, 18 of whom were African-American, or as the 1960 Census showed—99.8 percent white, and 0.0 percent "Negro."

One of his friends growing up, Barb Tilden—the first Barbie in his life—who lived 10 houses away from the Eckerts' modest, two-story, red-brick Cape Cod–style house, remembers him from their days at Washington Elementary School as "one of the cutest kids, nice, very quiet, and he was a little guy." The two went all through school together, were confirmed together, and his father was her dentist.

Another Washington Elementary School friend, Candy Purdom, lived three blocks from the Eckerts on South Parkview in Elmhurst's pleasant Crescent Park neighborhood, where beautiful elm trees once lined the streets until Dutch Elm disease destroyed most of them. Purdom and Bobby also went to Sunday School together at the nearby First Congregational United Church of Christ. "He reminded me of Timmy in the *Lassie* TV show," she says. But like others, she lost track of him when they went on to junior high and high school because "he was below the radar."

One of Eckert's close chums in elementary school and later was another future titan of industry. In 2002, Dave Fitzpatrick scored a $22 million package as executive vice president and chief financial officer of Tyco International in the wake of the scandal involving chairman Dennis Kozlowski, who was sent to prison for misappropriating more than $400 million of the company's funds.

In 1968, Eckert entered York Community High School as a freshman in the Class of '72, some 900 students strong.

While the rest of the country was in ferment—violent protests against the Vietnam War; the assassinations of Dr. Martin Luther King and Senator Robert Kennedy; riots in the streets of America's big cities; and the election of Richard Nixon as president—student life at York seemed in some sort of time warp.

Frank Canzolino, an honors student, observed,

If it was happening in the country, it sure as hell wasn't happening in this little suburb, a non-radical place. There were no demonstrations, nothing like that through my high school years.

Elmhurst was about as easy-going a place as you could possibly want to grow up.

As class member Glenn Balsis declares, "With few blacks, we didn't exactly have a balanced approach to life." Jackie Deshich Urso says many of the students at York were from families who were part of the "white flight from Chicago." She recalls that beyond a couple of black students in the Class of '72, there were only four Jewish students. "Elmhurst," she says, "was a white Republican conservative enclave."

It was in that kind of vacuum-sealed environment that the future leader of the world's largest toy company came of age. Many members of the class who were interviewed had no recollection of Bob Eckert as any kind of standout in high school. In fact, as they pointed out, he was virtually invisible.

In the 1972 yearbook, the only evidence of his attendance is the standard class picture. There is no indication that he was involved in any sport in a school known for its cross-country team; no involvement in music in a school known for its bands—although Eckert later confessed to *USA Today* that he became a fan of The Who, Led Zeppelin, and The Eagles while in high school; and no honor society involvement in a school that sent more than 90 percent of its graduates to colleges and universities. For a future leader of corporate America, Eckert was a virtual nonentity.

Of the successful York High graduates besides Eckert, the most remembered was "affable and bright" Ken Paulson, who became editor-in-chief of *USA Today*. Even though the newspaper covered Mattel and Eckert extensively in its business pages, Paulson says, "I didn't know Bob in high school. There were 800 of us in our graduating class and I don't think we've ever met."

Many of the students in the Class of '72 honors courses went on to prestigious schools like the University of Chicago, Harvard, Yale, and William and Mary. But Eckert took a different route. He went to the University of Arizona, a party school remembered during that time for its coeds with Farrah Fawcett hair and jocks in convertibles with CB radios. There, he earned a BS degree in the Class of '76, the year of the U.S. Bicentennial celebration. Within the school's enormous student population, Eckert seems to have been as invisible as he had been in high school.

He then went on to get his MBA in marketing and finance at Kellogg, joining Kraft upon graduation. At Kraft, it took him a decade to get his first vice presidency, in strategy and development in grocery products—and just about every two or three years thereafter he moved up the executive ladder until becoming president and chief executive.

Eckert himself later said in an interview after he became an industry leader, "You never would have predicted that I'd be a CEO someday I guess no one else would have, either."

■ ■ ■

Eckert did well with Mattel early on, and especially in terms of his own bank account—which quickly sparked criticism when it became public, especially in the wake of the furor over Barad's final paycheck.

Mattel offered him a three-year contract that paid him an annual base salary of $1.25 million, and an annual bonus equal to his salary, which could triple if he met prescribed goals. Another bonus was built into his contract—one that could pay him as much as $8 million over his first 36 months in office. Just by putting his John Hancock on the dotted line of his contract, he walked away with a healthy $2.8 million signing bonus. He received free shares worth $7.7 million, and options on 3 million shares that at the time had an estimated value of more than $11 million, with a strike price of almost $7 million. Moreover, if he was fired after three years, he'd get a pension worth $550,000 a year.

Beyond all of that, he was handed a $5.5 million loan that included tax gross-ups, giving it a true estimated worth, according to compensation expert Graef Crystal, "of around $11 million." The loan was presumably so he could purchase the fancy home he acquired in the spectacular Rancho Palos Verdes Estates above the Pacific. The house would eventually undergo what was described as a two-year decoration-and-renovation project overseen by his wife, Kathie, using a decorator known for her work in Las Vegas, the same one who had decorated former Mattel executive Diana Troup's house. Better yet, Mattel would eventually forgive the loan.

Writing in the *Los Angeles Business Journal*, Crystal called the deal that "the directors of Mattel fashioned" for Eckert as "equally galling" as the "obscene amount of severance" handed to Barad.

If he doesn't work out, shareholders will again foot an expensive bill for failure. Eckert's contract should be called "Jill 2," to use the fitting lingo of a Grade-B slasher movie. Nothing in its terms should give shareholders confidence that this is a company doing what it takes to dig itself out of its hole.

As it turned out, Eckert did even better than expected in the first seven months on the job. *Forbes* reported that he made "more than $12 million in salary and bonuses"—$4 million in bonuses and $7.7 million in stock awards.

■ ■ ■

Eckert's first big controversy at Mattel involved his staunch defense of Jill Barad's $50 million golden handshake. As the new CEO, who scored quite a glorious compensation package himself, he publicly stated that the Mattel board was "obligated to fulfill her contract" and even sweeten it in order to change leadership post-haste and "for the good of the company."

Eckert offered his Barad mea culpa some three weeks into his tenure at a meeting with shareholders who were furious at seeing the company's market value drop by $7 billion over the past year. They reportedly interrupted Eckert's presentation several times. He asked them to save their questions until he finished his presentation, but surrendered when many shouted at him until they were recognized. In the end, the shareholders who didn't sell off their stock had to wait it out and put their faith in Eckert.

Meanwhile, Barad, with her Mattel bounty, accepted election to a newly created seat on the board of Leap Wireless International, Inc., a wireless communications carrier, and a spinoff of Qualcomm. Leap's chairman and CEO, Harvey P. White, said Barad "will contribute strong strategic leadership and a track record of consumer marketing successes to Leap. Her track record . . . adds another dimension to our outstanding board." Incredibly, there was no mention in his announcement that Barad had just brought the world's largest toy company to its corporate knees. She also remained on the board of Pixar Animation Studios, Inc.

Although Barad had exited Mattel with a wad of dough, she did not receive as much as a farewell party from the company to which she gave so much of her life. Under better circumstances, there would have been a big, catered bash, but the security guards who were said to have escorted her out of the El Segundo headquarters for the last time weren't in much of a festive mood, and were just doing their job.

"After Jill had left the company she threw her *own* goodbye party because at Mattel she was just *out* the door," says Diana Troup.

About a year-and-a-half after she left the company, she had a party at her home where she invited her people who she really enjoyed the most to celebrate her career at Mattel, and that was wonderful. The people that were there for her at Mattel were the people that liked her, that did not say bad things about her, who genuinely did a great job for her. It wasn't like *I'm only going to have the crème de la crème.* Her assistant was even there. She invited people from lower level to upper level.

Barad also tossed a glitzy 50th birthday party for herself at a fancy restaurant. "We had to do something in the way of a little performance for her," says Troup. "It wasn't like she was Marie Antoinette and *please come and entertain me, do something special for me.* That was not from her, that was from her husband. So he got up there in a top hat."

At the same time, Troup, who had left Mattel because of her cancer, had joined Barad in a top-secret business venture, working out of her newly opened offices shared with her producer husband in Beverly Hills. "She couldn't do dolls because of her agreement with Mattel," says Troup. "We did something that was not toy-related, that was just *gorgeous* and *beautiful.*" But in the end, Barad made the decision not to market the product.

■ ■ ■

One of Eckert's big headaches, the troubled Learning Company, the purchase of which had resulted in Barad's ouster, was finally put on the block by Mattel in spring 2000 with a stern directive from the new CEO, who saw the company as a "distraction," to sell it at any cost.

He wanted a fresh slate. There were business media predictions that the interactive educational software company might sell for as little as $200 million, or about 5 percent of the $3.6 billion Mattel had paid. Credit Suisse First Boston was retained to handle the sale.

"Call it a learning experience," joshed *Forbes*.

Finally, in October of Eckert's first year, Mattel dumped the albatross from around his neck. A corporate turnaround firm, Gores Technology Group, purchased the company—amazingly for *no* cash and what was described as "an unspecified share" of future Learning Company earnings. Mattel even agreed to pay off a big chunk of the company's debt—a whopping $500 million. For the year 2000, Mattel's net loss for what was considered "one of the biggest corporate blunders ever" amounted to more than $430 million.

Moreover, as a result of shareholder lawsuits that were filed in 1999 and 2000 relating to Barad's atrocious acquisition—suits that charged mismanagement and breach of fiduciary duty—Mattel had to ante up a whopping $122 million.

But that was peanuts compared to the hell Bob Eckert and Mattel were about to enter as Barbie came face-to-face with the new world order of dolls—a street-tough, very sexy, and ethnic-looking pack that appeared to be putting Mattel's royal princess into retirement.

Chapter 15

# Barbie's Aging, Eckert's Making Excuses, and the Bratz Pack Is Booming

Through the early to mid-2000s, the Mattel CEO appeared to get Mattel under control. The reverse of Barad, he underpromised, overdelivered, trimmed the fat by cutting jobs, and kept the product line basic. Earnings were up and Mattel was starting to make money again. He appeared to be bringing stability to the long-volatile toy giant. Right below Oprah Winfrey, he was named one of the top 25 managers of 2001 by *BusinessWeek*.

As the magazine noted in a November 2002 story titled, "Mattel's New Toy Story," Eckert "believes he can take a lot of the guesswork

out by selling toys that make money year in, year out. . . . Eckert would
love a blockbuster toy. But he won't sacrifice steady growth to get it."

Evidently, Eckert knew coming in after the mess Barad had left
behind would be a challenge. As such, he concluded that Mattel needed
"to refocus on its core toy business—Barbie, Fisher-Price, Hot Wheels,
Matchbox." He also was aware that the world's largest toy company
with its 25,000 employees in more than 40 countries was too dis-
jointed, with a number of divisions. Worse still, the corporate culture
was horrific, with "discord and inefficiencies," and "an abundance of
contention and aggressiveness," with groups refusing even to talk to
each other.

It was clear, he believed, that Mattel's various divisions were working in "silos and were not very collaborative." As he put it, "There were
opportunities for improvement" and the "biggest one was in the area of
leadership development, and training programs in building leadership
capabilities." Workers, he believed, are not dummies. "They knew what
had to be done. It was management that stood in the way."

■ ■ ■

Under Eckert, Mattel appeared to be on an even keel, but soon growth
and profits began to slow once again.

By the middle of the first decade of the 21st century, Mattel was
again missing earnings targets, and Eckert was making excuses to Wall
Street analysts—the retail environment was too tough; higher gasoline
prices were keeping stay-at-home moms from taking the kids to the
local Wal-Mart to fill their shopping carts with Barbie dolls and Polly
Pockets, he bemoaned.

As *Fortune* observed in the article "To Thine Own Self Be True,
Barbie," "each quarter Eckert seems to come up with a new extenuating
circumstance to explain his profit problems."

As Christmas 2005 approached, the busty blond who was Mattel's
big earner, who made up a quarter of the company's sales, was flat—her
revenue was down for more than eight successive quarters. Gross sales
for Barbie worldwide had slumped to as much as 15 percent. "Our biggest challenge ahead," Eckert stated, "is reinvigorating the fashion doll
business . . . reinvigorating the Barbie brand. . . ." Moreover, Mattel

reported an $87 million loss on sales of $1.7 billion during the first six months of the year.

*Business Week's* headline told the story: NOT MUCH FUN AND GAMES AT MATTEL.

Evidently, Mattel could do without the flash and even the charisma of a Jill Barad, but creativity was the heart and soul of a great toy company—and that was one executive asset Eckert appeared to be lacking. As one Wall Street analyst pointed out at the time of his appointment, "Cheese, while a consumer product, is very different than toys which can be fad-driven."

■ ■ ■

Eckert had come into the job at Mattel with the staunch belief that for Mattel to continue to succeed and grow and keep shareholders happy, he had to return to its core products. Barbie was at the top of his list. But Barbie had begun to get long in the tooth, her age was showing, and the taste of little girls was changing. This new generation wanted toy hotties like they saw on MTV videos and in celebrity magazines. The likes of Britney Spears and Paris Hilton were their role models, not the dated, conservative image that Barbie still had. But Eckert and Mattel didn't appear to have the vision to gauge the changes in the taste of their prime girls' toys customers.

Suddenly, Barbie was being blitzed in sales by an upstart doll called Bratz, which down the road would lead to the biggest, most costly and vicious court battle over a toy in the history of the industry (more on that in Chapter 20).

Bratz was first brought to market in mid-2001 by MGA Entertainment, started by Isaac Larian, a young entrepreneurial Jewish Iranian immigrant who had come to America with $750 in his pocket.

The first Bratz Pack—Yasmin, Cloe, Jade, and Sasha, all with a "passion for fashion," according to MGA—were considered by Larian "not merely dolls but 'fashion icons' that look to the runways and what kids wear in and out of school for inspiration," as he later told the publication *Brand Strategy*.

With the dolls' bright-red lips as if injected with collagen, huge almond-shaped eyes, bubble butts, and erotic bellies extended from tight little tops, mysteriously ethnic and streetwise, they looked nothing like Barbie, and in fact were considered the "anti-Barbie" by Larian.

By Christmas 2001, to Eckert's dismay and concern, Bratz had become the top-selling doll brand in France, Spain, Israel, and Italy, and soon topped Barbie in Great Britain, and quickly began outselling Barbie in the United States. (Even worse, as Eckert and Mattel would eventually learn, the idea for the Bratz contingent had been developed by an ambitious young Mattel doll designer, Carter Bryant, who would become a key figure in the toy trial of the century. But that was still to come.)

The business magazine *Baseline*, in an article entitled "How Barbie Lost Her Groove," observed, "Girls who wanted attitude and ethnicity, not pert and pale [Barbie], bought $20 million worth of Bratz dolls in the first six months they were out." Bratz also won the People's Choice Toy of the Year award from the Toy Industry Association.

But that was just the beginning. As Christmas 2003 neared, MGA claimed that Bratz and its licensed products had a whopping $1 billion in sales.

By 2006, 125 million Bratz dolls had been sold worldwide, and global sales had reached more than $2 billion, still $1 billion below Barbie, but Barbie sales were continuing their decline and stagnation.

■ ■ ■

The only similarity between the slutty Bratz dolls and perky Barbie was the controversy the MGA line stirred. The Pack was attacked on all sides by parent organizations and other groups for promoting sexuality in young girls, along with materialism and consumerism.

With the popularity and sales of Bratz soaring seemingly out of the blue, Mattel—even with its "world class corporate intelligence system that consisted of teams of research scientists" working with business intelligence software—was caught completely off-guard and defenseless. The company's immediate red-alert response was to get a competitor in the stores as soon as possible, but under the many layers of bureaucracy and protocols at Mattel that emergency effort took some 14 months.

Mattel came out with a line called My Scene that included a trendier Barbie—more urban, more ethnic, more bling, and hotter— along with hip newcomers Madison and Chelsea. To Eckert's dismay, the brand didn't put a dent in Bratz's soaring sales. Worse still, it would spark a lawsuit several years later from Isaac Larian at MGA, who saw similarities with his Bratz girls, just as the original Barbie was much like the German Bild-Lilli that had also ignited litigation against Mattel.

Caught by surprise by the Bratz bombardment early in his reign, Bob Eckert found a scapegoat. He ousted 43-year-old Adrienne Fontanella, who had served for three years as president of the girls/ Barbie entertainment unit that included the My Scene rush-to-market concept.

Fontanella had been the discovery of, and anointed by, Jill Barad, to oversee the $1.8 billion world of Barbie, and other toys. Fontanella gave Barbie a slight breast reduction and less makeup.

Veteran toy industry analyst Margaret Whitfield of Stern, Agee, and Leach, who had been covering Mattel since the mid-1990s, told the author in April 2008:

> Adrienne did not react soon enough to this threat that Bratz brought to the company. Mattel should have undercut the Bratz doll big-time out of the gate with a Barbie that was priced so cheaply that no one would want to pay for Bratz. Or Mattel should have had a hipper design for girls six and up which is what Bratz's strong suit was.

> But there was no such action on the part of Mattel. In my view, Bob Eckert, overseeing this, did not react quickly enough. He's the kind of guy who probably lets things go too long before he intervenes.

> I have been disappointed in the evolution of Barbie under his reign. I believe that action should have been taken a lot sooner either to change the management of Barbie, or for Mr. Eckert to get involved a lot sooner than he did in making changes at the top and combating the Bratz invasion.

Fontanella's ouster was announced as part of Eckert's consolidation of the boys' and girls' divisions, placed under Matthew Bosquette, which mainly had to do with the beating Barbie was taking from Bratz in what was known as the Doll Wars.

Like other Mattel executives axed for poor performance, Fontanella got a hefty severance—$6.5 million, three years of health benefits, the forgiving of loans totaling a reported $3 million, but that's not all. Her golden handshake also included country club membership for three years, and even tax preparation counseling. She also got to keep the most prized doll she had on display in her executive suite—it wasn't Barbie, though her windowsills were lined with various Barbies—but rather a reproduction of Fontanella herself as a bride with a photograph of her bridesmaids in the background.

Whitfield points out that Bosquette, who was appointed by Eckert to succeed Fontanella, did even worse in his effort to compete with Bratz. "His solution was to go even edgier, and he developed that God-awful line called 'Flavas'—and that was a total bomb."

"Flavas"—as in "flay-vuhs," hip-hop, urban street pronunciation of *flavors*—meant "personal flavor and style." Armed with cell phones and soda cans and even a graffiti wall, the 10- to 11½-inches-high Flavas dolls—Kiyoni Brown, Happy D, Tika, Liam, Peebo, and Tre—sparked more criticism than sales. Detractors, and there were many—rappers and hip-hoppers among them—claimed the dolls stereotyped young African-Americans, and made fun of instead of complimenting the culture of hip-hop. Critics also pointed out that the Kiyoni Brown getup—a microminiskirt and halter top—made her look like a "video hoochie."

The *New York Times* in "A Makeover of a Romance" noted that Mattel's attempt to compete with Bratz by introducing Flavas was "like a desperate publicist trying to revive the moribund career of a Hollywood star."

On Wall Street, Flavas also raised questions about whether Mattel—read *Eckert*—had any handle whatsoever on the contemporary doll market with midlife-crisis Barbie still ruling the El Segundo roost, and the company's seeming desperation to battle the new kids on the block. In a story titled "To Lure Older Girls, Mattel Brings in a Hip-Hop Crowd," the *Wall Street Journal* in July 2003 reported, "In the 44 years since it introduced its bombshell Barbie, Mattel has rarely brought out a doll line to compete with her."

The toy industry trade magazine *TDmonthly* observed that in an attempt to counter MGA's juggernaut, "Mattel has done the unthinkable and created a competitor to its enduring Barbie line. . . . Mattel will have to hit the ground running to catch up with Bratz, which currently has 130 licensees worldwide" with hundreds of millions in projected sales.

And Flavas gave Isaac Larian a good laugh, too. "The only thing that's missing," he opined at the time, "is a cocaine vial. You think of Mattel, you think of Barbie and you think of sweetness. . . . This is like 'gangster Barbie,' and I think it's going to backfire."

He was spot on.

Faced with so much criticism and few sales, Mattel canceled the Flavas line a year after its introduction, and Eckert soon after booted Bosquette.

For many it's great to be hired by Mattel, and for some it's equally good to be axed, as Barad and Fontanella would attest.

Bosquette, who had been promoted by Barad during her ill-fated reign, walked away from Mattel with $5.4 million in severance—three times his annual salary—and received his bonus for the year. Moreover, the day he was fired, Bosquette secured a consulting deal with Mattel that gave him $1.5 million for two years—consulting services that, according to his agreement, "do not interfere with the consultant's personal and professional activities—as determined by the consultant."

A golfer, he also had his initiation fee paid to a country club, and got his leased company car for $100.

John Vogelstein, the head of Mattel's board compensation committee, took it on the chin from Graef Crystal who, in a piece for Bloomberg.com, declared, "If there's one thing that can be said about Vogelstein, it's this: He gives good severance."

And this was at a time when Mattel was once again facing what could fairly be called hard times.

Worse still, Mattel and Eckert were about to become entangled in a scandal that would make the Barad fiasco and the Ruth Handler scandal seem like child's play.

# Chapter 16

# Toy Terror 2007

To Bob Eckert, the toy giant appeared to be on a straight-and-narrow course at the start of 2007. Perky-breasted plastic Barbie, still the company's centerpiece, but seemingly running neck-and-neck with Bratz, had joined the age of the Internet, with a free website called BarbieGirls.com, allowing children in the 7-to-12 age group to create their own virtual characters, design their own room, and even customize their characters' outfits at a cybermall. The concept would also launch in about a dozen other countries, and Mattel had plans to hawk a $59.99 MP3 player to interact with the website.

At 48, Barbie was online with the likes of such new child pop-culture heroines as Hannah Montana, and that evil Bratz newcomer, who was giving her, or at least Eckert, palpitations.

But, as *Forbes* noted, Eckert "is making sure Mattel's impossibly blonde figurine, and its other classic brands like Hot Wheels and Fisher-Price, will stay on top 21st-century style." This included what the company termed *Premier Alliances*, connecting its iconic brands with major players in entertainment, sporting goods, clothing, and electronics—the likes of Time

Warner's Cartoon Network, the Walt Disney Co., and Universal Studios Home Entertainment.

Even better, Mattel had posted first-quarter 2007 profits in the face of analysts' forecasts for a loss—although U.S. sales for Barbie had dropped a troubling 21 percent, which Eckert blamed in part on a decline in "shelf space" in stores. In fact, Barbie was facing stiff competition from that upstart, freaky-looking doll called Bratz who had none of Barbie's old-fashioned glamour. But Eckert was confident that Barbie would again reign supreme. Barbie's losses were offset by strong sales for the preschool Fisher-Price brands and Hot Wheels.

"While not a particularly significant quarter within the seasonal toy industry," an optimistic Eckert noted, "our positive first quarter results are a good start to the year."

Little did he know.

■ ■ ■

"Friday the 13th" in any given year is considered by some an unlucky day, a good time to stay in and keep one's head down, if one believes in scary legends. Eckert had some last-minute work to clear up on Friday, July 13, 2007. He was looking forward to the weekend and a Saturday morning run, one of the ways he relaxed, and some quality time with his family in their spectacular multimillion-dollar home—paid for as a company perk—in the fashionable Palos Verdes Estates (long an enclave for Mattel honchos) overlooking the Pacific, south of the toy monster's El Segundo headquarters.

Eckert had hoped he could leave the office a bit early—he was not known as a workaholic—but his TGIF dreams were shattered when he was interrupted by one of his top lieutenants, Tom Debrowski. For Eckert, the dark myth of Friday the 13th was about to become stark reality.

As he recalled later, the first words he heard from Mattel's executive vice president of worldwide operations were "We have an issue."

Before the crises of high gasoline prices, bank and financial institution failures, government bailouts, and home mortgage foreclosures, there was Mattel's toy terror summer of 2007, when potentially deadly magnets and lead in paint in the company's most popular toys plagued parents and children, tarnishing the image of Mattel in the hearts and minds of the public, the media, consumer groups, and lawmakers in the nation's capital.

Eckert's problem had actually begun quietly a little over a month earlier, on June 8, when Auchan, a French direct importer, had tested for lead in paint on some of Mattel's preshipment toys destined for stores in France. Auchan had retained Intertek, an independent laboratory in Europe, to perform the test on a sample of toys manufactured for Mattel Asia Pacific Sourcing, known as MAPS, by Lee Der Industrial Company, Ltd. Lee Der was a vendor in the toy-manufacturing center of Guangdong province, in southern Communist China, the land of outsourcing and home of the largest toy-manufacturing industry in the world—the North Pole notwithstanding—where some 70 percent of Mattel's toys are made.

Lee Der Industrial was not a neophyte among the tens of thousands of vendors doing business for big American companies in the new and booming economy of China. It had been making toys for Mattel for 15 years, which included painting them.

Mattel's people in China, known as "product integrity employees," ordered shipment of the item halted and asked Lee Der to remedy the problem. On June 29, Mattel received what it thought was good news: A subsequent lead test by Intertek on another batch of the same toy proved negative.

Eckert would later testify before one of a number of congressional committees in the both the House and Senate probing the scandal, "The product passed the lead test. At that point, Mattel Product Integrity employees in Asia had reason to believe that Lee Der had solved any lead paint issue that it had."

But around the same time that lead in the paint was ruled out, a consumer telephoned Mattel's U.S. call center with a conflicting and more worrisome report. The customer had discovered lead paint in a toy using a home test kit. Mattel claimed later that that toy had been made by Lee Der. Children gnawing on toys containing lead in the paint can suffer headaches, stomach ailments, and death if large quantities of lead are ingested. Lead paint has been banned in the United States since 1978, because lead poisoning can trigger neurological problems, especially in children.

Mattel tried to replicate the same positive lead outcome without success.

As American families were about to celebrate the 4th of July 2007 holiday, unaware that some Mattel toys their children were playing with might be toxic and dangerous, a third test by Intertek for Auchan once again found high levels of lead in the paint on another sample of the originally tested toy in a different batch made by the Lee Der company.

In the following days, more toys with more lead in the paint were found, and Mattel's Asia operation notified Lee Der that it would accept no more of its product.

Incredibly, it wasn't until July 12—more than a month after the first lead paint was discovered in the test for the French importer Auchan—that Mattel's officials in Asia notified senior management in El Segundo.

The next day, what became known privately within Mattel as "Black Friday the 13th," Debrowski ruined his boss's weekend plans when he informed Eckert of the problem. According to the chief executive's subsequent testimony before the Subcommittee on Commerce, Trade, and Consumer Protection, "an immediate freeze of all shipments of suspect Lee Der products" was ordered.

On its own, Mattel began a quiet investigation to determine the cause and scope of the lead paint fiasco, the affected toys, whether any had been shipped, and the dates of production. The chief executive later asserted that the lead levels were traced to "yellow pigment in paint used on portions of certain toys" manufactured by the Lee Der company in what Eckert described as "a previously undisclosed plant" located in Foshan City, China.

Under the rules of the Consumer Product Safety Commission (CPSC), the watchdog agency responsible for keeping Americans safe from dangerous and defective products, companies like Mattel are required to report a potentially dangerous problem within 24 hours of its discovery. But Mattel had felt for years that it didn't have to abide by those guidelines, that it could police itself until it felt ready to file a report that could lead to a recall.

Finally on July 20—dozens of hours later—Mattel filed an "initial report" with the CPSC, which, like Mattel, would also come under a barrage of media fire and intense congressional scrutiny for inaction, understaffing—there was only one toy tester in the entire agency—and questionably close ties between agency officials and the industries it oversees, such as toys.

Mattel didn't file a "full report" with the CPSC until July 26, indicating what Eckert later described as the company's "desire to institute a fast track recall" of all products that Mattel believed "could contain impermissibly high lead levels."

The first 2007 mass recall of Mattel toys was on August 2, almost two months after the initial discovery of excessive lead in the paint. More than 80 types of popular preschool Sesame Street and Nickelodeon toys, among them Big Bird, Elmo, Dora, and Diego—almost a million units sold in the United States, the United Kingdom, and other countries around the world between May and August under the Mattel's subsidiary Fisher-Price label—were ordered returned.

Mattel offered a boilerplate apology to its millions of loyal and trusting customers in the United States, and gave Wall Street notice that the recall would cut pretax operating income by $30 million. But that was just the beginning of bad news for its stockholders—and its customer base.

■ ■ ■

Five days later, Mattel, in an apparent attempt to throw all of the blame about the recall scandal on China, chose to disclose to the world that the lead-tainted toys had been made by Lee Der Industrial, and that Mattel had ceased accepting shipments from the manufacturer.

Moreover, Mattel claimed it alerted its competitors to Lee Der's alleged misdeeds. A Mattel spokesperson never identified the competition by name, but asserted, "We do not consider safety to be a competitive advantage." Normally, in the $22 billion dog-eat-dog toy industry, one company wouldn't give ice away to another in the middle of a blizzard, so Mattel's decision to voluntarily share information about a vendor seemed rather curious.

The next day, in the wake of Mattel's revelation, the Chinese state media ominously announced that the country would "severely" punish those involved in the toy safety scandal, which in this case was Lee Der.

A Chinese quality control official was quoted as saying,

Concerning those involved in seriously conspiring to break the law, the parties involved will be transferred to legal authorities to be dealt with severely according to the law. The supervision bureau will increase its level of management, stop the export of

the goods in question and resume exports when qualifications
are completely overhauled.

In short order, Lee Der's export license was revoked, and the Chinese
government publicly revealed that a fake lead-free paint pigment had been
shipped to Lee Der by its paint supplier, sparking a government probe
into the sale of bogus lead-free pigment in China that then arrived on
toys in the United States and elsewhere, jeopardizing the lives of children.

Mattel's adverse publicity about the Chinese company then led to
another shocking and tragic development in the escalating toy scandal.

On Saturday, August 11, the Hong Kong businessman who owned
Lee Der Industrial, 52-year-old Zhang Shuhong, committed suicide. He was
found hanged on the third floor of his company's Foshan warehouse. An
employee told local reporters "our boss had two deep marks in his neck."

Zhang was reported to have spent the morning addressing some of
his 5,000 employees who were certain to be fired since the company
would lose as much as $30 million in business from Mattel because
of the scandal. These were workers who were lucky to earn $3 a day,
and many lived in tenement-like tiny rooms within the factory. The
few-and-far-between toy assemblers working in the United States
made at least $18 an hour. But there weren't many toy-making jobs
left in America. As was Japan when Barbie was first produced in 1959,
China was now Mattel's go-to country for cheap labor.

After Zhang's death, a Chinese newspaper, the *Southern Metropolis
Daily*, reported that the company had gotten the disputed paint from a
firm run by a close friend of Zhang's, and that Zhang felt that he had
been betrayed.

The *New York Times*, in a lengthy story titled "Scandal and Suicide
in China: A Dark Side of Toys," observed that Zhang's suicide "read
like the latest twist in a morality play," and noted that Zhang

> . . . was a victim . . . of his own duplicitous suppliers, of China's
> faulty supply chains, and the pressures of its loosely regulated
> brand of capitalism, where Chinese entrepreneurs feel squeezed
> between Western companies' appetite for cheap goods and the
> fierce local competition to satisfy it. . . . Zhang was one of

the hundreds of thousands of entrepreneurs who had helped make China into the world's factory floor, providing the inexpensive goods that fill the shelves of Wal-Mart and Target.

The prestigious *Guardian* newspaper in London reported, "The finger of blame has also been pointed at Mattel for apparently failing to enforce safety standards in its supply chain. . . ."

While Mattel claimed it owned and controlled a dozen factories in China, it was contracting with as many as 40 other vendors in 2007. In 2002, the last Mattel manufacturing plant in the United States, part of the Fisher-Price division, was closed. By 2007, an estimated 70 percent of Mattel's toys were made by low-paid workers in China, and some, such as the Barbie doll, were produced in Indonesia, Mattel stated, with additional Barbie accessories made in China. Other Mattel toys are made in Mexico and elsewhere—but none are reportedly produced in the United States.

Three days after the suicide, on August 14, Mattel "suffered another blow," as the *Financial Times* noted, when it announced its second enormous recall of the summer. This recall involved some 9.3 million toys sold in the United States and 11 million in foreign countries. In all, they included popular Barbie, Polly Pockets toys, and *Cars* movie items manufactured in China—using Mattel specifications. Millions of the toys were made with tiny magnets that could seriously injure or kill a child when swallowed.

And they already had.

In its recall press release, however, Mattel gave more precedence to the lead paint found on 253,000 of the *Cars* die-cast vehicle line—the Sarge character. It wasn't until the fourth paragraph that the larger and more serious recall of toys with the magnets was mentioned. Mattel would be accused of purposely burying the more massive recall of dangerous-magnet toys, which had already caused injuries to children—and at least one child's death involving a different toy manufacturer. One such critic, Dara O'Rourke, an assistant professor of labor and environmental policy at the University of California, Berkeley, charged that Mattel "really mixed these issues," and accused the company of playing public relations.

(As early as 2005, long before the toy terror summer, two young-sters, one in Indiana and the other in Colorado, had swallowed mag-nets that were part of the very popular Mattel Polly Pockets brand. The children became extremely ill, almost died, and required emergency surgery. To avoid a public scandal, assert lawyers representing the fam-ilies, Mattel quietly made financial settlements with the families. The horrific experiences of the children and their families are detailed later in this book.)

With all hell breaking loose, Eckert later told *Fortune*, "I had no idea this was the beginning of what turned out to be a long summer for us in the toy business."

And long it was. Before the end of 2007, Mattel and its subsidiary, Fisher-Price, were forced to have a total of five recalls of some 20 mil-lion toxic and dangerous toys mostly manufactured in China, including 675,000 Barbie accessories, in which lead paint was discovered. A con-gressional request for a sixth recall was denied by Mattel.

The legal limit for lead in paint is 0.06 percent, but Mattel toys recalled in 2007 had as much as 11 percent lead, which was caused by the manufacturing process of its vendors in China. Recalled magnetic toys that caused injuries to children, such as Mattel's popular Polly Pockets brand, however, were the result of poor design by Mattel.

*Forbes* headlined the international scandal, CHINESE TOY TERROR, and *USA Today* declared, "Mattel's Stellar Reputation Tainted."

Those two stories were typical of the worldwide coverage, and of the panic the recalls sparked among outraged and frightened parents. In the story "After Stumbling, Mattel Cracks Down in China," the *New York Times* reported that one mother angered by the series of recalls showed up at Mattel headquarters with a car loaded with the compa-ny's playthings and demanded that someone in authority go through them to see which were dangerous and which were safe; Mattel claimed none were problematic.

Nevertheless, "the blow to Mattel's public reputation was substan-tial," the *Times*' story observed. The indignation of parents was exem-plified by an irate father in Belgium, who angrily commented on the *Times of London* website:

I am so glad this has come to light before Christmas when so many more of these toys would have been sold. I am sick and

tired of the greed. Please have a conscience. If you don't I hope
your company has to close down.

■ ■ ■

Toy recalls, however, might not be effective at all because very few of the
products ever get returned. That was the shocking conclusion of a study
published at the height of the Mattel imbroglio in the August 2007 issue
of the peer-reviewed journal *Injury Prevention*. Keri Brown Kirschman, an
assistant psychology professor at the University of Dayton, and a specialist
in pediatric injury prevention, found that many dangerous, recalled toys
wind up on online auction sites and at flea markets.

"Today we're thinking about Mattel, we're thinking of Fisher-Price,
because the recalls are in the news," Kirschman said, "but three years
from now, when we go online to buy toys, we won't be thinking about
recalls." The researcher said that when she went online she found toys
for sale recalled in the late 1990s. "A concern for current Fisher-Price
and Mattel recalls is that these products will linger in second-hand ven-
ues long after the publicity dies down."

One of the most knowledgeable hands-on experts on toy testing
and recalls is Robert L. Hundemer, who, for almost three decades until
his resignation in January 2008, was the CPSC's "sole full-time tester
for toys on the market in the United States." Until his retirement at
the age of 61, Hundemer worked out of grubby facilities in a 1950s
building whose rundown condition, including rodent infestation, he
describes as being like "a ghetto," although it's what he calls "the toy
lab for all America—for all of the United States Government." Before
he left the agency, when the Mattel scandal was in the headlines daily,
Hundemer had become a symbol of CPSC's lack of teeth in performing its investigative and enforcement duties due to insufficient funding
and personnel dating back to Reagan Administration budget cuts.

In his many years of experience dealing with unsafe and dangerous
toys, Hundemer states unequivocally that "recalls are not effective. The
CPSC *knows* they're not. The return percentage of recalls is very low,
below 10 percent. We don't really know how many toys are returned or
disposed of. We've never done a study." (During the 2007 recalls, Mattel
said it planned to recycle as many components of returned toys as

possible, but also noted that historically only about 6 percent of recalled toys are actually returned by consumers.)

Hundemer also reveals another important aspect of recalls—that they are actually *negotiated* between a manufacturer like Mattel and the CPSC. "Recalls are not an edict decreed by the CPSC," he asserts.

> You have to negotiate with the manufacturer for the wording of the recall. It's a legal process. The CPSC just doesn't go out and say, "Okay, you've got to recall these products." If you have to negotiate the wording of the recall with the other side, it's sometimes a time-consuming process. If it took four months or six months for the recall to take place, all that time the public has been exposed to the hazard. It's like the magnets, which were out there for well over a year, a year-and-a-half, before the problem became known. It's a failure of our system—a failure of prevention. Recalls are not a success story.

By the time recalls get into the public domain, the child may have outgrown the product, or the toy may have been broken and discarded, notes Hundemer, who also learned in his many years as the government's toy tester that with an expensive toy "parents measure the risk versus the reward. If it's a favored product, a lot of times parents are reluctant to discard it." Moreover, he believes that despite the publicity recalls generate in the media, "Most people aren't product geeks, so the recall just kind of passes their knowledge. The attention span is very short in all of America—and unless you are a consumer geek, recalls aren't effective."

Hundemer advocates "third-party certification" in order to make certain toys are safe, such as the kind of independent laboratory used by the French company that touched off the flood of Mattel recalls in 2007.

> You have to have meaningful independent certification by a disinterested party of a product in production, not one that's cherry-picked by the manufacturer. That's what I would want. That's my requirement. Mattel did their own certification. Obviously, they didn't do a good enough job.

But Hundemer is also critical of the manufacturing process in China and the mindset involved. "The fact of the matter is the only thing the Chinese really understand is the Yen," he maintains.

They have children, but is their eye as keen as ours when it comes to safety? Hell, no. Do the Chinese workers have the same environment as in the United States? No. Do they have the same pollution standards as in the United States? No. Do they have the same health standards as the workers in the United States? No. So why would they care about the toys they make? If they're not that concerned about their own people, where do you think we rank?

Hundemer's assertion that there were ties between the CPSC and the industries the commission oversees became public in the midst of the recall scandal.

The *Washington Post* disclosed that Hundemer's boss, Nancy Nord, the agency's acting commissioner, and the previous chairman, Hal Stratton, under whom Hundemer also worked, had taken dozens of trips at the expense of the toy industry and others that the agency regulates. "Some of the trips were sponsored by lobbying groups and lawyers representing the makers of products linked to consumer hazards," the *Post* reported in its story, "Industries Paid for Top Regulators' Travel."

In February 2006, for instance, the Toy Industry Association, the trade and lobbying group for Mattel and other manufacturers of playthings, paid for Nord's travel, meals, hotel stay, and even her parking so she could attend the annual Toy Fair in New York. This was later viewed as a probable conflict of interest, if not just plain bad judgment on her part.

As with Mattel's Eckert, Nord came under fire during heated congressional hearings. Nancy Pelosi, the speaker of the U.S. House of Representatives, called for President Bush to fire Nord, whom he had appointed. She had previously worked in public relations at Kodak.

The allegation about her close industry ties, and a letter Nord sent to lawmakers, which (incredibly) criticized a proposal in the Senate to increase CPSC's authority, infuriated members of Congress. Pelosi, for one, declared that anyone who doesn't think the agency needs more resources "does not understand the gravity of the situation and does not understand the concerns that America's parents have for the safety of their children."

# Chapter 17

# An Outrageous Apology

O n August 21, within a week of the second massive recall by Mattel, the company faced its first major legal challenge in the escalating scandal. A Philadelphia lawyer, Jeffrey Killino, an expert in dealing with problems resulting from Chinese-manufactured products, filed a class action suit in Los Angeles County Superior Court.

He took the action in an effort to compel Mattel to pay for lead testing for "possibly millions" of children who might have been affected by the company's lead-tainted products. After the first two recalls, families around the country began contacting him, fearing the lead in Mattel's toys might have damaged their children.

"The families were so irate, and so sad," Killino asserts.

They were saying, "We put these toys in our kids' hands and we don't even know which ones have lead. Is my kid sick? Is my kid going to get hurt?" You want to give your kid every benefit in life, and instead of giving them every benefit, you give them a toy and you're giving them poison. There was nobody who wanted to profit from Mattel's problems. They wanted the right thing done. They wanted Mattel to take responsibility for having their kids tested, for paying for any medical bills. Those were their concerns and they didn't want it to happen ever again to anybody else. If you put a lead-painted toy in contact with a child, every pediatrician is going to say that the child has to be tested no matter what.

What Mattel did wrong was put toxic toys in kids' hands. So who should pay to get the kids tested to see if they've got lead in their system? In my estimation, Mattel put profit before safety. When the problem arose and they got caught, they stalled getting the word out to parents as soon as possible, and then they should have tested the kids as soon as possible to see if they had any lead. Mattel just cared about controlling the situation so they could get their [2007] Christmas toy sales.

One of the youngsters Killino alleges was injured by Mattel's lead-tainted toys was three-year-old Kevin Ryan Fisher, of Chicago, whose parents joined in the class action suit. In the spring of 2007, the tyke's mother, Beth Fisher, noticed extreme changes in his behavior. "He just was very, very hyper and then he would get lethargic," the mother of four says. "It got terribly bad in the late summer, when he wasn't speaking very well. He only had two- or three-word sentences. He would get very angry. He would have meltdowns. He was really tired. His appetite decreased. In my gut, I knew there was something wrong."

It was then that the Fishers read about the Mattel recalls and saw a report on ABC's *Nightline* about the lead-tainted toys. She took her son to his pediatrician and was shocked to learn from blood and urine tests that he showed "a seriously high level" of lead in his system, according to Killino. "Lead had settled in his bones, his brain, and his tissues," 33-year-old Beth Fisher says.

She soon determined that Ryan had been eating the painted hair off of his Diego toy, part of the popular Dora the Explorer line imported from China by Mattel's Fisher-Price division, located in East Aurora, New York. It was one of the Mattel toys in the August 2 recall. "Ryan ate the hair off it," his mother says. "He used to sleep with the

Diego. He also had Monkey Boots, which is part of that line, and he ate the boots off of it. I would try to get the toys and take them out of his mouth. I didn't realize they were toxic. I had a lot of faith in Mattel."

Faced with a toxic toy situation, Fisher called Mattel's advertised recall hotline to get a list of the toys that had been recalled and to see what the company was doing for people who had been affected. The response surprised her.

> I called right after I found out Ryan was lead-poisoned. They told me to send the toys to them and then they would give me a voucher to buy the same toys. The representative then asked me whether I would continue to buy Mattel and I said, *no!* I asked to speak to a manager and she said the manager wasn't available. They obviously weren't going to acknowledge that their toys were the cause of my child's lead poisoning.

She says she joined the lawsuit because she feels that

> Mattel should pay for testing children for lead. I'm hoping that Mattel takes some responsibility for the damage they have done to these children. I'm very angry at what has happened to my child. I am a very vocal person, so everyone I know now knows my story, and a lot of people I know do not now buy Mattel toys because of what has happened to Ryan, and the fear of what might happen to their children.

■ ■ ■

After the first two recalls, Mattel went into deep-crisis mode. The recalls created a public relations disaster for the company and increased trade tensions between the United States and China. In full-page ads that ran concurrently with the second recall in the *Wall Street Journal*, *New York Times*, and *USA Today*, Eckert offered a mea culpa. In the ad, which pictured three children playing, Eckert, the father of four, said:

> Fellow parents. Nothing is more important than the safety of our children. Our long record of safety at Mattel is why we're one of the most trusted names with parents. And I am confident that the actions we are taking now will maintain that trust.

Mattel went further and produced a videotaped apologia by Eckert that aired on Mattel's website, promising things would get better. The media reaction to Mattel's spin was not positive, as exemplified by a CNN reporter who stated that "damage control is now the name of the game at Mattel, both on Wall Street and Main Street, USA." Eckert told CNN, "I'm disappointed, I'm upset, but I can ensure your viewers that we are doing everything we can about the situation."

Eckert made the TV rounds. On ABC's *Good Morning America*, he was berated by co-anchor Chris Cuomo, who suggested that the CEO's push for profits by manufacturing toys in China had endangered children. "Every batch of toys we're producing meets our rigorous standards and we're testing every batch of toys before it's released to the retail chain," Eckert maintained.

An editorial, "Toy Story: Mattel's Recall, and China Bashing," in the *Wall Street Journal* observed: "Parents will decide in coming months how much they trust products made for Mattel in China. . . ."

*Time* called Mattel's PR campaign a "punch-drunk performance."

In the eyes of the world media, the U.S. Congress, and the public, Bob Eckert became the latest international CEO poster child for corporate mistrust, accused of everything from misleading the consumer to stonewalling lawmakers in Washington who were suddenly—in the face of headlines and constituent indignation—working to enact new laws to tighten toy testing and safety.

"Why Eckert wasn't forced to resign is something I don't understand," declares Bob Hundemer, the former CPSC toy-tester-turned-industry-gadfly, who notes,

Corporate ethics start at the top. Eckert set the tone for Mattel's corporate mantra. He's arrogant. He was all apologetic, saying, "Yes, it was our fault; we're going to stand up and take responsibility." He said that on one hand, but on the other hand, he didn't take any *personal* responsibility at all.

Officials of the Chinese government responsible for the safety of its products—China produced 86 percent of all of the toys sold in the United States in 2007—were furious that Mattel was placing the blame for the recall scandal on its manufacturers.

Li Changjiang, the country's quality watchdog chief, claimed that 85 percent of the Mattel toy recalls were due to Mattel design faults—the toys made with tiny magnets that kids were ingesting—and 15 percent of the toys were considered unsafe because of the use of dangerous lead in paint. He noted that Chinese exports in the first half of 2007 to the United States were up by 17.8 percent, and by more than 30 percent to the European Union, declaring that "these figures show fully that Chinese products are popular all over the world. . . . More than 99 percent of our goods meet standards. Demonizing Chinese products, or talking of the Chinese product threat, I think is simply a new kind of trade protectionism."

A spokesman for China's General Administration of Quality Supervision, Inspection and Quarantine further stated that Mattel "should improve its product design and supervision over product quality. Chinese original equipment manufacturers were doing the job just as importers requested, and the toys conformed with the U.S. regulations and standards at the time of production."

Since the Mattel recalls started, China had come under intense criticism from the likes of U.S. Sen. Christopher J. Dodd, the Connecticut Democrat, who had gone so far as to propose suspending all toy imports from China. His idea might have been taken seriously, because still more trouble was brewing.

Just as the long Labor Day 2007 holiday ended and children were headed back to school, another Mattel recall shattered the expectations of the public, the media, and members of Congress, now out for blood, that the toxic toy danger had subsided.

On September 4, the CPSC and Mattel announced that 844,000 toys containing excessive amounts of lead were recalled. Three Fisher-Price toys and a number of Barbie accessories—a whopping 675,000—were named. Mattel claimed the recall was part of its ongoing investigation that was promised after the August recalls.

With the latest recall, *CBS News* reported that Mattel's "reputation took another hit," and noted that the company "could face an uphill battle convincing consumers about the safety of its products. . . ."

Eckert was now about to put a plan into effect that would give Mattel an even bigger black eye.

■ ■ ■

Faced with increased criticism and anger from Chinese officials, who refused to have their country take the blame for all of Mattel's recall problems, Eckert did something extraordinary—he sent an emissary to Communist China in the third week of September, just after the third recall, to offer what the *Financial Times* called "a humiliating public apology." This ignited yet another firestorm from consumer groups and politicians—this time complaining that Mattel was kowtowing to China.

The decision infuriated outspoken Senator Charles Schumer, the colorful senior Democrat from New York, who blasted Mattel: "It's like a bank robber apologizing to his accomplice instead of to the person who was robbed. Mattel's playing politics in China rather than doing what matters."

Congresswoman Rosa DeLauro, a Connecticut Democrat, says,

I almost couldn't believe it when Mattel apologized to the Chinese. I was angry, because it reflected for me that they must have been told, "Hey, you're going to have real trouble with your production," with the labor issue, whatever it was. What really bothers me is that Mattel remains more concerned with the cost of doing business than with the safety of our children.

But precisely what Mattel's apology meant was "caught up in translation," noted the *Washington Post*.

On the face of it, Mattel's Tom Debrowski, who first broke the bad news to Eckert about the lead paint issue some two months earlier, appeared to have been sent to Beijing to offer regrets for harming the reputation of Chinese manufacturers. After all, Mattel was locked into China for about 70 percent of its toy manufacturing, and needed to restore goodwill. As the *Post* observed in "Mattel and China Differ on Apology," Mattel "has every interest in maintaining a good relationship with China, even as it must shore up the confidence of its customers."

*Time* magazine pointed out that "Mattel needs China just as much as China needs Mattel, and it cannot afford to jeopardize its relationship."

Eric Johnson, a management professor at the Tuck School of Business at Dartmouth, an expert on the U.S. toy industry's dependency on China, noted that Mattel needed "Chinese industrial capacity for its toys," and said that Mattel didn't want to lose its "significant investment of their own capital. I suspect that Mattel has a vested interest in expanding into the Chinese market as well." He said the public apology by Mattel "is all about saving face and a private apology wouldn't have done that for China. They really needed this public apology."

Former government toy tester Bob Hundemer asserts,

> Eckert had to apologize . . . because he offended them, and the fact of the matter is without China there is no Mattel—none at all. He was just being a politician. Eckert sent his guy to China and said, "Gee, I really offended you guys and I'm sorry I did that. I didn't mean it to sound the way it did." Eckert had to kiss the ass of Congress and now he had to kiss the ass of the Chinese.

According to the state-run New China News Agency, Debrowski "apologized personally" to product quality chief Li Changjiang "for the massive recall of made-in-China toys due to design flaws committed by itself." Debrowski was quoted as telling Li:

> Mattel takes full responsibility for these recalls and apologizes to you, the Chinese people, and all our customers who received the toys. . . . [The] vast majority of those products that were recalled were the result of a design flaw in Mattel's design, not through a manufacturing flaw in China's manufacturers. We understand and appreciate deeply the issues that this has caused for the reputation of Chinese manufacturers.

The *Financial Times* called the meeting "carefully stage-managed" and observed that the apology was "in stark contrast" to U.S. Senate testimony a week earlier by Eckert, who had indicated the recalls were the fault of outside contractors in China. "We were let down," he stated. The newspaper declared, "Beijing has bitten back" and termed Mattel's apology "astonishing."

Mattel immediately complained that the meeting had been "mischaracterized" by the Chinese, and challenged reports in the media. Blaming the messenger, Mattel asserted that Debrowski was just repeating what had been stated to consumers—that Mattel design issues, not

Chinese manufacturing, had caused the dangerous problems with the magnetic toys.

Mattel further claimed it was apologizing to consumers in China, not manufacturers, and issued a press release saying, "Since Mattel toys are sold the world over, Mattel apologized to the Chinese today just as it has wherever toys are sold."

The Xinhua News Agency, which had a reporter present at the Li-Debrowski powwow, maintained it was a "personal apology" to the Chinese government. In an editorial titled "An Apology at Last," the *Guangzhou Daily* declared that "the impact on the innocent Chinese workers who have been made to pay for others' mistakes has been deleterious." The paper said the apology had come too late, "but at least it addressed injustice against toys made in China."

To many, Mattel's statements and contradictions seemed like so much corporate doubletalk.

■ ■ ■

Immediately in the wake of the apology brouhaha, embattled Mattel was faced with another embarrassing lawsuit, this one from shareholders who felt injured by the ongoing scandals. The derivative lawsuit named as defendants a dozen current and former directors, including chief executive Eckert, for delaying reports of product problems to the CPSC, some dating back to the 1990s, and other alleged wrongdoing. The suit was filed on October 10, 2007, on behalf of the Sterling Heights Police and Retirement System, a pension fund in Sterling Heights, Michigan, which owned 23,600 shares of stock worth more than $530,000 at the time. The suit was filed in Delaware, where California-based Mattel is incorporated.

In a report about the lawsuit on his news program on CNN, the outspoken populist Lou Dobbs declared, "My gosh, on nearly every level, this Mattel operation is failing the American consuming public."

The suit accused the company of breaching fiduciary duties by flaunting the CPSC laws, and alleged that Mattel executives and board members made insider profits by dumping large amounts of Mattel shares. "Since 2001, the CPSC has fined Mattel twice for 'knowingly' withholding information regarding problems that created an unreasonable risk of injury or death," according to the court filing. The shareholders claimed that that has been "Mattel's way of doing business."

According to the lawsuit, four members of the Mattel board of directors sold more than $33 million in stock from January through mid-May 2007, and noted that the "timing of these sales is highly suspicious given that the selling defendants sold their shares while Mattel possessed reports of defective products but before the defects were reported to the CPSC." Mattel, however, said it didn't learn of the lead paint issue until June.

Declared Jay Eisenhofer, the attorney representing the Sterling Heights pension fund:

> While no one is accusing Mattel of intentionally bringing shoddy and dangerous toys to market, our suit makes the case that the company has repeatedly shirked its responsibilities under the law to come clean with regulators, consumers and investors when problems have arisen with its products that could jeopardize public safety, especially when those problems could lower sales and put a dent in earnings.
>
> By consistently refusing to abide by federally mandated rules governing disclosure of product safety issues, Mattel has failed its stockholders and regrettably used its illegal, drawn-out reporting to mislead investors as well as to cover up profit-taking by company insiders. Those actions add up to a breach of trust in the extreme, especially since Mattel's disclosure violations placed millions of children at risk of serious injury. This is a most unfortunate "Toy Story."

(As of the fall of 2008, the case was still pending. Any proceeds from the suit were to be paid by the directors to Mattel, not to shareholders, as is standard in derivative suits.)

■ ■ ■

Mattel had its fourth and fifth hellish recalls of 2007 in less than three months. The fourth recall involved a smaller number of toys—55,500 Go Diego Go products containing high levels of lead in the paint, which had been sold mostly in the United States, Great Britain, Ireland, and Canada.

By the time of that recall, on October 25, Mattel, more than six decades old, had established what it called an Office of Corporate Responsibility because of the scandal.

There was a fifth recall on November 6 of some 155,0000 Laugh & Learn Learning Kitchen toys imported from Mexico by Mattel's Fisher-Price division, because pieces of the faucet or the clock hands could detach. This posed a choking hazard to young children, according to the CPSC. The agency reported having received 38 instances of small parts separating. There were two reports of children gagging on pieces, one of a child who started choking, and one of an actual choking occurrence. Fisher-Price offered customers a free repair kit.

Mattel's problems continued into 2008, when a controversy over a blood pressure cuff in a Fisher-Price toy medical kit that had high levels of lead was disclosed in the December 2007 issue of *Consumer Reports*. Acting on the revelation, Illinois Attorney General Lisa Madigan urged parents immediately to take the item away from their children. Fisher-Price acted quickly to remove the toy from store shelves in Illinois, and offered consumers safe replacements.

But Mattel refused calls from Congress for a nationwide recall of the toy, contending that while the cuffs had "higher than anticipated" levels of lead, the plastic part had met American and European standards. The number of toys affected was in the thousands.

On January 29, 2008, more than 50 lawmakers sent a letter to Eckert, declaring, "If this product is too dangerous for the children of Illinois, it is too dangerous for children in the rest of this country."

One of the key drafters, Congresswoman Rosa L. DeLauro, a senior member of the House Appropriations Committee, told Eckert, "we are disturbed by your lack of action. . . . We find this response to be deficient."

The letter quoted Eckert's words back in September, when he offered "my sincere pledge . . . that we will do the right thing." DeLauro and her colleagues asked him to

> . . . review your pledge and act accordingly. . . . [W]e challenge you to live up to your words and set a standard for the entire

industry by completely eliminating the use of lead in all of the children's products manufactured by Mattel. When parents purchase a product from your company, they are not just purchasing a toy—they are putting their trust in an established brand that has historically been believed to provide merchandise that is safe for their children. We urge you to live up to this reputation.

■ ■ ■

The recalls of 2007 weren't the first to point to dangerous toys unintentionally produced by Mattel, or by its overseas suppliers. Unsafe and risky products go back as far as the founding Handler era.

Fred Adickes, who in the late 1960s wore the hat of Mattel's product development manager of boys' toys, had with the help of an industrial designer, Floyd Schlau, discovered that a pink liquid called Plastisol, which was used in the manufacture of dolls, became rubberlike when heated at a low temperature.

They soon developed die-cast metal molds in the shape of insects and other objects into which the Plastisol, renamed *Plasti-Goop*, was poured and then heated over a small electric heater. Mattel marketed the toy as "Creepy Crawlers," which was a huge moneymaker. "They sold like crazy," Adickes says. But production was discontinued over safety concerns about children playing with the small electric heater to heat the goo. An updated and safer model was later marketed.

On the website Feelingretro.com, where nostalgic memories good and bad are posted by fans of 1960s and 1970s toys, commenters recalled the horrors of Mattel's Creepy Crawlers. "I remember the nasty, plastic smell while they cooked," wrote one. Another observed, "I can't believe we had these kinds of toys unsupervised, and didn't die or end up horribly maimed."

In 1967, Adickes was looking to follow up on the success of Creepy Crawlers to impress Ruth and Elliot Handler, and make another bundle for Mattel. "I thought, 'Well, we've got the heater. I'll bet we can make something kids can eat.'" On the way home he picked up a box of Aunt Jemima's pancake mix, some food coloring, and mixed it all up and put the green concoction into one of the small molds, and turned out a little green pancake shaped like a horned toad.

I brought him to the product conference, put him on the table in Jack Ryan's office, and Ruth and Elliot were there. I said, "This is something we might do." I took out this horned toad and bit the head off and chewed it up and swallowed it. Ruth stood up and said, "My God, that's incredible!"

But the Father of Barbie wasn't impressed, because one of the successes of Creepy Crawlers was that they wiggled. Ryan suggested that Adickes develop such an edible that did wiggle. "I almost gagged and thought, 'Ugh, I've never tasted anything in my life that I wanted to eat that would wiggle,'" recalls Adickes. "But Jack came up with gelatin that would wiggle and it was brought out by Mattel as Incredible Edibles."

In *Dream Doll*, Ruth Handler recalled taking Incredible Edibles to the New York Toy Show and writing

. . . tremendous orders . . . [we] geared up to make millions of the sets. . . . Kids went wild, too, after seeing our fantastic commercial that featured boys and girls dropping disgustingly wiggly "worms" and "bugs" into their mouths.

According to Adickes, "We sold about $50 million worth before it had to be taken off the market because it was unsafe." As Ruth Handler termed it, "the roof caved in."

Horrifyingly, diabetic children were becoming ill because the starch in Incredible Edibles turned to sugar in their stomachs. While there was no Consumer Product Safety Commission in those days, the Food and Drug Administration ordered Mattel to remove Incredible Edibles, which had been labeled "sugarless," but did not take into account the carbohydrate content.

"In the FDA's eyes, our 'sugarless' labeling might be misleading," Handler stated.

"No one at Mattel foresaw that problem," observes Adickes. "After we got the reports of the kids becoming ill—I don't think there were any deaths—Incredible Edibles had to be withdrawn, and all the product that had been shipped had to be relabeled."

As part of a negotiated deal with the FDA, Mattel hired temporary workers to go to every toy store and wholesaler in the country and paste a label on every Incredible Edibles box, warning diabetic children about the product's carbohydrate content.

Ruth Handler called the FDA's demand "a scary incident," stating that it would have been "catastrophic" for Mattel if all the toys had to be recalled.

According to Adickes, "Mattel had a responsible attitude as a company, but they also had a very strong legal department and I'm sure the legal department gave some big advice in a hurry, and so they responded properly as a corporation should."

Aside from the more serious diabetic issue, commenters on Feelingretro.com registered sour memories about the taste of Incredible Edibles. Noted one: "My most vivid memory of Incredible Edibles is making some after [it] was past its prime and throwing up for hours afterwards. It was absolutely vile-tasting stuff." Another wrote, "I loved the licorice flavor! I'd forgotten about the nasty mint. Gross stuff! And, for me, the tutti-frutti was barely tolerable."

Another Mattel toy considered dangerous to children during the Handler years had a name that virtually boomed "serious ear damage"—the Sonic Blaster. It looked like a military bazooka that a child pumped with air, causing a loud explosion heard "a block away" when he or she pulled the trigger. Like Incredible Edibles, Sonic Blaster was a huge hit for Mattel when it was introduced at the annual Toy Fair. "The trade fell all over us," Ruth Handler boasted later. "They ordered and ordered, and we shipped and shipped."

But the FDA ruled the toy caused noise pollution and potential damage to children's eardrums and ordered Mattel to recall thousands of them sold in the United States. Mattel tried unsuccessfully to bargain with the federal agency because, according to Ruth, "We still didn't believe the product could injure children's ears." She subsequently unloaded the toy at a fire-sale price to an Australian manufacturer who thought the Sonic Blaster would pass his government's regulations. It didn't.

One of Mattel's early toys, its very successful Jack-in-the-Box, blinded a boy when the coil spring broke loose and struck him. In the wake of the accident, the Handlers named an executive to the post of quality control and product safety, and began torture-testing its toys.

"I have always been proud of the fact that we were the nation's leader in toy safety," she crowed.

# Chapter 18

# "Like Something Out of *The Exorcist*"

W hile lead levels in the paint of Mattel toys ignited most of the media frenzy, public fear, and congressional indignation in 2007, the company's magnetic toys were the more dangerous, such as Polly Pockets. The tiny magnets could be easily ingested by children, severely injuring them, or in the case of another company using similar magnets, causing death.

The hands and feet of the Polly Pockets dolls, which are several inches tall, are made of a bendable plastic and have tiny magnets embedded in them, as do the Polly Pockets soft rubberized fashion accessories, which have magnets glued to them. The dolls were originally distributed by a British company, Bluebird Toys, which was purchased by Mattel in 1998. Mattel redesigned the toy and introduced a collector brand called Fashion Polly!

The untold stories of some of the injured underscore the horrific toll toys such as Mattel's Polly Pockets, with their $\frac{1}{8}$-inch-diameter magnets, have taken—until they were redesigned again by Mattel in the wake of tragic incidents.

Seven-year-old Paige Kostrzewski was a huge fan of Polly Pockets, and so were all of Paige's friends in their blue-collar Indianapolis, Indiana, neighborhood. They carried the very-portable toys wherever they went and played with them in each other's homes.

Polly Pockets had a virtual cult following among the 6 to-8-year-old set, due to Mattel's heavy promotion. Paige's mother, Misty May, an hourly warehouse worker with a brood of four, usually picked up the latest Polly Pockets set for her daughter at her local Kmart. The cost was $15 to $20 a pop, a considerable wallop to her pocketbook, but worth it in order to keep her baby girl happily busy at play.

Monday, July 11, 2005, was payday for Misty May, and right after work, she went to the store and bought Polly Pocket! Quik-Clik Boutique, for Paige's collection of about a dozen Polly Pockets scenarios. This one had a "magic dressing room" to allow Polly to change quickly in to a new outfit.

Paige also was a Barbie collector—the basic doll now cost at least three times her original 1959 introductory price of $3—and the previous Christmas, the child had found four new Barbie dolls gift wrapped under the tree. Mattel was a part of her young life, and therefore Paige Kostrzewski represented millions of little girls who were a new generation of Mattel toy loyalists. Mattel was a brand name their parents trusted. But that was before Paige almost died.

Two days after Paige got her new Polly Pockets, the child began acting strangely. "She just started running around and not acting herself, and by the next day she didn't want to eat," says Misty May.

> She wasn't complaining of any pain or anything, she just wasn't feeling well. I called our doctor and was told that as long as she was keeping fluids down she was fine. I thought she had a cold or the flu coming on. But then, by Thursday evening and Friday, she wouldn't drink anything, and then late Friday and early Saturday she starting puking green stuff, like something out of *The Exorcist*. It was gross.

By Sunday morning, Paige had gotten worse, vomiting when she wasn't sleeping, and not eating or drinking. Frightened, Misty May put her very ill daughter in the car and took her to the emergency room at

Indianapolis's Wishard Memorial Hospital, a county facility. Misty May described her daughter's symptoms, but none of it made sense to the doctor on duty. "We thought maybe because she and her brother like to wrestle that maybe he kicked her too hard in the stomach," she says.

The ER doctor ordered an x-ray of Paige's stomach, and the results were shocking.

"The picture showed metal foreign objects in her body," says Misty May. "I was thinking that maybe she swallowed coins or something. I was freaking out. I asked Paige, and she said, 'No, Mom, I do not put coins in my mouth.'"

Paige was transferred from Wishard across the street to Riley Children's Hospital, considered one of the Midwest's top centers for pediatric care and research. Further emergency tests were conducted to determine the liquid she was throwing up. The findings were horrific. The child's intestines had been punctured, causing toxins from her bowels to seep through her body, which could cause other major organs to shut down and kill her.

"They told me flat out that Paige required emergency surgery or she was going to die," says Misty May. "I was actually freaking out. I couldn't think straight. I was trying to figure out what she could have swallowed to do this to her. Paige had the surgery within a couple hours of being at Riley. They moved four people out of the way to get her into the operating room for the surgery, which lasted almost three hours."

When the operation was over, the surgeon, Dr. Thomas Rouse, handed Misty May a bottle in which he had placed two tiny, but powerful, magnets that had got stuck in different parts of her daughter's intestine, causing two punctures.

> The surgeon showed it to me, and I looked at him and I said, "I know exactly where they came from. They came from her Polly Pockets—out of the clothes of her Polly Pockets doll." I brought in the toy to show him the next morning. He was surprised, especially being that I had just bought the toy on Monday and she was sick by Wednesday.

Before the life-threatening event, Misty May had no concept that cute little Polly Pockets posed potentially fatal danger to her daughter, or any other child who played with the fast-selling toy.

Paige knew not to put things in her mouth or chew on things. The toy was new. I didn't think the magnets would fall out, or that they would fall out just like *that*. As soon as Paige woke up, I asked her what had happened. She told me she was putting the doll into the little boutique and that her hands were full so she stuck the outfits between her lips. I was like, Paige, if you swallowed these you should have come and told me the minute you swallowed them, and she said, "Mom, I didn't even know that I swallowed them."

Because of the accident, the child spent two weeks in the hospital, missed six weeks of the new school term, couldn't do any physical exertion, and the visible scar caused her embarrassment. She had to watch what she ate, and required an annual checkup. Her medical bill was $31,786.69, paid by Medicaid because the family could ill afford health insurance.

Misty May tossed out all of the Mattel toys before Paige got home from the hospital, and since the incident has refused to purchase anything from Mattel, she says. She thought about what would have happened if her youngest, who was one year old at the time, had been the victim. "I thought, what if this happens to somebody else's kid, and what if they are too late in getting them to a hospital? I lost a child before and I couldn't imagine going through that again—or somebody else going through that."

It was at that point that she decided to talk to a lawyer. As it turned out, her aunt was a housekeeper for Gordon Tabor, a prominent Indianapolis attorney who specialized in product liability cases. He met with Misty May three or four days after Paige's surgery. Tabor conducted an investigation "questioning the safety of this product" and made his determination. "There was no doubt that those two magnets had come from the Polly Pockets product," he says. "Those magnets are small and powerful and when they attract they catch the bowel wall in between them. It shuts off circulation, and causes necroses of the bowel, resulting in a hole in the bowel."

Before taking any action involving Mattel, Tabor closely watched Paige's case because "there was a question after her dismissal from the hospital about what her permanent condition was going to be, and whether or not she would regain full bowel function."

Tabor says he soon learned that Polly Pockets wasn't the only product that used these or similar magnets.

We spent time going to Wal-Mart and Kmart looking at products off the shelf, buying products, bringing them back to our office, playing around with them, and doing our own in-house investigation. I have a granddaughter in Florida who was the same age as my client and I called my daughter and asked if she had ever heard of Polly Pockets, and she said, "Yes, Madeleine has two of them. All of her friends have these dolls. They are a very, very hot item." I told my daughter to take those products away from her. At that point, I felt we've got a product here that is exposing a lot of kids, so we've got to take some action.

He also contacted the Consumer Product Safety Commission to determine whether there had been any other similar cases of children swallowing magnets, from Polly Pockets or otherwise. His contact information and the issue he was asking about went into the commission's database.

There was one big problem facing Tabor in the Polly Pockets matter. Because of questionable tort reform in 1995, the Indiana product liability law didn't favor the consumer as it once did, a change that came about as a result of intense lobbying by big corporations and trade associations. "They dumped a ton of money into Indiana, and it sailed through," he explains. "We had great consumer law until this onslaught from all this money coming from out of state. The American Manufacturing Association threw a ton of money, and that brings in the toy manufacturers, the drug manufacturers, the whole shooting match."

Rather than pursuing what would have been a complicated legal procedure in Indiana because of the tort reform, Tabor retained a lawyer friend in California, who, by coincidence, had had dealings with an outside law firm that had represented Mattel in the past. He told him, "I think I've got a bear by the tail." Rather than file a lawsuit against Mattel, Tabor decided to have his co-counsel make contact with Mattel's lawyer and see where it went.

■ ■ ■

It was now the summer of 2006, almost a year since Paige Kostrzewski had swallowed the magnets that could have killed her, when an attorney for Mattel arrived in Indianapolis to interview the child, her mother, and the surgeon in Tabor's offices—where also on display was the Polly Pockets in question, with the two destructive magnets.

While it was unusual for Tabor, who'd been in practice for almost four decades, to allow a probable defendant's attorney to have an informal interview with a client, he felt, "I had nothing to lose because there wasn't any question that the magnets caused the injury. I had no fear. Mattel wouldn't be sending a high-powered lawyer halfway across the country before a lawsuit is even filed unless they had a concern over this product."

Tabor "absolutely" believed that Mattel in 2006 was hoping to keep the whole matter quiet, reach an amicable settlement without a lawsuit, and avoid the attendant national publicity that could hurt Polly Pockets sales and place a dark cloud over the company.

"Mattel had to figure that at some point the Feds were going to get involved, and so was the media," Tabor says.

> As a human being, you have to keep in the back of your mind that the product is potentially harmful to many, many others. As a lawyer, you have to take care of your client first, and then you have to put on your white hat. We weren't going to settle the case without a representation by Mattel that they were going to take action of a curative nature with the toy.

Mattel negotiated for several more months before a confidential settlement was quietly reached.

Misty May says it wasn't until May 2007—a couple of months before the summer of toy terror began—that she received the settlement check. While she was under orders not to disclose the amount, she says that Paige will "get to go to college and buy a house and a car." But she also had to pay her medical bills out of the settlement, reimbursing Medicaid, plus paying reduced attorney fees.

What are her feelings about Mattel?

"Polly Pockets should have been recalled when my daughter had her surgery and almost lost her life," she maintains. "I don't care for Mattel because of the stuff my daughter had to go through, and Mattel made us feel like they didn't give a crap."

Once the case was settled, Tabor says he learned that the magnet problem was the result of a Mattel design flaw rather than a Chinese manufacturing quality control issue. "Mattel drew up all the specifications," he notes.

As did Misty May, he came away with a bad taste concerning the biggest toy company in the world. "I'm very disappointed in Mattel," he declares.

> In early 2006, when Mattel had information of my case, I know damn good and well that they had their research and development people looking at these magnets. But did they comply with the federal requirements of reporting to the Consumer Product Safety Commission so CPSC could get out an immediate warning to the public? I don't believe so. I never saw it. I have to fault Mattel for that.

> After notice of my case, the magnet problem was to be taken care of. There was to be a voluntary recall. These products were supposed to be taken off the market. Mattel knows they had the same design, the same magnet, in other toys in addition to Polly Pockets, and they sort of got the information out piecemeal, a PR campaign—don't slam the public with a whole bunch of information, just give them a little here, a little there.

> Do I think Mattel was a good corporate citizen? Hell, no, particularly in light of who the consumers were—young children. There is an additional moral responsibility to the manufacturer of a product that is being utilized by children. They are more susceptible to incurring the wrath from a dangerous product than an adult would be. There was a special moral responsibility, in addition to whatever federal regulations apply to them, for Mattel to respond promptly. I don't think they did.

Shortly after the secret settlement with Paige Kostrzewski was finalized, just before Thanksgiving 2006, Mattel and the CPSC recalled 4.4 million Polly Pockets products after at least three children, including Paige, suffered serious injuries from swallowing the magnets. By then, the agency charged with keeping Americans safe from dangerous products knew of some 170 cases of the small magnets coming out of the recalled toys. But the agency had no idea how many others—hundreds? thousands?—might have swallowed the magnets, suffered symptoms, but luckily escaped injury. The CPSC, which would come under intense congressional and media scrutiny in 2007, noted that the Polly Pockets recall did not include sets then currently on store shelves because of a redesign by Mattel.

At the time, Ed Mierzwinski, consumer program director for the U.S. Public Interest Research Group, a nonprofit consumer advocacy group in Washington, said Mattel needed better safeguards. "They should have never allowed it to happen in the first place. They have a responsibility to avoid recalls."

Little did he and the rest of the world know that the worst was still to come.

# Chapter 19

# Keep It Out of the News!

Lavina and Chris Bowman of Rock Spring, Wyoming, bought Polly Pockets for their three-year-old daughter, Kelli, because the little dolls and accessories kept her happy; therefore, the Bowmans, like millions of other parents, kept Wal-Mart and Mattel happy, because as soon as a new Polly Pockets showed up on the shelves, the Bowmans would buy it for her.

"She saw them in the store aisle and right away she wanted them," Lavina Bowman says. "So I thought, well, buy them, it'll shut her up," says the jovial young mother, who worked with battered women. "She used to play with them all day long, play with them in the bathtub, even."

Kelli's six-year-old brother, Devlin, a first grader, wanted no part of the girls' toy. He was a Hot Wheels man, one of the millions of boys who played with the fast little cars from Mattel. Like Paige's family in

Indiana, the Bowmans of Wyoming were devoted to toys by Mattel—a company they trusted.

It was in December 2005, however, when their blind brand loyalty suddenly changed.

The Christmas tree was put up in the living room right after Thanksgiving, and the Bowmans had already done their holiday shopping, which included a few more Polly Pockets dolls for Kelli.

Shortly before midnight on the bitterly cold night of December 7, 2005, a night that will live in infamy for the family, Devlin Bowman awoke screaming in pain. "I thought it was going to be a really tough night," says his mother, who was eight months pregnant at the time, "because it was flu season, and I thought we were going to be dealing with the flu."

Devlin told his mom he had a really bad tummy ache and that he needed to throw up. She didn't think anything was unusual when he vomited.

> Kids get sick, they throw up. But I couldn't take his temperature because he was writhing around on the floor, grabbing his lower stomach in pain. When he started doing that, I was pretty sure it wasn't the flu, and just to make sure, I got him a drink that should have calmed his tummy down a bit and it didn't.

When the drink came up, too, the frightened Lavina Bowman turned on the computer and went to WEBMD.com to "plug in his symptoms and get some advice." It was too late to call the family doctor. When she rated the pain her son was experiencing, the computer's advice was to take him to the hospital.

Because it was 30 degrees below zero outside, Bowman bundled up to face the frigid Wyoming night and warm up the family's 1999 Chevy Suburban. "Thank the Lord," she recalled thinking to herself, "the truck turned on right away. I had to heat it up for a half hour."

Meanwhile, in the house, Devlin's pain intensified.

> He just kept on screaming, there was so, so much pain. I knew whatever was happening was over my head. I bundled him up and put him in the backseat. He was still writhing and gagging, and he had to hang his head out the window but there was nothing left to throw up. He stayed like that for the seven-mile trip to the emergency room.

At Memorial Hospital of Sweetwater County, the emergency room personnel gave Devlin priority over others waiting for treatment because the child was in agony. Placed in a bed, he was given a morphine drip. "The emergency room doctor was moving pretty fast, so I knew this was serious." An x-ray was inconclusive, so he was given a CTScan around 2 A.M. and the picture "showed something metallic in his intestines." The doctor suggested that maybe Devlin had swallowed a BB, but Lavina Bowman rejected that diagnosis because the Bowmans didn't own a BB gun.

Meanwhile, the morphine wasn't working to reduce the pain. "They could only give him so much, so he had to be in severe pain for 10 or 15 minutes before they could give him more, and that really sucked."

Around three o'clock in the morning, with no idea what was going on with the Bowman boy, and because there were no pediatric surgeons in Rock Springs, and no high-end hospitals in the state, the emergency room physician called for Life Flight, Wyoming's only emergency air transport service, to fly the severely ill child by helicopter to Primary Children's Hospital, in Salt Lake City.

Because of the severe cold, the helicopter was grounded. Around five o'clock, a call was placed for an ambulance, which had to be warmed up. "I had to wait while Devlin was on the morphine drip screaming with pain every once in a while."

It was around seven in the morning when the ambulance began the 185-mile, three-hour trip to Salt Lake City, with Chris Bowman, who worked on an oil-drilling rig, and daughter Kelli, following in the Suburban. "Devlin went from passing out from the morphine to waking up screaming." In the ambulance, he was given the highest dose possible of morphine to keep him from writhing around for fear his intestines might rupture and he'd bleed to death internally. "He was out cold and that was really scary. I spent the whole ride staring at his face."

In the ambulance with her was an EMT who could see how worried she was. He told her, "If your boy starts losing his stats, I have something that reverses the morphine."

The ambulance arrived at the hospital about 10 o'clock in the morning on December 8. The doctors, alerted that he was on the way, needed to let the boy's morphine wear off so they could better diagnose his system, which was a nightmare because Devlin's pain was even more severe. "By then I had to get a hold of myself and sort of put on my mean mommy face and just make him calm down because you can't lose it. I had to tell him he'll be fine, that the doctors were going to fix it."

More time ticked by. The emergency room staff reexamined him, and the radiology staff took more x-rays and another CTScan. "I had the pictures with me from the first hospital. I told them to look at those, but they were like, no, we want new ones, and that just took all kinds of time. They needed to see for themselves what they needed to do for treatment."

By late afternoon on December 9, a huge team of surgeons had been assembled at the teaching hospital to deal with the frightening case. Suddenly, the boy's intestines began to swell and he had to be rushed into emergency exploratory surgery. Because he was barely dosed with morphine at that point, it took three nurses to put a breathing tube down his throat. "He was fighting them tooth and nail."

During the two-hour operation, the surgeons had to cut the boy wide-open, not knowing what they were faced with. Inside, they found two Mattel Polly Pockets magnets. Unlike little Paige Kostrzewski, Devlin Bowman's intestines fortunately had not been perforated, but the magnets had made him deathly ill.

Exhausted, Lavina Bowman was seated in the waiting room outside of the operating room when the surgeon rushed in. "Devlin's fine," he told her

> . . . but he's like, you gotta see what we found. He had the magnets in a little jar with a lid on it and he took the lid off and said, "Hey, watch this," and he pulled the two magnets apart and they went skipping back together. He's like, this is amazing how powerful these little magnets are, and he was going off on that. He asked me if I knew what they were, and I knew they were from the Polly Pockets. Those were the only toys with magnets that we had. They're just itty bitty, smaller than a pencil eraser.
>
> The surgeon had never seen them before and his reaction was he wanted to get my permission to write about them in a medical journal so that other doctors could read it and recognize the symptoms faster because swallowing them is an emergency

situation that can perforate the intestines and a child can bleed to death internally—not to mention the excruciating pain.

After surgery, Devlin was placed in a private room, kept on drugs intravenously to keep him from being nauseated, given a morphine drip and a catheter, and was not permitted anything to eat for several days, even intravenously. "It was no fun," says his mother. Devlin's parents stayed with him through the four-day hospital ordeal after the surgery.

Back at home, the Bowmans tossed all of the Polly Pockets play sets in the trash with the help of Kelli, who realized how the plastic toys with magnets almost killed her brother.

Lavina Bowman theorized that the magnets had come loose from the water in the tub, where Kelli played with her Polly Pockets. If there were any more loose ones in the house, she couldn't find them because they were so small.

■ ■ ■

While Lavina Bowman was in the hospital after giving birth to her baby in early January 2006, she heard that there were lawyers "who can sue to change things." The first one she called, from a big Salt Lake City firm, said he would not take on Mattel. Three others told her the same thing:

> "Your boy didn't die, plus this is Mattel you're talking about. No way." They said they only take cases they know they can win, and they didn't think they could win against the very litigious giant of the toy industry. Mattel is so big that they're intimidating. I was thinking, "So people have to die before we can fix things."

Then she heard about an attorney in the state of Washington who had just won a big magnetic-toy case, similar to the one involving Devlin. "So I gave it one more chance and sent him a really terse e-mail," says Lavina Bowman. "I wrote, 'My son got wounded by magnets, too. It was from Polly Pockets from Mattel, and if you want to take the case here's my e-mail address.'"

Sim Osborn, headquartered in Seattle, responded within a day.

In the realm of product liability, in particular involving dangerous magnets in toys, Osborn was considered the go-to guy. When he went to the Toy Fair in New York in 2008 to nose around, the chief executive of one of the major companies called him the "anti-Christ."

Osborn earned a national reputation in October 2006 by winning a $13.5 million settlement paid out to 13 families from a toy company called Mega Brands. In all, he represented 15 families in nine states whose children had been injured from swallowing tiny magnets that had fallen out of sets of the company's popular Magnetix brand, a building set of plastic pieces with magnets encased inside.

Tragically, one of the victims, 22-month-old Kenny Sweet Jr., of Redmond, Washington, died on Thanksgiving Day 2005—within the same timeframe that the Mattel magnets injured Paige Kostrzewski and Devlin Bowman. In the Sweet case, an autopsy showed that the magnets had pinched closed the toddler's small intestine, tearing a hole in the intestine wall, and leaking toxic bacteria into his bloodstream.

"It's been the hardest year of my life," said Kenneth Sweet Sr., the boy's father, at the time of the settlement. "The fact is we would much rather have our son. There's nothing that could ever replace him. I still walk by his picture everyday and even though I think it's weird, I kiss his picture and tell him I love him." His wife, Penny, said that having taken on a big toy company and won had given her "a sense of relief. I'm at peace with everything."

In agreeing to the settlement, Mega Brands did not admit any wrongdoing, but issued a statement saying, "We deeply regret these events and have taken proactive measures to ensure the safety of our products."

Mega Brands was forced into another recall in March 2008, because of magnets that could detach from the flexible parts of the company's toy animals, vehicles, and building sets. The recall occurred after 19 reports of magnets coming loose, including a case of a 3-year-old boy who required medical treatment to remove a magnet from his nasal cavity, and a case involving an 18-month-old boy who was found with a magnet in his mouth, which was not swallowed.

Following the first Polly Pockets recall by Mattel after the Paige Kostrzewski case was settled, Sim Osborn, representing the Bowmans, filed a personal injury lawsuit against Mattel on November 21, 2006, seeking damages for medical bills and for the emotional harm caused the family from Devlin's ordeal.

Within a few weeks, an attorney with the law firm of Lynberg & Watkins, in Los Angeles, one of a number of outside firms that represent Mattel, appeared at Osborn's office. According to Osborn, "He was straight upfront. He said, 'Look, Mattel wants to settle this case. Let me go look at the child and let's talk.'"

As in the Kostrzewski case, Mattel wanted to avoid the public glare of a trial, Osborn believes. Moreover, he was a tough opponent.

"Frankly, I had a very good track record against Mega Brands, had done very well, and made a lot of headlines, so Mattel wanted to settle and avoid all of that," he says. "Look what happened to Mega Brands stock after we filed the lawsuit. It went from around $27.00 to $5.00. Right after the Sweet case was filed they had lost $257 million in market cap, and it continued to go down as I kept filing cases."

Osborn recalls the lawyer saying,

> "Mattel doesn't want to drag this out. Their toy hurt someone. They want to settle. They want to get this behind them." And it was good advice on Mattel's part, and on their lawyer's part, because we kept Magnetix in the press for so long and that raised awareness to the dangers of magnets. I think Mattel may have learned from what happened in those other [Mega Brands] cases. They may have been scared. They may have just felt it was better to handle these kind of cases expeditiously because the longer it drags out, the more time it's in the public eye, and the more press there is. So it went very quickly.

Mattel's agreement to settle with the Bowman family was announced on March 20, 2007, according to news accounts. This was some three months after Osborn filed suit, and before the big recalls started. The actual monetary settlement was kept confidential. Mattel did not admit liability. Osborn chuckles about how quickly the case was resolved. "They were scared shitless. They had to [settle quickly] because of what happened in the Magnetix case."

■ ■ ■

Among the scandalously enormous number of recalls of Mattel products during the toy terror summer of 2007 were more Polly Pockets and related accessories on August 14—Mattel's second recall in two weeks—involving more than 9 million "made in China" toys. Besides the 7.3 million Polly Pockets play sets recalled, other toys with magnets included 683,000 Barbie and Tanner play sets, 345,000 Batman Magnetic Action Figure sets, and one million Doggie Day Care magnetic toys.

Osborn closely followed the recalls, and later observes,

> Mattel kind of hid the second Polly Pockets recall in with the lead paint, and the media jumped on the lead paint. Looking at it in the abstract, it was pretty good PR on Mattel's part. Have you ever heard of a kid dying from lead poisoning from playing with a toy? Have you ever heard of a kid horribly injured from some lead paint? No. But you get two magnets in your belly and you can die.

In January 2008, Mattel's beleaguered Bob Eckert, in an interview with *Fortune*, was asked why the lead paint and magnet issues were put together in the same public recall announcement—even though the bigger recall was for the magnets. In the article, he did not seem to directly answer the question. Moreover, he didn't acknowledge Mattel's quick settlements with the children in Indiana and Wyoming. Instead, he mentioned that a child had "ingested a magnet from one of our competitor's toys," and put a positive spin on the tiny magnets, declaring that they "allow toys to become quite magical for children. Unfortunately those magnets tried to find each other in the child's intestines, and that changed how the entire toy industry viewed these magnets." He then went on to boast that Mattel had developed a system

> . . . that permanently locks the magnet in place. We thought it was so much better than any other system that we said, we should tell parents if they have toys we made over the last five years that don't have the benefit of today's technology, we want them back. We started developing the new technology in January 2007 [after the Indiana and Wyoming cases were settled]

and it was the industry standard in May. The events dictated that August was the time to make the announcement.

(A number of attempts by the author to secure an interview with Eckert for this book were unsuccessful, either directly through his office, in telephone calls with his assistant, through e-mail correspondence with his office, or subsequently with a public relations representative for Mattel.)

In a series of interviews with the author in March 2008, Osborn expressed distrust that safeguards were in place as expressed by Eckert because

> . . . there are still thousands of toys out there with millions of magnets from old sets. Somebody's going to bring their toddler over to the boss's house, and the boss's wife is going to bring down the can of Polly Pockets toys her daughter used to play with and there's going to be some loose magnets in there, and then another kid's going to play with them and the magnets are going to come out.

Hopefully, it will never happen again, and hopefully, there's enough public awareness about it. But we have had cases despite people knowing, and despite the huge publicity generated by all these lawsuits and recalls.

■ ■ ■

Under the rules of the Consumer Product Safety Commission, Mattel and other manufacturers are supposed to report within 24 hours any claims of products that might have hazardous defects.

But, as stated in Chapter 15, Mattel hasn't always followed that rule to the letter. Instead, the company takes its own good time, sometimes months, to make the required disclosure. The big recall in August 2007 of Polly Pockets and other Mattel toys with dangerous magnets fell into that category—one of at least "three major cases" since the late 1990s of late reporting, as the *Wall Street Journal* reported in a front-page story in September 2007 that was titled "Safety Agency, Mattel Clash Over Disclosures."

According to the newspaper, Mattel "collected scores of complaints for months before disclosing them" to the CPSC. "At times, Mattel officials have considered possible remedies before making an initial report to the agency disclosing safety concerns."

The *Journal* story paraphrased Eckert as saying in an interview that "the company discloses problems on its own timetable because it believes both the law and the commission's enforcement practices are unreasonable. Mattel said it should be able to evaluate hazards internally before alerting any outsiders, regardless of what the law says."

Eckert maintained that the government and industry gadflies often take incident reports and blow them out of proportion, and he asserted, according to the *Journal*, that even if the reports numbered in the hundreds there still wasn't enough evidence to label a toy unsafe.

Eckert said the CPSC's 24-hour rule of reporting an incident that could possibly expose a hazard was a "standard [that] might apply to almost anything. It's very easy for anyone to apply the word 'could' backward."

Eckert emphasized that Mattel was not withholding information from the CPSC, and that the issue in question was whether the company reported a problem "in a timely manner. We are allowed to investigate" before turning over consumer complaints.

Mattel was fined by the CPSC at least twice since 2001 for "knowingly" hiding product problems that, according to the agency, "created an unreasonable risk of serious injury or death." Such fines are normally less than $2 million per incident. The agency stated that the cases had been settled—without Mattel's acknowledging any wrongdoing or admitting there was a defect in the toys that were recalled. While the CPSC didn't identify the toys in question, the scenario of the outcome was strikingly similar to the Bowman and Kostrzewski cases, which were quickly settled by Mattel.

Eckert's comments to the *Journal* sparked outrage. Before a U.S. Senate committee, one of a number in both Houses that put Mattel and its chief executive on the hot seat in Washington during the recall summer of 2007, Sally Greenberg, the senior product safety counsel for the powerful Consumers Union, termed his assertions "disturbing" and "telling," coming from the head of the world's leading toy company.

Maureen Keene, writing on the website Made (Deadly) In China, said,

Oh, Mattel. I held such high hopes for you. You seemed to be different from other toymakers. Maybe I bought into the hype of Mattel setting the gold standard for doing business in China. Maybe it simply stems from my childhood love of all things Barbie. Either way, CEO Robert Eckert's attitude toward product safety tears it. . . . My only remaining hope where Mattel is concerned is that consumers will make a statement against the company's irresponsible business practices this holiday season and boycott Mattel and its subsidiary Fisher-Price. It's on consumers now—if we buy as usual, companies like Mattel will continue conducting (dangerous) business as usual.

■ ■ ■

Considering all of the heat and criticism Bob Eckert took, 2007 turned out to be a pretty good year for him. Not only did he stay in power during the scandal-riddled year of recalls with the support of Mattel's board of directors, but he received an enormous raise to boot—a whopping 68 percent more than 2006. His total compensation package was valued at more than $12.2 million compared with $7,278,178 the previous year.

In a filing with the Securities and Exchange Commission, Mattel stated that Eckert received a salary of $1.25 million, and nonequity incentive plan compensation of $7.1 million, of which $5.7 million was earned at the end of what was termed a three-year "performance period" on December 31, 2007. He also received stock and option awards with an estimated value of $3.4 million. Other compensation included $213,350 for the personal use of Mattel aircraft and more than $116,000 in company contributions to a deferred compensation plan.

Mattel didn't fare as well as the boss did in the first two quarters of 2008. Analysts were shocked and investors were spooked when Mattel reported a net loss of $46.6 million in the first quarter—the company's first quarterly loss in three years—compared to net income of $12 million a year earlier, much of it blamed on the recalls. Sales of the flagship Barbie doll brand were flat. Eckert warned of price increases. The headline in *Playthings*, the industry trade magazine, blared, MATTEL FUMBLES. . . . To make matters worse, Mattel's main competitor, Hasbro, the world's second biggest toymaker, beat expectations. In Mattel's second quarter, Barbie sales continued to fall as the 50th anniversary of the brand drew closer, and the company experienced a 48 percent decrease in profit.

The third quarter of 2008 wasn't good, either. And with the U.S. and world economy in a deep, horrific recession, Wall Street analysts were painting a bleak picture for 2008 Christmas toy sales. But CEO Eckert put up a brave face, telling analysts in a third quarter conference call, "There will be a Christmas and Mattel toys will be under the tree." Still, CNNMoney.com ran a headline declaring, TOY MAKERS BRACE FOR TOUGH HOLIDAY SEASON . . . BATTLE FOR PARENTS' DOLLARS LIKELY TO BE TOUGH.

Just a few weeks later, the optimistic Eckert morphed into the Scrooge of Christmas Past when Mattel announced in early November that 1,000 jobs worldwide—about 3 percent of the workforce internationally—were being cut in response to the economic turndown of 2008. Some 8 percent of the professional and management staff, many at the El Segundo world headquarters, also faced a bleak, jobless holiday as Mattel was preparing to celebrate Barbie's big 5–0.

(In mid-December, the company agreed to a $12 million settlement with 39 states to settle the 2007 lead-tainted toys investigation, and also agreed to lower the acceptable level of lead in toys, and to keep better records of lead screenings. A company statement said its move "demonstrated its commitment to children's safety.")

In China, Mattel also faced serious, new economic problems. A major factory that made its toys, Smart Union Group (Holdings) Ltd., in Guangdong, had closed its doors in October 2008 because of the financial crisis in the United States. The company's 8,700 employees were left jobless. With the Chinese economy also in turmoil, some 3,600 toy factories were shuttered. As the Associated Press reported: "Economic upheaval in the U.S. is already changing and shrinking China's vast manufacturing hub in . . . Guangdong, long regarded as the world's factory floor. However, factory closures will not just be a China problem—shoppers will feel the effect in malls and stores across the U.S. and Europe."

If 2007 was the toy terror summer, Mattel's summer of 2008 was a knockdown, drag-out court battle between Barbie and Bratz.

# Chapter 20

# Don't Diss Barbie, and the Toy Trial of the Century: *Bratz vs. Barbie*

When it comes to Barbie, Mattel has always been extremely litigious. While the company has every right to defend its trademark and legitimately protect its sacred product, it often hurls lawsuits around that have a chilling effect on artists, writers, small businesses, and others if it perceives the slightest negativity or criticism—directly or indirectly—toward the doll.

At times, even just the use of the name *Barbie*—unrelated in any way to the iconic plaything—can set off Mattel's enmity, resulting in legal action and causing distress and expense for the unsuspecting and the innocent.

Barbie Anderson-Walley perfectly fit the profile.

A clothing designer in Calgary, Alberta, Canada, she special-ized in fetish wear—latex outfits and handmade corsets with a gothic influence—and sold undergarments under the label "Lingerie By Barbie." She named her store after herself. Her place of business was called Barbie's Shop, and Anderson-Walley had a website advertising her apparel, called Barbiesshop.com. None of her commerce had any-thing whatsoever to do with the Barbie doll, or with any other toy.

She'd been quietly and peacefully doing a modest business when in January 2004 her world was turned upside down and her ability to make a living put in jeopardy when she received a cease-and-desist order from Mattel demanding she stop using the Barbie name in her business. She couldn't believe what was happening, laughed it off, and called her parents and asked them to deal with Mattel since it was they who started calling her Barbie as a nickname when she was a child rather than her given name of Barbara.

Mattel asserted that it owned a website called Barbieshop.com. But Anderson-Walley's site was called *Barbiesshop.com*. On the advice of her local attorney, she had bought the domain because it was available. The problem for Mattel was the similar website names, though the spelling was different—Anderson-Walley's had two *s*'s.

Nevertheless, in an effort to escape from what she considered Mattel hell, Anderson-Walley offered to sell her Web address to the toy monster for $30,000 to cover its costs and the investment she'd have to make in devising a new one. Playing its usual hardball, Mattel declined the offer.

With Mattel now after her, friends recommended that she had bet-ter retain a lawyer—that Mattel wasn't kidding around. And Mattel wasn't. In July 2004, the company sued her to enforce "its rights in its famous trademark Barbie against defendant's acts of cybersquatting, infringement and dilution with respect in that mark."

The 14-page suit—*Mattel, Inc. vs. Barbara Anderson a/k/a Barbie Walley*—was filed in the U.S. District Court for the Southern District of New York, more than 2,000 miles from Calgary, making it even more difficult for Anderson-Walley to defend herself since her local attorney at the time was not licensed to practice in the Empire State.

As the real-life Barbie says in May 2008,

Mattel likes to think that they own everything that has the name Barbie. But they don't, so they don't like that reality. After I was served with the court papers, I tried to call Mattel a couple of times. Never, ever once in the whole two years this case went on did I get a real voice. I always got put on hold, or got an answering machine, or was told "Someone will get back to you." All I wanted to say was, "What are you thinking? You cannot be serious—as if my tiny business up here is making some kind of dent in your big doll world."

However, Mattel declared in a court memorandum, "This is a simple case of Internet piracy."

Anderson-Walley eventually found a New York attorney, Linda Joseph, who by coincidence had done intellectual property legal work for Fisher-Price before Mattel acquired the company. In her research, Joseph discovered that Mattel's attorneys in the case, the New York firm of Perkins & Dunnegan, had actually been using a private detective, named in court papers as Michael Falsone, to comb the Internet looking for any entity using the Barbie name in business. "He had been involved in a number of cases by Mattel going after people," says Joseph. The law firm is one of a number that Mattel uses.

Based in New York City, the shamus placed an order for an item from Anderson-Walley's shop, and had it shipped to Manhattan, where the lawsuit was filed. As Linda Joseph notes, "Mattel is located in El Segundo, California, and they sued her in New York City. It couldn't have been more inconvenient. It was basically an effort to make it difficult for her to defend."

In the end, after Anderson-Walley had racked up thousands of dollars in legal fees and a couple of years of stress and anxiety, U.S. District Judge Richard Conway Casey, prior to discovery, threw out Mattel's case on a motion to dismiss filed by Joseph asserting lack of personal jurisdiction. The jurist noted that Mattel took legal action "on a single sale" from Anderson-Walley's website that was ordered by the PI, Falsone, and shipped to New York City. Casey also pointed out in his order to dismiss that "Mattel has had some success with its strategy of using its private investigator to create circumstances giving rise to personal jurisdiction over alleged cybersquatters in the past." He noted that the court action was "nothing more than an attempt by" Mattel "to manufacture a contact" with the court.

Long after the case concluded, Joseph observes, "Mattel just didn't want her to use the name Barbie even though that is her real name. There wasn't any way that anybody was going to associate the adult-type things she was selling with Barbie dolls."

In Calgary, at her parents' home, on the eve of Barbie's 50th anniversary, there was a trunk filled with one of Barbie Anderson-Walley's favorite dolls when she was a little girl: Barbie. But after her David-and-Goliath run-in with the world's largest toy company over the Barbie name, she's decided never to do business with Mattel. "I have a grandson who loves Hot Wheels, but now I won't buy them for him because they're made by Mattel."

The cases involving the Barbie's Shop owner and others like her were small potatoes, though, compared to the court battle in 2008 that would have hundreds of millions of dollars on the line, and pit Barbie against her most serious competition ever.

■ ■ ■

Before he fathered the Bratz dolls, Isaac Larian, the founder of MGA Entertainment, had already made a fortune virtually overnight by acquiring American distribution rights to Nintendo's Game & Watch series in the late 1980s. MGA, which stood for Micro Games of America, sold $22 million worth of the gizmos that seemed to have kids from Tuscaloosa to Tokyo hypnotized.

When that craze died, Larian needed a new toy on which to cash in.

Enter 31-year-old Carter Bryant, a baby-faced, creative fashion, hair, and makeup designer for the Barbie line who worked for Mattel during the Barad era from 1995 through 1998, and then again from 1999 through 2000, the latter period when Bob Eckert had come to power.

Bryant had been hired at Mattel by then–design head Margo Moschel, who says, "I gave him the assignment to create sketches and drawings for a brand-new Barbie and I handed him something from *Women's Wear Daily* and said, 'This is the look I want.'"

That look, or close to it, may have been the inspiration for what eventually became Barbie's nemesis, Bratz, though the slightly built, blondish-haired, mild-mannered Bryant would offer other scenarios for the Bratz creation when he became the central figure in the *Barbie vs. Bratz* case.

Bryant, who had aspirations of becoming a songwriter before he got into the doll world, had signed two separate employment agreements with Mattel, as have all Mattel designers and inventors since the early Handler years, giving the toymaker full and complete rights to everything he conceived. Those agreements would become important legal issues down the road when MGA and Mattel went head-to-head in court.

Like all creative types in the highly competitive and aggressive corporate culture of Mattel, Bryant was always looking for ways to create a better-selling look for Barbie, but, even more, he was determined to come up with the *next* Barbie—seemingly an impossibility. Many others had tried and failed over the years. But Carter Bryant wanted to be a star. He wanted fame and riches.

In October 2000, he officially went to work for Isaac Larian at MGA, as so many other Mattel employees had done because they felt their creative freedom at the world's largest toy company had been inhibited.

Somewhere along the line, the all-American Barbie designer showed the Iranian toy entrepreneur his sketches that became the Bratz line. But precisely *when* he made his presentation, directly or indirectly, or before or after he joined MGA, would be among the key questions and important evidence that would later be argued in the toy trial of the century: *Mattel vs. MGA Entertainment.*

■ ■ ■

As with Ruth Handler, who had trouble early on convincing her male colleagues that the world needed a more adult-looking doll with breasts, similar to the cutouts her daughter played with, Carter Bryant did not exactly bowl Isaac Larian over with his concept of doll beauty. These dolls looked nothing like Barbie, which Larian felt was the image required to win first place and generate billions of dollars in the marketplace. These were Britney Spears–looking trollops. Why would girls care? But that's exactly why they did, as it would turn out. They idolized the future tabloid train wreck and others of her ilk.

"To be honest, to me it looked weird—it looked ugly," Larian later recalled thinking after seeing the Bratz drawings.

Luckily, the best and the brightest, at least regarding whether a toy was hot or not, was visiting his office that day—his 11-year-old daughter, Jasmin. Larian, who did lots of market research with kids, trusted her judgment and asked her what she thought of those weird-looking harlots sketched on paper.

"I saw this sparkle in her eye that you see in kids' eyes," he noted some years later. "They talk with their body language more than their voice. And she says, 'Yeah, it's cute.' I said, 'Okay, we'll do it.'" He said he thought, "If Jasmin thinks so, so will other kids."

And sure enough, they did.

From the first day Bratz hit the store shelves in the United States and overseas, sales of the Pack immediately skyrocketed—girls loved them—soaring to the 200 million mark by 2007, with global sales estimated at over $2 billion.

■ ■ ■

Between 2004 and the big trial in 2008, lawsuits were fired back and forth between MGA and Mattel like political campaign barrages between Sarah Palin and Barack Obama in the presidential race of 2008. The competition between the two toy giants—and MGA, by the middle of the first decade of the new millennium, could now fairly be called a giant—had become ugly and fierce.

The first such lawsuit, filed by Mattel against Carter Bryant and 10 other unnamed defendants on April 27, 2004, charged breach of contract, breach of fiduciary duty, breach of duty of loyalty, and unjust enrichment and conversion. In layman's language, Mattel accused Bryant of taking his designs to MGA while still in Mattel's employ and thus violating his contract. Bryant didn't back down, and filed a countersuit. His claim was that Mattel's confidentiality agreement was illegal and covered too much territory. Under it, he asserted, he couldn't even tell his own mother the names of his office colleagues.

Mattel then fired the big guns and amended its lawsuit to include MGA and Isaac Larian, alleging in 58 pages of tough legal talk that the House of Bratz

> . . . intentionally stole not just specific Mattel property, such as Bratz designs, prototypes and related materials, but also a vast array of trade secrets and other confidential information that comprise Mattel's intellectual infrastructure.

The *New Yorker*, in a December 2006 piece called "Little Hotties," about the Doll War, quoted Larian as saying,

> This lawsuit just proves that Mattel is desperate. They are living in a fantasyland. They wish they owned Bratz. . . . We will continue to beat them in the marketplace in the old-fashioned American way, through better product innovation, better sales, and better marketing.

Chuck Scothon, general manager and senior vice president of Mattel's girls' toys division, responded by telling the *New Yorker's* Margaret Talbot, "Barbie will be around for another 47 years. The same can't be said for the competition." He never uttered the initials *MGA*.

The second volley came from MGA against Mattel's My Scene. Larian claimed My Scene was a ripoff of Bratz—from the multiethnic looks to the clothing and even down to the boxes in which the girls appeared on toy store shelves.

The suit also accused Mattel of engaging in unfair competition and intellectual property infringement. Larian's lawyers alleged that Mattel was attempting to "muscle MGA out of the business" and accused Mattel of "serial copycatting." They asserted that Mattel's iconic doll "does not 'play nice' with others (particularly her competitors), and needs to be taught to 'share' (at least in the fashion doll marketplace)."

Even more, MGA claimed that Mattel had actually bought up the supply of hair that both Bratz and Barbie have on their little heads. Mattel denied all of the allegations.

Naturally, Larian didn't think much of Mattel, which he believed was "too busy with corporate politics and suing people," he told the London *Times* magazine. Referring to Bob Eckert, he declared,

"Mattel's boss comes from the cheese industry. They don't see that selling cheese and toys are very different. It's kind of sad that instead of innovating, the world's top toy company is imitating. . . . [M]aybe it's time for Barbie to retire."

■ ■ ■

A funny thing happened on the way to the trial in the summer of 2008.

With potentially billions of dollars hanging in the balance, the opposing lawyers got into a pre-court tussle—not over *Barbie vs. Bratz*—but rather over hotel rooms.

Mattel's prime outside attorney, John Quinn, a pit bull in the courtroom who over the years had been described variously as "tenacious" and "swashbuckling" and had once boasted, "I suspect we're hated," was all set on having his legal team from the firm of Quinn Emanuel Urquhart Oliver & Hedges luxuriously ensconced in lovely rooms at the historic landmark Mission Inn, in Riverside, California, where the trial was to be held.

But when he tried to book the rooms he was shocked to learn that Larian's top litigator, Tom Nolan, of the prestigious global Skadden, Arps, Slate, Meagher & Flom law firm—a Doberman pinscher in the courtroom—and his team had already claimed the rooms, and that MGA even had the temerity to have the hotel contractually agree to ban the Quinn team from staying in the Mission Inn facility.

Security and sabotage were the reason given: MGA's lawyers were concerned that Mattel's lawyers might by chance get their hands on case files and faxes during the trial.

Quinn, whose more than 100 partners each made $3 million annually on average, according to *The American Lawyer*, and were allowed to dress in jeans, T-shirts, and flip-flops, went to the jurist who would be presiding over the actual trial, U.S. District Judge Stephen Larson, to rule that the contract with the hotel was unenforceable and to allow the Quinn Emanuel law firm team to stay there. The judge didn't think it was in his domain to get involved in the hotel-room war. However, the Mission Inn's legal team noted that there was a clause in the contract with MGA that gave the Quinn team the right to book rooms through an outside travel agent, rather than with the hotel itself.

It seemed that the Doll War was now playing second fiddle to the skirmish over where the Mattel lawyers bedded down. While some of Quinn's team were booked into the Mission Inn, where rooms went for as much as $2,000 a night, Quinn himself and most of his trial colleagues stayed at the nearby Marriott, where the highest-priced room was $350 a night, and where Quinn felt the facilities were better for long hours of trial work.

The first day that the opposing lawyers were at the Mission, a package of legal documents meant for a Quinn colleague was mistakenly delivered to the room of a Skadden associate. In the end, according to the *Daily Journal*, the full battalion of the Quinn legal team was happily booked into the Marriott.

Another bizarre development arose when an anonymous letter was sent to Larian at his office that stated ominously: "We have learned some disturbing information that may be of concern to you." The strange, rambling missive, postmarked May 21, 2008, claimed that two named Mattel executives "have collaborated to spy on you and your family at your home and your children's school." The letter was signed *Shalom*, meaning *peace* in Hebrew. MGA turned over the letter to the judge, who had it sealed. But the letter was subsequently posted on MGA's website along with a reward of $10,000 for information leading to the sender and proof that the assertions made were true. "Please come forward," the company pleaded. Mattel denied the allegations in the letter after the *Los Angeles Times* ran a story about the episode.

■ ■ ■

On May 19, 2008, a week before the start of the copyright infringement trial, which would last seven weeks, Mattel suddenly settled its case with Carter Bryant, who, according to testimony from Larian, was paid more than $30 million in royalties from MGA for his work on the Bratz Pack. Mattel, which had sued him for $35 million, dropped its breach-of-contract claims. The Mattel-Bryant settlement, which had come out of the blue, was kept secret by the judge. On hearing the news, MGA declared, "Mattel has finally acknowledged that its suit against Carter Bryant was without merit," and looked forward to facing Mattel in court. Bryant, however, was ordered to testify at the trial.

A month before the settlement, the judge had ruled that the agreement between Bryant and Mattel gave the company the right to make claims on any "ideas, concepts and copyrightable subjects" that Bryant had developed during his employment.

The federal intellectual property trial began on May 27 in U.S. District Court, Central District of California, with lawyer John Quinn asserting that MGA was in the doll-making minor leagues when it decided to take on Barbie with Bratz, a concept Mattel claimed was developed by Bryant while he was in Mattel's employ. "This explains how a small company that never designed a fashion doll was able in a short period of time to come up with a doll that became a global hit," Quinn told the court. He also charged that Larian had ordered his employees to keep Bryant's name a top secret to avoid any legal entanglement with Mattel.

MGA's lawyer, Tom Nolan, in opening arguments, claimed that Bryant's drawings were similar to 1998 magazine ads that the designer said had inspired him, and that Mattel now wanted to "grab back" the lucrative idea that was conceived before Bryant returned to his job at Mattel. The lawyer promised that Bryant's mother and his life partner, Richard Irmen, would testify that Bryant had made the drawings before he came back to Mattel.

Nolan also noted that there was never a coverup of Bryant's name at MGA, and that it was "common knowledge" in the toy industry that he was involved with Bratz. Nolan also argued that Mattel was too paralyzed by bureaucracy to come up with a similar idea.

"MGA took the risk and brought Bratz to the retail market," he told the jury, "and Mattel is not entitled to what they didn't think of." As for Bryant's employment agreements with Mattel, Nolan asserted they were "not a lifetime sentence."

The California trial received the attention of the world media, as far away as New Zealand, because both Barbie and Bratz were competing international icons.

"Clinton vs. Obama it may not be," observed *ABC News*, "but the battle of Barbie vs. Bratz is a showdown that could net hundreds of millions of dollars for the world's largest toy maker [Mattel]."

On the stand, Larian testified that he didn't see a problem if Carter Bryant had done some work on Bratz while employed by Mattel, but he noted he understood that Bryant had come up with the original idea between jobs at Mattel.

In his testimony, Carter Bryant, the star witness, acknowledged under questioning that he had sketched some of the Bratz while still working for Mattel, and that for a mockup of the doll he had used little boots that belonged to Ken and possibly a Barbie body. He said he had found a plastic doll head in a trash bin at Mattel while he was still employed there, made up its face, put hair on it, and used it as the prototype doll that became Bratz, based on his own original idea and conceived when he was not employed by Mattel.

Bryant claimed that in 1999 he had sent a Bratz drawing to an artist agency to see if there was any interest. He testified he didn't "have the foggiest idea" that Bratz would become so enormously successful—a $2-billion-a-year product.

Under oath, he said, "I didn't do the drawing while I was at Mattel."

But he acknowledged that he had done some finishing work on his drawing at Mattel, and while still there had meetings with other toy companies, during which he met Isaac Larian. He testified that Mattel was never offered his idea, but that he offered it to MGA and another toy firm, and even used a Mattel fax machine to communicate with MGA.

Moreover, he said he asked some co-workers at Mattel for their help on Bratz without revealing that work wasn't for Mattel. "I didn't think it was a big deal." He said he was never certain that MGA was a Mattel competitor, only that MGA was a "toy company. I didn't know how big they were." He asserted, "I had no idea they'd ever compete with anything Mattel did."

During his grilling, he said he never really understood or consulted with a lawyer about the Mattel employment agreements he had signed that covered such items as developments, designs, know-how, and data, and that precluded him from assisting "in any manner any business" that was a competitor of Mattel's. Such agreements are widely standard in creative businesses. He said that while he worked at Mattel he had heard "a general rumor" that Mattel employees "moonlighted" for other toy companies.

Mattel's lawyers claimed that Bryant had used a software program called "Evidence Eliminator" on his laptop to scramble and erase files in an effort to hide work he had done for MGA. MGA's lawyers said Bryant had bought the software to stop "popups" that were of a pornographic nature because he was worried someone else might use his computer.

"Dressed conservatively in a dark suit and a pale yellow shirt, his cherubic face mild behind arty wire-framed eyeglasses, Bryant seemed like an unlikely perp in a high-stakes intellectual property battle," observed *BusinessWeek*.

■ ■ ■

The year 2007 had been Bob Eckert's worst since he was named CEO at the start of the decade as he faced the lead-and-magnet recall scandal that put a dark cloud over Mattel and caused company losses into 2008. On top of the toy terror imbroglio, he had another headache. Bratz had surpassed Barbie, becoming the top fashion doll, at least for one quarter. With the toy terror issue fading in the headlines, and with Congress passing legislation to hopefully avoid such problems in the future, Bratz and the trial appeared to be Eckert's biggest headache in the summer of 2008.

Although the two men had never met, Isaac Larian was clearly Eckert's nemesis in the doll wars, and Larian felt he had every reason to gloat. "The consumers have spoken," the MGA boss boasted. "Bratz is the clear No. 1 fashion doll in the U.S.A. and we intend to stay at No. 1," he told the toy industry magazine *Playthings*. "We will keep that pace and increase it with product innovation and marketing."

Before Eckert took the stand, the equities analyst Margaret Whitfield observed to the author, "Basically, the Barbie brand has been significantly truncated to the point where it's only 6 percent of U.S. sales. Mattel lost the market share they once held. If this case had come to trial a few years back it might have made a big difference for Mattel, and certainly taken some of the momentum out of MGA if they were forced to pay out significant dollars. There's no question that Bratz put a dent in Mattel—a major dent. We're talking tens of market share points."

Whitfield also told *Forbes*, "Mattel just doesn't have the dynamism it had in the '90s."

Having been on the political, media, and public hot seats in the lead-and-magnet scandal, Eckert was now called to testify in the most important court case in Mattel's history, one that in the best-case scenario would turn over the Bratz copyrights and profits to Mattel.

As the boss of the world's largest toy company, he did not come across as being on top of things. He conceded that the first time he had ever heard of Bratz was "probably in the fall of 2001," when the doll was offered for sale in Spain. At the same time, he testified that he didn't think the toy business was more competitive than the processed cheese business he had overseen at Kraft Foods. "I view businesses like these to be very competitive. Both the cheese business and the toy business."

He acknowledged that he saw nothing wrong with holding secret recruitment meetings with employees still working for other companies— this in the face of Mattel's assertions that Bryant had violated Mattel's contractual agreements by allegedly having dealings with MGA while still working for Mattel. Eckert admitted under examination by MGA's lawyers to having two such personal meetings with a Disney executive, Tim Kilpin, whom he personally interviewed to head Mattel's boys' division, and who was hired by Mattel as general manager of both the girls' and later the boys' toys divisions.

Asked by MGA's Nolan, "Do you think it is wrong to recruit executives from competitive toy companies?" Eckert responded, "No, I don't think it is."

Some of the evidence introduced by Mattel's lawyers was based on news accounts regarding the origins of Bratz. Larian had testified that he had been misquoted in some of those stories.

Under questioning, however, Eckert seemed to undermine Mattel's case when he acknowledged that he had given a 2004 commencement address at the UCLA Anderson School of Management during which he made note of a survey that found that journalists were "sloppier, less professional, less moral, less caring, more biased, less honest about their mistakes" than in earlier years. It wasn't on a par with Spiro Agnew's famous attack on the media, calling the press corps "nattering nabobs of negativism . . . an effete corps of impudent snobs," but by mentioning the survey in his talk Eckert demonstrated a media bias, the MGA attorneys attempted to show.

When Eckert joined Mattel, a year before Bratz was launched, he felt that morale at the company was very low, as was the stock price, he testified. "There were certainly morale issues at the company," he said under questioning by Nolan. But Eckert emphasized that he was "pleasantly surprised" about how proud employees felt about the company. (Coincidentally, while the trial was underway, Mattel proudly learned it had been named one of 2008's "Best Places to Work in Los Angeles," according to an annual survey conducted by the *Los Angeles Business Journal*. Mattel had ranked 13th in 2007, and had moved up to 9th place among large companies with 250 or more employees.)

An article Eckert had written for the *Harvard Business Review* in 2001 was introduced into evidence that appeared to contradict his testimony about the rosy picture at Mattel when he joined. In it, Eckert declared, "Mattel had lost its focus. It was losing up to a million dollars a day. . . . Mattel was borrowing money to stay afloat," and several top executives "had left" the company. Eckert had denied in testimony that Mattel suffered from a creativity problem, but as the news agency Reuters reported, he "backtracked after Nolan showed jurors an interview in which the CEO said the 'struggling' company 'needed to focus on creativity.' "

On Thursday July 10, 2008, the attorneys gave their summations and the case went to the 10-member jury. Nolan told the panel, "For 40 years Barbie was the only doll in town, and then Bratz came in and knocked her off her pedestal." Quinn argued that MGA knew all along that Bryant was under a Mattel contract when it decided to proceed with the Bratz line. "They helped him because they needed a successful product," the lawyer told the jury. "MGA was with him [Bryant] every step of the way."

Quinn's colleague, Bill Price, pointing at MGA, said, "There is a right way and a wrong way to compete, and what you did here is cross the line."

A week later, Mattel declared victory when the jury, appearing to reject practically all of MGA's defense, returned with a verdict that the Bratz Pack was born while Carter Bryant was employed at Mattel, that all but four of Bryant's drawings were sketched while he was a Mattel designer, and that even the name *Bratz* was conceived while he was at Mattel.

In "Mattel Prevails Over MGA in Bratz-Doll Trial," the *Wall Street Journal* observed,

> The verdict could reshape the fashion doll market, which has focused on the intense rivalry between Barbie and the edgier Bratz line. . . . MGA might be forced to surrender royalties to Mattel, or even the rights to produce Bratz dolls.

The *Los Angeles Times* described the verdict as "a personal blow to Larian" in the story "Mattel Wins Important Verdict in Bratz Dolls Case." But Larian didn't see the verdict as a knockout punch. He claimed that Mattel had "succeeded in confusing the jury. . . . [T]he case is not over yet. . . . I can say confidently that we will prevail."

Eckert, though, called the verdict "a triumph," and declared, "What MGA did was wrong." In a prepared statement, he said: "This is a victory for all the hard-working people at Mattel who come together to create many of the most beloved toys for children. It is also a victory for all those who believe in fair play."

But the case was far from over. The second phase, which began after a short break, involved the penalty against MGA, a decision to be made by the jury.

Suddenly, it all seemed to explode.

Near the end of the deliberations, Juror No. 8 was reported by another member of the panel as having made an ethnic slur against the Iranian Jew, Isaac Larian. In setting a hearing to determine whether the case should continue or end in a mistrial, Judge Larson said in a court order that the juror's husband, a lawyer, had told her that his own Iranian clients were "stubborn, rude, stingy . . . thieves, and have stolen other persons' ideas." The judge called the comments "grossly inappropriate," but noted that all the jurors clearly indicated "that the remarks would have no effect" on them and did not influence their decision on a penalty.

Nolan immediately asked the court for a mistrial, and Judge Larson dismissed the offending juror. Mattel, in a statement, called the incident "very unfortunate," but noted that the trial "has been and will continue to be about Mr. Larian's and MGA's wrongful behavior. Nothing changed that."

A few days later, the judge rejected the mistrial motion, declaring that the juror's dismissal was an adequate remedy. Larian called the decision "very disappointing." Mattel said it was pleased. Nolan said MGA would appeal to the Court of Appeals for the Ninth Circuit, but in a two-page opinion the appeals court ruled that intervention wasn't warranted.

Two weeks later, the jury awarded Mattel as much as $100 million—far less than the $1.8 billion Mattel had demanded. Mattel's stock jumped a dime on the news. In the second quarter of 2008 alone, Mattel reported spending more than $16 million on the case. The judge would have to decide the exact amount. MGA said it was $40 million, not $100 million, contending that the jury may have duplicated awards on three claims.

MATTEL WINS SKIMPY DAMAGES IN BRATZ DOLL CASE, trumpeted the headline in the *Los Angeles Times*. The paper noted, "Mattel won the big battles in the Barbie vs. Bratz trial, but it may have lost the financial war."

The toy market analyst Margaret Whitfield declared, "MGA wins on this one, big time. That amount maybe just covers Mattel's legal expenses, with a little left over."

The jury foreman, a retired school custodian, said he felt Bryant had "pulled the wool over everyone's eyes."

The opposing lawyers said they'd appeal the verdicts.

Eckert said his company was "pleased that the principles of fair play and fair competition that prompted Mattel to bring the suit in the first place had prevailed."

Isaac Larian said, "I feel happy. We're going to go home, pray, and have a bottle of champagne. It was painful for myself and my family when in closing arguments they were calling me names like a liar and a thief."

But Larian's seeming optimism—with the help of God and some Dom Perignon—would soon turn. Mattel had some shockingly unexpected maneuvers planned.

■ ■ ■

In mid-November 2008, Mattel's lawyers asked the court to actually ban MGA from producing any more dolls in the Bratz line, and further asked that the court order Bratz products impounded and destroyed. MGA's lawyers fought the demand. The judge put off making an immediate decision, and declared that any court order wouldn't kick in until after the Christmas holiday in order to spare retailers hit by the dreadful economy.

A commenter with the nickname "Babs," and an ironic sense of humor, wrote on a *Wall Street Journal* blog:

> Now I shall have to move out of my Crystal palace and into a van down by the river. Competition is NO FAIR! I want a monopoly! I want to be the only fashion doll on the market! Why should I, Barbie, have to compete in the marketplace? You're all being mean to me! Wah! Wah! Wah!

But as it turned out, Barbie, always Mattel's heroine, won the day.

There would be no need for her to move into a van. Far from it. In a sudden bombshell decision just three weeks before Christmas, Judge Stephen Larson handed Mattel a gift-wrapped present extraordinaire in the form of a shocking order that rocked the toy industry: Isaac Larian's MGA would have to stop selling Bratz dolls, and the jurist banned the company from using the Bratz name. He decided that literally hundreds of Bratz products infringed on copyrights owned by Mattel.

Declared Larson: "Mattel has established its exclusive rights to the Bratz drawings and the court has found that hundreds of the MGA parties' products—including all the currently available core female fashion dolls Mattel was able to locate in the marketplace—infringe those rights."

Going even further, the judge ordered MGA, in the court's December 3, 2008, permanent injunction, to recall all Bratz dolls from the marketplace—and destroy "specialized plates, molds and matrices" used to manufacture the dolls. The only bit of relief for MGA was that Judge Larson stayed his order until early 2009, when Barbie would have much more to celebrate—her immense victory over those pouty-lipped upstarts—than just her big 5-0.

A Mattel lawyer called the decision "a pretty sweeping victory," and the company's stock rose several dollars on the news.

Larian was furious and announced he'd appeal, He wanted the judge's order stayed until what could be a lengthy appeals process was over. His goal, he stated, was to allow MGA to "maintain the over 1,500 people" the company employed "and continue to give our customers a product they desire."

But, as one scribe glibly noted, "Barbie has regained control of the dollhouse."

On its website, CNN asked readers whether it was fair for Bratz to be taken off toy store shelves. Of the 80,198 who initially voted the day after the court decision, about 52 percent in the unscientific poll said yes, and 47 percent voiced a no.

Naturally, Bob Eckert was overjoyed with the court's decision. But with good news sometimes comes bad. A day after Mattel beat MGA, Eckert learned that his other corporate nemesis, Hasbro's boss, 45-year-old Brian Goldner, who had joined Hasbro around the same time as Eckert came to Mattel and had transformed the world's No. 2 toymaker, had been named MarketWatch's CEO of the Year.

As one veteran Mattel executive noted, "In corporate America you win some and you lose some."

There were cliff-hangers galore throughout the trial, and the biggest one—at least in MGA's favor—came two days before the New Year 2009 was rung in when a surprise decision by the judge gave the Bratz girls a last minute reprieve, at least for a while it appeared. It was almost like a scene from old Hollywood when the governor calls the prison warden just before the executioner zaps the mad-dog killer with 20,000 volts. Instead of a February 11 deadline set for Larian to pull all of his Bratz products off store shelves, the jurist indicated at a hearing that he might permit retailers to continue to sell Bratz products through the end of 2009, according to Tom Nolan, the MGA lawyer.

About to go to the toy far in Hong Kong to hawk the latest Bratz line, Larian enthused it was "a good day for MGA, its employees and Bratz." He told the news agency Reuters that he would continue to "pursue our appeal rights" and expressed confidence that MGA would eventually keep the rights to Bratz.

Mattel remained mum about the way things had suddenly turned, but the company did file a motion accusing its arch-rival of questionable sales tactics and untimely financial disclosures.

Like the furious conflict that had broken out between Hamas and the Israelis at the start of the new year, the battle between Mattel and MGA never seemed to end, and was certain to continue into and after Barbie's 50th. It appeared the old girl would still have to compete with those sexy young upstarts—though Mattel revealed at year's end that it had begun a makeover of the iconic Barbie brand, even changing the doll's classic look in advertising, all to make her fashionable once more.

# Author's Note
# on Sources

Since this is the first objective and independent book about Mattel, I had the enormous task of tracking down dozens of knowledgeable, credible sources.

While over the years there have been numerous published reports about the world's largest toy company, none have gone into the kind of detail necessary for a candid, in-depth, objective portrait of the kind I set out to write.

One book that gave me a kick-start into the company's history, though often self-serving, was *Dream Doll*, written by Mattel co-founder Ruth Handler, now deceased.

That said, I would like to point out that I have attempted to clarify in the text of the book the sources I have used. All quotes by people interviewed by me, or my researcher, Caroline Walton Howe, are written in the present tense ("she says," "he observes"). See the acknowledgments.

Quotes from other sources such as magazine articles, newspaper stories, and books (see the Selected Bibliography), are written in the past tense ("he maintained," "she declared").

For example, all the direct or indirect quotes attributed to Ruth Handler, who died in 2002, came for the most part from her book, or from interviews with her in various newspaper and magazine articles, or from people to whom she spoke and whom I interviewed. The same is true of quotes attributed to such present and former Mattel executives as Robert Eckert and Jill Barad.

As for quotes attributed to the Father of Barbie, Jack Ryan, his words come from audio tape recordings made mostly at seminars in 1988 sponsored by the organization Invention Convention. The recordings were graciously made available to the author by Stephen Paul Gnass, founder of InventionConvention.com and executive director of the National Congress of Inventor Organizations.

Over the decades since Mattel's incorporation immediately after World War II, the company has been the subject of thousands of articles. Controversies, scandals, toy announcements—everything from mundane quarterly earnings reports to front-page blockbusters—have received coverage in daily newspapers and weekly and monthly magazines, and in recent years, on the Internet.

Many of those reports, combined with my firsthand interviews, were particularly valuable for my research, and for writing a cohesive, readable, and balanced story.

I've attempted to cite these published sources by name where applicable in the context of this book's chapters. Among them, in no particular order of importance, are: the *Wall Street Journal*, the *Los Angeles Times*, the *New York Times*, the *Washington Post*, *USA Today*, the *Financial Times*, the *Los Angeles Business Journal*, *Time*, *Newsweek*, *BusinessWeek*, *Fortune*, and *Esquire* (and the various periodicals' related websites). Their reportage has been admirable.

# Selected Bibliography

Florea Duhaime, Gwen, and Glenda Phinney. *Barbie® Talks*. San Jose, CA: iUniverse.com, Inc., 2001.

Gabor, Zsa Zsa, and Wendy Leigh. *One Lifetime Is Not Enough*. New York: Delacorte Press, 1991.

Handler, Ruth, and Jacqueline Shannon. *Dream Doll: The Ruth Handler Story*. Stamford, CT: Longmeadow Press, 1994.

Horowitz, Jay. *Marx Western Playsets*. Sykesville, MD: Greenberg Publishing, 1992.

Jamison, Kay Redfield. *Night Falls Fast: Understanding Suicide*. New York: Alfred A. Knopf, 1999.

Kerr, Barbara. *Strong at the Broken Places: Women Who Have Survived Drugs*. Chicago: Follett Publishing, 1974.

Leffingwell, Randy. *Hot Wheels: 35 Years of Speed, Power, Performance, and Attitude*. St. Paul, MN: MBI Publishing, 2003.

Lord, M.G. *Barbie, The Unauthorized Biography of a Real Doll*. New York: William Morrow, 1994.

Miller, G. Wayne. *Toy Wars*. New York: Times Books, 1998.

Sweet, Roger, and David Wecker. *Mastering the Universe: He-Man and the Rise and Fall of a Billion-Dollar Idea*. Cincinnati, OH: Emmis Books, 2005.

# Acknowledgments

A book of this scope—profiling an enormous, dynamic, creative, and iconic international public corporation, as Mattel is—required the cooperation of a wide range of sources, from secretaries to top-level executives. My goal was to paint an objective portrait of the world's largest toy company—the House of Barbie, Hot Wheels, and many other toys that have brought joy to generations.

But from the start of my research, Mattel, to my surprise, declined to offer any assistance. I found this quite curious because, when it suits corporate purposes, the company offers up access to newspaper, magazine, TV, and radio reporters. In my case, a virtual brick wall was put in place. Telephone calls were made and e-mails were sent by this author to the office of the CEO and chairman, Robert A. Eckert, but those were passed on to Mattel's corporate public relations people, who offered no assistance in the end. I began to wonder why. What, if anything, were they hiding?

I began my research on this book at a horrific time for Mattel—in the midst of one of the worst crises the world's largest toy company had ever faced in its long and storied history—the toy terror scandal of 2007, when millions of Mattel and its Fisher-Price-division toys were being recalled for dangerous defects.

Lead had been found in the paint of toys manufactured for Mattel by its vendors in China and millions were recalled. Mattel toys containing tiny magnets were also recalled. Whereas the magnet toys were manufactured in China, the problem with them resulted from their design in the United States. In both cases, though, children could have faced serious injury. As this book documents, children who swallowed the magnets from toys made by Mattel and at least one other company did suffer serious injury. There was at least one death of a child reported, not attributable to a Mattel product. And parents claimed that lead had caused health problems for their children. Lawsuits were filed.

As a result of the scandal, Mattel put on a major public relations campaign in an effort, often unsuccessful, to calm millions of irate parents. The U.S. Congress began holding hearings, and the media blared headlines that didn't make Mattel happy.

I was told by sources close to the company that Mattel wouldn't cooperate with the author of a book, especially one that it couldn't control, a book that was unauthorized, and particularly at the height of a scandal. That is not to say that Mattel controls what magazines and newspapers write about it. It's just the opposite. However, this wasn't going to be a one-off article, but rather an entire book that would get into the dark nooks and corners that Mattel might not feel comfortable seeing revealed in print.

In fact, the first question one of Mattel's top corporate public relations people asked me during a brief telephone conversation was, "Who's talking to you? Who's giving you information?" He wanted to take names, and the thought that ran through my journalistic mind was, give him names, and they'll most likely be looking for new jobs. Some months later, that same public relations official sent me a friendly e-mail announcing that he had left Mattel and joined another corporation.

Despite Mattel's internal reluctance, or outright refusal, to give me on-the-record access to key executives, I was able to interview dozens upon dozens of people who were with Mattel virtually from the beginning to the present. With candor, they spoke openly about the corporate culture, and the personalities that have driven Mattel over the years. Almost everyone spoke on the record and without setting ground rules. I respected the requests of the very few who wanted anonymity. You know who you are.

With that said, I offer my heartfelt thanks to all of the following, who were candid and forthright, who opened doors for me, who took time out of their busy lives to help me tell the story of Mattel. I could not have done it without you:

Elliot Handler, Derek Gable, Stephen Gnass, Roger Sweet, Margo Moschel, Nancy Zwiers, Nancy Hudson, Sim Osborn, Gordon Tabor, Gun Sunderson, Rita Rao, Norma Green, Diana Troup, Lynn Rosenblum, Diana Ryan, Roger Coyro, Annie Constantinesco, Gun Sundberg, Misty May, Lavina Bowman, Cliff Annicelli, Virginia Smith-Rader, Fred Adickes, Bob Hundemer, Dr. Marvin Klemes, Dr. Pamela Harris, Steve Dubin, Norma Green, Kitty Bernharth, Marvin Barab, Carol Spencer, Linda Joseph, Barbara Anderson-Walley, Jim Marshall, Aldo Favilli, Ruby Knauss, Dr. Kay Jamison, Glenda Phinney, Gwen Florea, Bill Smedley, Gene Kilroy, Janos Benne, Anne Zielinski-Old, Margaret Whitfield, Denis Bosley, Loretta Bosley, Magda Ryan, Candy Purdom, Gigi Peters, Glenn Balsis, Jackie Deshich, Michael Hilliger, Dan Hanck, Frank Canzolino, David Wecker, David Niggli, Kim Compton, Rep. Rosa DeLauro, Beth Fisher, Jeffrey Killino, Warren Braren, Dr. Irene Kassorla, William Bessire, Tom Forsyth, Ann Thompson, Erik Lotke, Deborah Davies, Jay Horowitz, Ron Goodstein, Susan Stern, Robert Passikoff, Dr. Alan Oestreich.

I'd also like to thank my editors at John Wiley & Sons, Debra Englander, who got it from the start, and Kelly O'Conner, who has grace with the pencil, and style all the way. My agent, Jeremy Katz, was a champ throughout.

If for some reason I missed offering an appreciation for your help, please accept my apology.

# Index